# FREEDOM OF RELIGION
# AND THE SECULAR STATE

**Blackwell Public Philosophy**
Edited by Michael Boylan, Marymount University

In a world of 24-hour news cycles and increasingly specialized knowledge, the Blackwell Public Philosophy series takes seriously the idea that there is a need and demand for engaging and thoughtful discussion of topics of broad public importance. Philosophy itself is historically grounded in the public square, bringing people together to try to understand the various issues that shape their lives and give them meaning. This "love of wisdom" – the essence of philosophy – lies at the heart of the series. Written in an accessible, jargon-free manner by internationally renowned authors, each book is an invitation to the world beyond newsflashes and soundbites and into public wisdom.

**Forthcoming**

# FREEDOM OF RELIGION & THE SECULAR STATE

## RUSSELL BLACKFORD

**WILEY-BLACKWELL**

A John Wiley & Sons, Ltd., Publication

This edition first published 2012
© 2012 John Wiley & Sons, Inc.

Wiley-Blackwell is an imprint of John Wiley & Sons, formed by the merger of Wiley's global Scientific, Technical and Medical business with Blackwell Publishing.

*Registered Office*
John Wiley & Sons Ltd, The Atrium, Southern Gate, Chichester, West Sussex, PO19 8SQ, United Kingdom

*Editorial Offices*
350 Main Street, Malden, MA 02148-5020, USA
9600 Garsington Road, Oxford, OX4 2DQ, UK
The Atrium, Southern Gate, Chichester, West Sussex, PO19 8SQ, UK

For details of our global editorial offices, for customer services, and for information about how to apply for permission to reuse the copyright material in this book please see our website at www.wiley.com/wiley-blackwell.

The right of Russell Blackford to be identified as the author of this work has been asserted in accordance with the UK Copyright, Designs and Patents Act 1988.

*Library of Congress Cataloging-in-Publication Data*

Blackford, Russell, 1954–
    Freedom of religion and the secular state / Russell Blackford.
        p. cm. – (Blackwell public philosophy ; 11)
    Includes index.
    ISBN 978-0-470-65886-4 (hardcover : alk. paper)—ISBN 978-0-470-67403-1 (pbk : alk. paper)
    1. Freedom of religion.   2. Religion and state.   I. Title.
    BL640.B63 2011
    201'.723–dc23

                                        2011024992

A catalogue record for this book is available from the British Library.

This book is published in the following electronic formats: ePDFs ISBN 9781118153291; Wiley Online Library ISBN 9781118153321; ePub ISBN 9781118153307; Mobi ISBN 9781118153314

Set in 10/12 pt Sabon by Toppan Best-set Premedia Limited
Printed and bound in Malaysia by Vivar Printing Sdn Bhd

1   2011

*Dedicated to freedom, reason, and tolerance . . . and to all who labor on their behalf*

# CONTENTS

CHAPTER ONE

MOTIVATION AND OVERVIEW

# Introduction

Religious freedom is not just one liberal freedom among others. As Rex Ahdar and Ian Leigh remind us, it is the prototypical liberal freedom, a cornerstone of modern political rights.[1] At the same time, however, its nature is disputed. Exactly when should we say that people possess religious freedom? When should we say that the freedom has been denied? Importantly, how does it relate to modern notions of secularism – and to other key freedoms such as freedom of speech?

Each day, we see passionate struggles over the concept. Patients refuse life-saving medical care – for themselves or their children – and invoke religious freedom in their defense. If a sick child dies after her parents deny her standard treatment, should the parents be criminally liable? Rival litigants strive to keep evolutionary biology out of the high-school science curriculum, or try to make sure it is taught. Strangely enough, *both* sides to this dispute invoke freedom of religion. Heated debates take place over concepts of blasphemy, over female dress, over religious displays on public land, over laws that enforce religious moralities. Churches seek exemptions from urban planning codes, claiming a freedom that others construe as religious privilege. Indeed, the very same churches and communities that claim to be marginalized can be seen by others as powerful and oppressive.

If religious teachings encounter severe criticism, or religious leaders receive scorn or mockery from their opponents, is that an *exercise* or a *violation* of religious freedom? What if a government tries to disarm a violence-prone apocalyptic sect? Is this a legitimate activity to protect citizens from harm, or an illegitimate encroachment on religious exercise?

*Freedom of Religion and the Secular State*, First Edition. Russell Blackford.
© 2012 John Wiley & Sons, Inc. Published 2012 by John Wiley & Sons, Inc.

What if a government agency or a private corporation prevents its employees from wearing turbans on the job – or burqas, or yarmulkes, or conspicuous crosses? In all these situations, both sides of the debate may claim that they favor "true" religious freedom. Neither side will admit to being opposed to freedom of religion, but surely both cannot be right. Religious freedom can't be all things to everybody, yet quite opposed policies are often pursued in its name.

In what follows, I consider religious freedom in historical and philosophical perspective. Somewhere at the core of the concept lies the fear of overweening government power, used to impose a favored understanding of the world – or another, transcendent, world – or to persecute those with a different understanding. As John Locke complained in the seventeenth century, the secular sword of government has been wielded to destroy unwanted doctrines, faiths, and sects. As Locke knew well, many heretics have been imprisoned, tortured, and often burned at the stake.

Historically, disagreement with the state's preferred religion has often been met with ruthless force. As we look back, we see that this was sometimes successful; other times, it proved to be futile. Inevitably, it brought human costs, and in many times and places these were on a grand scale, as with the thirteenth-century Albigensian Crusade, in which hundreds of thousands of people died, many of them openly massacred. Even this was dwarfed by the European wars of religion in the sixteenth and seventeenth centuries. For the sake of one or another religious orthodoxy, men (and sometimes women) have been driven to terrible acts of destruction and cruelty.

Finally, around the seventeenth century, Western governments began a long process in which they slowly stepped away from religious impositions and persecutions. Here, then, is the beginning of religious freedom – in essence a freedom from persecution or the imposition of another's religion. From this process grew the modern secular state and the turn toward liberalism.

## Liberal Democracies

The process continues, and the outcomes to date have been patchy. The concept of religious freedom is still fiercely contested, even in the relatively secular nations of Europe, North America, and the developed world in general. Many citizens of those countries argue, on various grounds, that their freedom of religion is endangered or incomplete. In others, such as prominent nations in the Middle East, Western ideas of religious freedom, including the freedom to change religions or reject religion entirely, are not even given lip service.

I do not aim, in this study, to investigate freedom of religion on a global scale. That is a huge topic, and I can do no more than touch on some aspects here and there, where relevant. Perhaps another occasion will arise. Instead, I shall focus on the intersection of religion, law, and politics in contemporary liberal democracies. In particular, I will explicate a concept of the secular state, revising and updating John Locke's views from the seventeenth century. Even this limited task has endless ramifications, and it's not helpful that the concept of liberal democracy is itself a blurred and contested one.

On some strong conceptions there may be no pure liberal democracies. A conception like that will be far too narrow for my needs, but we can identify some necessary features. The concept includes at least some system of popular elections, together with various protections from the arbitrary or oppressive exercise of government power. Though governments are elected and responsive to the views of the people governed, that does not entail that they exercise a tyranny of the majority. Rather, there are limits to what governments may legitimately do, even with majority support: limits that offer a zone of protection for minority interests. These limits or protections may include written constitutional provisions, but the strongest may be rather less formal. They may involve widely understood political principles that guard the liberty of citizens. For example, there is a principle in modern Western societies that punishments should not be inflicted arbitrarily, but solely in accordance with generally applicable laws that are enforced through procedurally fair processes.

Again, whether by constitutional provisions, political principles, or a mix of both, the reach of government power may be limited in various respects. In particular, it may be established or understood that only certain kinds of justifications ought to be offered for coercive laws. At one extreme, it might be thought that no society is truly a liberal democracy unless it enacts coercive laws only in compliance with John Stuart Mill's harm principle. This is essentially the idea that an individual's liberty may rightly be abridged, through the exercise of social or political power, only in response to acts that cause certain kinds of harm to others.[2] At a later point, I'll elaborate and defend the harm principle, or at least a version of it that seems faithful in spirit to Mill's account. However, no country in the world would be a liberal democracy if this required rigorous adherence to the harm principle. All jurisdictions enact at least some coercive laws that are justified to the public on other grounds – even if those laws and grounds are controversial within the jurisdictions concerned.

Strict application of the harm principle would be too purist as a necessary condition for liberal democracy. Nonetheless, the latter idea involves at least some acceptance of reasonable social pluralism by those with the power to enact or enforce coercive laws. The "liberal" part of "liberal democracy" implies a degree of restraint by the apparatus of the state. It will be reluctant to impose any template, or narrow set of templates, for the good life. Instead, the assumption is made that many ways of life are at least tolerable, and perhaps even valuable. No attempt should be made to suppress them by means of fire and sword, as Locke would have put it: that is, by the state's coercive power. While the governmental apparatus of a liberal democratic society will be used for a variety of ends, including the deterrence of certain behavior, most ways of life are accommodated to the extent that social peace allows.

Thus, even though no modern society adheres strictly to the harm principle, not just any society qualifies as a liberal democracy. To do so, it must combine a democratic process for choosing the government of the day with significant reluctance to restrict the liberty of citizens (and others legitimately resident in the jurisdiction) to act as they wish with the resources available to them. Moreover, where individuals' personal lives and life plans are at stake, including their ability to express themselves freely, have consenting sexual relations, and make reproductive decisions, the state apparatus of a liberal democracy is particularly solicitous of freedom of choice, unless a compelling reason can be found to do otherwise.[3] Whereas many other political arrangements involve the coercive imposition of a comprehensive view of reality favored by the state, liberal democracies aim to provide a framework in which people with many differing views can live in harmony, or at least with mutual forbearance.

It seems to follow that no political formation meeting the minimal requirements to qualify as a liberal democracy would be motivated to persecute citizens (and relevant others) on the ground of religion. But as I'll explore in the following chapters, life is not so simple.

## What is Religion, Anyway?

To this point, I have been using the words "religion" and "religious" as if they are unproblematic, but that is not so. We may question whether what we know as religion is a unitary phenomenon: is Christianity really the same sort of thing as Buddhism, for example, and are non-literalist forms of Christianity the same sort of thing as those which treat the Bible as historically and scientifically accurate? Are any of the well-known modern religions really the same kind of thing as ancient polytheism, or even more ancient forms of spirit worship? Do theistic religions and non-theistic ones really belong in the one category?

Many scholars and courts of law have struggled with the concept of religion, and there is no perfect definition either for the purposes of the law or for those of scholarly fields such as anthropology. In Lecture II of the series that constitutes *The Varieties of Religious Experience*, William James doubted that an exact definition was possible,[4] while Frieder Otto Wolf has recently suggested that the concept of religion is "most deeply imbued and tainted by Euro-centrism and naïve assumptions derived from an often unilaterally simplified Christian tradition." He adds:

> It is, indeed, doubtful that there is any meaningful common denominator between the "everyday magical practices" of an indigenous tribe, Judaic obeisance to the commandments of God to be found in the Tora, the practice of Sunni Islam based on the Qur'an, of Sufi mysticism, of Jainism, of Shintoism, or of Buddhism.[5]

Robert Wright indicates that there is (arguably) no specific concept of religion in hunter-gatherer societies, since their various spirits and gods are seamlessly continuous with the observed phenomena of nature. Such societies' "religious" beliefs and rituals are tightly interwoven into everyday thought and action, and are not clearly distinguished from a non-religious sphere of activity.[6] Charles Taylor makes essentially the same point: in the oldest societies, religion was so ubiquitous that it was not even noticeable as a separate sphere.[7]

Does this mean that "freedom of religion" is a meaningless expression (along with such expressions as "secularism," which seem to contrast with religion in some way)? If so, what were the historical disputes about – the struggles between monotheistic religions and pagan polytheism, for example, or those within Christianity? Untold millions of people have fought, killed, or died, tortured or been tortured, in the name of religious correctness. Or so it appears. Was there nothing that these events had in common? More generally, should we confess that that we don't know what we're talking about when we use such words as "religion" or such expressions as "religious persecution," "religious freedom," and even "comparative religion"? Surely that can't be right.

No matter what definition is adopted, there will probably be marginal cases. Still, the concept is not so vague as to be useless for the practical purposes of social and legal policy in contemporary liberal democracies. James's efforts in *Varieties of Religious Experience* provide one good starting point, and a more modern one can be found in Taylor's monumental study, *A Secular Age*.

With considerable misgivings, James settled on a loose definition, for his purposes, referring to the feelings, acts, and experiences of individuals in solitude "*so far as they apprehend themselves to stand in relation to whatever they may consider the divine.*"[8] As he acknowledged, this definition then raises a question about what is meant by the word "divine." "The divine," he concluded, "shall mean for us only such a primal reality as the individual feels impelled to respond to solemnly and gravely, and neither by a curse nor a jest." He then felt it necessary to add that religion involves a special kind of "happiness in the absolute and everlasting."[9] Moreover, even this is somewhat vague, and James took a slightly different tack at the beginning of Lecture III, where he characterizes the "life of religion" in its "broadest and most general terms" as consisting in "the belief that there is an unseen order, and that our supreme good lies in harmoniously adjusting ourselves thereto."[10]

Writing mainly of the Abrahamic traditions of the West, but with perceptive comparisons to Buddhism, Charles Taylor explains religion in terms of belief in an agency or power that transcends the immanent order – by which he means the operations of the natural world. For Taylor, religion relates to "the beyond," to an otherworldly order of things, but not in just any way. He posits three specific dimensions. First, religion asserts that there is some higher good or ultimate end beyond ordinary human flourishing. Second, it includes the possibility of personal transformation, to ensure that the higher good is achieved. This, in turn, involves the existence of a transformative and transcendent power. Third, the religious account of our possible transformation involves a sense of human life extending beyond "this life."[11] Taylor's analysis is easily applied to Christianity, where the crucial transformation involves salvation through Jesus Christ (however this is explained by different theological systems).

Taylor claims that the political organization of pre-modern societies was connected to, based upon, or guaranteed by some kind of adherence to, or faith in, the otherworldly order. As far as it goes, this is plausible, though it needs to be qualified (and soon will be). His project is to describe and explain the historical change from political and social structures founded on religion to the modern Western state, where religiosity (or otherwise) is largely private, and governments pursue goals that are purely worldly or secular (I'll use these words interchangeably); where religious belief is, at least to some extent, in decline; and where, in any event, religion is neither forbidden nor compulsory.

For Taylor, the central issue is how religion became a mere *option*, a sort of menu item, after such a long history of dominance in societies where disbelief seemed virtually unthinkable. By contrast, I am concerned with neither the intrinsic plausibility, or otherwise, of religion nor how irreligion became a live alternative; my real concern is the relationship between religion and state power. Nonetheless, I find Taylor's understanding of religion useful. We can work with its key ideas: an otherworldly order of things and an otherworldly dimension to human lives; an ultimate good that transcends worldly kinds of flourishing; the possibility of spiritual transformation, such as the Christian idea of salvation; and the existence of transcendent and transformative powers, such as the Abrahamic God.

As already mentioned, this conception of religion is very apt as a description of Christianity, so much so that Wolf might consider it tainted by Christian thinking. It might prove less useful when applied to certain other religions that have a presence within liberal democracies. However, most of the dimensions described by Taylor are recognizable in the well-known religions of ancient and modern times. In particular, the well-known religions seem to involve an order that transcends the natural, or immanent, one, something *otherworldly*. Again, they involve some kind of power connected with this otherworldly order, as well as a relationship between the otherworldly order and our own lives and conduct. This is not unlike James's ideas of "happiness in the absolute and everlasting" and harmonious adjustment to the unseen.[12]

Note, however, that much in the ancient polytheistic traditions deviates from Christianity. Not only was pagan polytheism syncretic and, in its fashion, tolerant; it often placed far less emphasis on personal transformation. Jonathan Kirsch explains this well in the context of ancient Rome, where the priestly ceremonies were never intended to meet the citizens' "intimate spiritual needs." Instead, they were meant to earn divine favor: "the life and health of the emperor, the safe arrival of grain ships from Africa and victory in battle for the Roman legions against the barbarian tribes threatening the border provinces of Western Europe and the armies of the Persian Empire." Thus, the ruling classes of Rome regarded the traditional religious rites "as a civic duty and an essential component of statecraft."[13] Though otherworldly powers and agents were invoked, it was for communal purposes, rather than to enhance the spirituality of the individual. This is typical of the ancient state religions, though not of the various mystery cults that multiplied and prospered in antiquity.

Accordingly, it is something of a distortion to think that ancient Rome was founded on faith in an otherworldly order. There was certainly a connection, but transcendent powers were invoked by the state mostly as an adjunct to its concern with success and prosperity in this world.

## Religion in the Courts: The *Scientology* Case

From time to time the courts have faced the issue of what counts as a religion, or better, "What, for legal purposes, is a religion?" Not surprisingly, they have struggled to produce an uncontroversial definition. In considering the issue from an American perspective, Kent Greenawalt argues for a flexible and context-sensitive approach, though he also emphasizes that there are many systems which are indisputably religious, and that we are not without appropriate information when we make our judgments. We can start with undoubted or paradigm examples of religions, then "determine how closely an arguable instance of religion resembles these."[14] When we identify some things as undoubtedly religious, we don't apply a theoretical definition; rather, we look to certain elements of belief, practice, and organization:

> These may include a belief in God or gods; belief in a spiritual domain that transcends everyday life; a comprehensive view of the world and human purposes; a belief in some form of afterlife; communication with God or gods through ritual acts of worship and through corporate and individual prayer; a particular perspective on moral obligations that is derived from a moral code or from a conception of a divine nature; practices involving repentance and forgiveness of sins; "religious" feelings of awe, guilt, and adoration; the use of sacred texts; and organization to facilitate the corporate aspects of religious practice and to promote and perpetuate beliefs and practices.[15]

The High Court of Australia has provided an especially influential and oft-cited case, one which looks closely at such elements. In *Church of the New Faith v. Commissioner of Pay-Roll Tax (Vic)* ("the *Scientology* case"),[16] five members of the court considered whether the Church of the New Faith, that is Scientology, was a "religious institution." If so, it was exempt from pay-roll taxation in the state of Victoria. With some reservations about how the question had been framed in the lower courts, the High Court judges accepted that their task was one of determining whether or not Scientology was a religion, or at least whether the set of beliefs, practices, and observances that were in evidence on the record could be properly described as a religion.[17]

This, in turn, required the judges to frame a legal understanding of "religion." In the event, all five of them held that Scientology was a religion for such purposes as pay-roll tax exemption, though they produced three separate judgments with somewhat different reasoning. Each of these drew upon decided cases from the US Supreme Court to construct a relatively expansive concept of religion, certainly not confining it to monotheism or even to belief in a god or gods. Mindful of the tolerant or syncretic practices of some actual (and incontrovertible) religions such as Hinduism, the judges did not insist that a religion, to qualify as such, must claim to be the one true faith to the exclusion of all others.

Acting Chief Justice Mason and Justice Brennan emphasized that their task was not an academic exercise in comparative religion but "an inquiry into legal policy."[18] This required them to consider the essential features or indicia of religion that had attracted legal freedom or immunity in Western countries such as Australia. They identified a legal policy of maximum freedom for citizens to respond to abiding and fundamental problems of human existence: our destiny; the meaning of our existence; and the explanation for the existence of the phenomenological universe. Having noted the availability of reason-based approaches, involving science, philosophy, and other secular disciplines, they distinguished religious approaches to these problems:

> For some, the natural order, known or knowable by use of man's senses and his natural reason, provides a sufficient and exhaustive solution to these great problems; for others, an adequate solution can be found only in the supernatural order, in which man may believe as a matter of faith, but which he cannot know by his senses and the reality of which he cannot demonstrate to others who do not share his faith. He may believe that his faith has been revealed or confirmed by supernatural authority or his reason alone may lead him to postulate the tenets of his faith. Faith in the supernatural, transcending reasoning about the natural order, is the stuff of religious belief.[19]

For Mason and Brennan, then, legal policy protected freedom of belief in a supernatural (or otherworldly) order, where these beliefs were used to address fundamental problems of human existence. After further discussion, their judgment settled on two criteria, which it described as "belief in a supernatural Being, Thing or Principle" and "the acceptance of canons of conduct in order to give effect to that belief." They observed that these criteria might vary in their relative importance between different religions. Indeed, the tenets of a religion might give primacy to one particular belief or one particular canon of prescribed conduct. Likewise, religions and individual adherents of a religion might differ in intensity of belief or intensity of commitment to canons of conduct.[20]

Justice Murphy took a broad and pragmatic view of what should be accepted as a religion for legal purposes. While noting that some so-called religions were merely hoaxes, he added that this should be the legal conclusion only in extreme cases. On his approach, the categories of religion were not closed, but he provided a non-exhaustive list of sufficient, rather than necessary, grounds for an institution or other such body to be accepted as religious. Thus, any organization that claimed to be religious should be accepted as such if: (1) its beliefs or practices revived or resembled those of earlier cults; (2) it claimed belief in a supernatural being or beings, such as gods or spirits, whether they were visible, invisible, or abstract; or (3) it offered a way to find meaning and purpose in life. He specified that, "The Aboriginal religion of Australia and of other countries must be included."[21]

With some expression of trepidation, Justices Deane and Wilson sought to develop a conception of religion from empirical observation of accepted religions. They identified four or five indicia that they considered helpful in deciding whether a set of ideas or practices amounted to a religion for the purposes of the law: (1) ideas and/or practices involving belief in the supernatural (a reality extending beyond what can be perceived by the senses); (2) ideas relating to humanity's nature and place in the universe, and its relationship to the supernatural reality; (3) acceptance by the adherents that the ideas require or encourage them to observe standards or codes of conduct, or to participate in practices with supernatural significance; (4) the adherents forming an identifiable group or groups; and possibly, (5) their perception of the collection of ideas and/or practices as constituting a religion.[22]

All three judgments identified a supernatural element in religion, though Justice Murphy placed less emphasis on this: in particular, he would have been prepared to identify a religion wherever he saw an organization that considered itself religious and offered teachings about life's meaning or purpose. Perhaps he was correct, for the practical purposes of the law, to extend "religion" that far. Nonetheless, it appears plausible that the central cases of religion involve an otherworldly or supernatural order, much as described by Taylor and by most of the judges who have contributed to existing case law. If so, we can distinguish thoughts and worldviews that are confined to *this world*, however counterintuitive some of its elements and mechanisms may turn out to be when examined scientifically, from those that also describe another order of things. The latter are central to the phenomenon of religion.

For somebody socialized in a pervasively religious society, such a distinction might not be clear, but it is adequate for the purposes of public policy in liberal democracies. Even if the hunter-gatherers described by Wright, and alluded to by Taylor, do not distinguish a specifically religious sphere of life, contemporary legislatures and courts can take note of, and attempt to protect, their belief in transcendent agents and powers.

## Religion and its Conflicts

Religions are not merely systems of belief that postulate the existence of an otherworldly order, complete with transcendent agents and powers. Importantly, these agents and powers make demands and produce transformations. They typically require worship, and they often set comprehensive standards for a believer's conduct and way of life. Some religions may, admittedly, divorce everyday questions of how to lead a good life from questions of how to propitiate the gods, leaving the former to philosophical inquiry, the secular law, and shared social understandings. Such was often the case with ancient polytheisms. But most religious systems include codes of morality. These are often comprehensive and burdensome, sometimes impossibly so. Moreover, they may cause the believer difficulties if compliance with them violates the secular law, raising questions about the legitimacy and wisdom of coercing conscience. A different set of questions arises if religious believers argue that the secular law ought to enforce their moral code, even on non-adherents.

Issues relating to religious freedom stem from the combination of religion's otherworldly claims; its supernaturally mandated standards of conduct; its typical concern with the transformative power of the other world; and its rejection, or at least deprecation, of what it sees as merely worldly standards of human flourishing. These aspects can place religions in conflict with individual non-adherents, with the state, and with each other. Such conflicts defy resolution, since rival claims about another world and its manifestations in this world are not easily verified or falsified.

In observing this, I don't claim that religious beliefs lie entirely outside of scientific investigation, or that religion can always (or even usually) be reconciled with our knowledge of the immanent order. On the contrary, advancing scientific and humanistic knowledge may, over time, render some religions quite implausible. If a religion makes sufficiently specific claims about how the other world interfaces with this world, it may become open to outright scientific refutation. Science already investigates very small, very distant, and very ancient events, drawing conclusions about mechanisms that are not directly observable. In doing so, it reasons about the effects of these events on present-day, medium-sized things that fall within our sensory range. Transcendent agents or powers could be approached in the same way if enough information were offered as to how their activities are supposed to affect this world.

But in practice that's not how it usually goes. Any erosion of plausibility takes place over time. Religious beliefs are resistant to any simple, decisive refutation, and not only because otherworldly phenomena are undetectable with the ordinary senses and scientific instruments. In practice, belief is not abandoned merely because events in the natural world turn out differently from what might be predicted by secular reason if it took claims about the otherworldly order literally. Of course, major scientific theories can also be resistant to change, and the evidence for or against them can be ambiguous, as in the late sixteenth and early seventeenth centuries, when the case for heliocentrism was incomplete. In such a situation, however, an extensive body of theory may eventually be rejected as anomalies pile up to embarrass its proponents. By contrast, if transcendent powers fail to produce their warranted effects upon the immanent order, religious apologists will find many ways to avoid embarrassment. If, for example, a god or spirit fails to answer prayers as advertised, it might be explained that this is a capricious god, a god with mysterious reasons, or a god that refuses to be tested.

Accordingly, religious claims that seem highly implausible, when contemplated from outside, may be more resistant to falsification than even the most well-entrenched scientific paradigms. Even if philosophically decisive arguments can be brought against a particular religious viewpoint or doctrine, some adherents will prove to be more committed to their cherished beliefs than to whatever canons of philosophical reason are relied upon. In all, there is no practical prospect of employing secular reasoning to produce short-term resolutions of clashes between rival religious claims. Some individual adherents may be persuaded by scientific or philosophical arguments to change their beliefs, but this is certainly not typical. There is no realistic prospect of arguing adherents out of their religion en masse.

At the same time, religious adherents may feel that much is at stake, not least their own spiritual salvation, if they defect. The upshot is that suppression of a religion will gain little assistance from secular reason, and will depend on the brutal application of force. What's more, even the most rigorous persecutions will often fail. Secular rulers would be wise to accept this as a reality that limits their options whenever conflict arises between religions or between religion and the state.

A number of related points should be noted here. First, one religion or another may make many demands of its adherents and other parties, including the state and its officials. Because religions so often look to an ultimate good that differs from, and allegedly transcends, ordinary human flourishing, they can sometimes recommend, or even insist upon, behavior that appears irrational, perhaps counterproductive, from a purely secular standpoint. That might not be a problem if the religiously motivated behavior is required only from adherents, and if it is mainly self-regarding. Obviously, however, there is room for conflict if religious adherents pursue other-worldly goals that clash with the secular goals of others, or with the goals of adherents to rival religions.

Second, the state may have many policies and programs that bring it into conflict with at least some of its religious citizens. These policies and programs may involve no persecutorial intention, yet lead to outcomes that are experienced as, or "feel like" persecution. What, for example, if devout Christian parents in the United States of America, who may be Bible literalists, find that their children, attending a state school, are being taught that the earth is billions of years old and that human beings evolved from earlier primates over a period of millions of years? This sets up a situation where the state's action is in direct opposition to the parents' efforts to teach their children the literal Genesis account of creation. This is just one example. There are countless situations where state actions that are not intended to be persecutorial may be *experienced* as if they were.

Once again, the use of scientific reason does not bring an easy resolution. If scientific reason suggests that some claims made by a particular religion are simply false, the reply may be that scientific reason is being employed in bad faith, or even that it is methodologically corrupt.

Third, many of these situations can, however, be turned around and viewed from the state's perspective. Well-established scientific findings do, indeed, contradict the Genesis narrative unless it is given some kind of nonliteral interpretation – perhaps as an allegory – or treated as a culturally significant narrative that is open to many interpretations. We all have an interest in high-quality education for children, and it might be added that children themselves have an interest in learning about the true nature of the universe in which they find themselves. If that is so, the question changes: Why should the wishes of parents stand in the way of these secular interests, when the state acts for reasons that have nothing to do with religious hostility or a spirit of persecution?

After all, decision-makers within the apparatus of the state would pursue the same educational policies whether Bible literalists existed or not. These decision-makers are not interested in imposing a comprehensive worldview, religious or otherwise, or in stamping out heresy. Their aim is to provide students with some understanding of scientific method, plus knowledge of the most important and robust findings of scientific investigation. I'll return to this example in Chapter 8.

Fourth, there are also many situations in which individuals who do not subscribe to a religion experience it as *imposed* upon them by the state, even if that is not the intention of the state's decision-makers. The latter may act for many reasons, such as enforcing traditional morality, keeping social peace, or merely allaying inchoate "public concerns." But those explanations may appear seriously inadequate to the individuals affected. Traditional morality can be inextricably intertwined with religious doctrine; social peace can be threatened by interest groups who have religious motivations; and "public concerns" may often originate from religious sentiment.

Consider laws that criminalize homosexual conduct or otherwise disadvantage homosexuals. Those who actually bear the brunt of these laws may experience them as tyrannical, no matter what the subjective motivation of the legislators might have been. The law may seem even more tyrannical if some, or many, legislative votes were based on religious injunctions against homosexual conduct. If some gay men and lesbians allege that religious doctrines – doctrines to which they don't adhere – are being imposed upon them, they are not stretching the truth very far. Similarly, it would be objectionable if a Muslim-controlled legislature banned the eating of pork and drinking of wine for all in the jurisdiction.[23] It would be natural for non-Muslims to complain that their religious freedom had been violated, that they were being forced to live their lives in accordance with a religious doctrine that they did not, perhaps could not in honesty, accept. Plainly, it would be easy to multiply such examples.

To skip ahead to Chapter 5, this may not be the sort of situation that is readily justiciable. It can't necessarily be precluded by constitutional provisions relating to freedom of religion (though other provisions, perhaps relating to equality or sexual privacy, may become relevant). Be that as it may, a situation like this is closely related to issues of religious freedom.

Even this is not exhaustive of the problems that can arise with religion within a liberal democracy. What, for example, should we make of liberal democracies, such as the United Kingdom, in which an established church continues to function? Is this an unacceptable imposition of religion, or is it merely a tolerable anachronism, or even a beneficial tradition, with no real impact on religious freedom? Perhaps it's of more concern that governments commonly enact laws to restrict freedom of speech in relation to religion, banning or constraining what is seen as blasphemy or hate speech. This might, for example, prevent Christians and Muslims from expressing certain traditional views of each other or each other's doctrines. Christians and Muslims provide an obvious example, but we can imagine religions that have a history of even greater mutual hostility (let us say, Zeusists and Mardukites). Should they shut up about each other? Should the law require them to?

From one viewpoint, blasphemy enactments and the like might be seen as *protections* of religion. It might also seem that some of the most hateful kinds of religious recriminations are no loss to society or the marketplace of ideas. Nonetheless, blasphemy enactments, or laws proscribing "hate speech," might also be experienced as unnecessary restrictions on religious speech and legitimate discussion of religion. The social effect of any such enactment will depend on its exact content and best interpretation, but there is an obvious danger to freedom of speech, and to freedom of religion itself, if (1) some religions profess doctrines *about each other*, and (2) some people are legally prevented from asserting or teaching them. If the Zeusists once broke away from the Mardukites, whom they now regard as benighted and hell-bound, shouldn't they be allowed to say so? What if their holy book contains such an anti-Mardukite doctrine? Should the holy book be prohibited? But if the Zeusists can't teach what's in their holy book, isn't this a significant restriction on religious exercise? And if that's so, what does it require to justify the restriction?

Again, what should we say about practices that are currently banned, or at least not recognized by law, but are permissible within, or even encouraged by, a particular religion? A classic example is Mormon polygamy, which was crushed in the United States in the nineteenth century. *Muslim* polygamy provides a current example: how should this practice be regarded in a liberal democracy? Should it be criminalized? Given a special accommodation (as an exception to the ordinary law of marriage)? Treated as legal (with whatever benefits that might entail) without being recognized as marriage? Or what? And what about "ordinary," that is monogamous, Muslim marriages? If a marriage between two devout Muslims breaks down, should they be permitted to settle disputed issues, such as property rights and custody of children, in accordance with Sharia law? If not, why not? Where does the public interest lie in a case such as this?

These are among the many current issues relating to freedom of religion in modern liberal democracies.

## The Plan

The chapters that follow consider current issues in detail, although Chapters 2 and 3 mainly provide historical context. In Chapter 2 I consider the persecutorial attitude that religion, not least Christianity, has often displayed. The main emphasis is on events in the Roman Empire and Christian Europe, leading up to the key seventeenth- and eighteenth-century debates over religious freedom. Chapter 3 then focuses more closely on the model of church–state relations developed by Locke. This includes Locke's famous pronouncement that the state is concerned with the things of this world (hence, not with transcendent powers or spiritual transformations).

In Chapter 4 the focus is on the *imposition* of religion. Among the issues that arise here are the effects of formal religious establishments, such as still exist in many European countries, and the propriety of religious or anti-religious speech by governments. Chapter 5 deals with a related aspect: whether the state should impose moral requirements that are supported by, or entangled with, religious doctrine. In Chapter 6, by contrast, I emphasize the vexed question of *accommodating* religion. Within liberal democracies, it is seldom suggested that any religion should be persecuted, except perhaps in some extraordinary set of circumstances. However, there are many cases where state action that is not motivated by hostility nonetheless feels like persecution. When, if ever, should the state acknowledge this and be accommodating? Should it ever grant a right of conscientious objection, based on religious grounds, to laws of wider application?

Many of the cases that have occupied the time of the US Supreme Court have involved nothing like dramatic persecutions, but have generated practical difficulties and anxieties. They include, for example, the burden of city zoning regulation on religious groups. Zoning normally has a secular and non-persecutorial motivation, but it may cause sufficient inconvenience to feel like persecution. Should exemptions be built into city regulations? If not, should they be crafted by a court or tribunal with power to protect the free exercise of religion?

I turn, in Chapter 7, to the private power exercised by religious organizations and related communities. It is one thing to suggest that the state allow for freedom of association, and that it defer to the choices of individuals, including religious adherents, to arrange their own affairs freely and consensually. But is this always realistic? Should the state sometimes interfere in the seemingly "private" activities of religious organizations and communities?

Chapter 8 deals with the important relationship between freedom of religion and the interests of children. It is one thing to claim religious freedom for oneself; it's another to exercise it in a way that may harm others or negatively affect their life opportunities. When it comes to children, the state has an interest in assuring their welfare, even if this involves overriding the preferences of parents. But how far does this interest go? An obvious conflict arises if secular concepts of children's flourishing are not compatible with parents' visions of an ultimate goal such as spiritual salvation or conformity to the will of a god. How should this be resolved?

In Chapter 9 I turn to another vexed relationship, that between religion and freedom of speech. The main issue here is what can be referred to broadly as religious vilification laws: laws designed to protect believers from incitements to hatred or offense to their sensibilities. I am critical of such laws and the threat that they pose to freedom of speech on matters relating to religion.

Chapter 10 briefly draws together the threads of a complex argument. Here, I sum up my views, which take Locke's vision of a secular state to what seems like its logical conclusion. *Pace* Locke, however, there is sometimes room for accommodation of religion, even where this conflicts with the policies behind purely secular laws. At the same time, the interests of the religious must bend to a large degree, to allow the state to protect citizens' worldly interests. Exceptions to general and neutral laws must be confined closely and crafted with care, balancing the interests that may be at stake in any particular case.

I will, throughout, illustrate the issues and arguments with a mix of imaginary and real examples, commenting on decided cases where it seems helpful. Although this book is certainly not intended as a study of American constitutional law, but as a broader philosophical inquiry with implications beyond any one country, the complex jurisprudence of the US Supreme Court is a rich resource. I will draw on it frequently, but also on cases from other jurisdictions as appropriate (as with the High Court of Australia's useful discussion of religion in the 1983 *Scientology* case, considered above).

The American courts are, of course, charged with protecting the First Amendment, which includes the so-called "Establishment Clause" and "Free Exercise Clause." Together, these read: "Congress shall make no law respecting an establishment of religion, or prohibiting the free exercise thereof." Notoriously, it is difficult to reconcile all the decided American cases – even those that are still good law. They feature striking changes in legal doctrine, fine conceptual distinctions, and puzzling divisions among the judges on the nine-member bench of the Supreme Court. Despite the impressive erudition of US judges, they have yet to develop a body of stable and reliable doctrine relating to the Establishment Clause and Free Exercise Clause.

Nonetheless, they have engaged carefully with many of the key issues. Their reasoning shows a high level of intellectual sophistication, and merits careful philosophical study, so long as this does not distract us from the larger picture.

## Conclusion

Issues relating to freedom of religion are important and intransigent. Many of them are also topical and controversial. If one thing is clear, it's that religion itself is not going to wither away any time soon, despite the impact of the scientific revolution, the Enlightenment, Darwin, and the social iconoclasm of the 1960s. While church attendances declined in most Western countries during the twentieth century, and there has been some rise in the proportion of non-believers even in the relatively religious United States, many people in the West still base their worldviews, life plans, and ultimate values on faith in an otherworldly order. Religious lobbies continue to seek prohibitions on conduct that they consider immoral, whether it be abortion, stem-cell and therapeutic cloning research, or physician-assisted suicide. They also seek exemptions from many laws of general application.

Meanwhile, Western secularism is confronted by new challenges, most notably from various forms of political Islam – some with ambitions to extend Sharia law universally. The most radical forms of Islam take a hard line against secularism, modernity, and all forms of liberal thought. How should the secular state respond to opponents who deny its political legitimacy?

The issues I've foreshadowed in this chapter are a daily source of contention, often involving deep commitments and arousing strong emotions. It can be fascinating to observe how different groups line up in specific debates. The opponents are not, in all cases, religious adherents on one side, pitted against ardent secularists or atheists. There can, instead, be shifting, sometimes unlikely, alliances. For example, atheists who wish to engage in robust criticism of religion can sometimes find themselves allied with evangelical Christians in resisting laws that restrict "hate speech" or "vilification." The evangelical Christians may be prepared to accept robust criticism of their own views as a fair price for the right to preach the gospel fearlessly, including the freedom to criticize non-believers and rival religions or churches.

In the past, battles over religion were fought with swords and guns and armor, with dungeons, fire, instruments of torture, and the hangman's noose. In many parts of the world, things have not changed much, though theocratic regimes are now equipped with army tanks, explosive missiles, and fighter planes. Within the liberal democracies of the West, conflict over such issues sometimes inspires violence on the streets. Most often, however, the opponents fight it out in courtrooms, the mass media, and the new medium of the blogosphere. There is no sign that the contention will go away, but all too often it sheds more heat than light. This study attempts the opposite, but some of its conclusions are bound to be controversial. Nobody, I expect, whether religious or secular, will be comfortable with all of them. So be it, for that's the nature of the subject matter.

To make intellectual progress, we must understand how Western liberal democracies reached this point. Let us now put the issues in a broader perspective.

# Notes

1  Rex Ahdar and Ian Leigh, *Religious Freedom in the Liberal State*, Oxford University Press, Oxford 2005, p. 1.
2  J. S. Mill, *On Liberty*, 1st pub. 1859, Penguin, London 1974, p. 68.
3  H. L. A. Hart, *Law, Liberty, and Morality*, Oxford University Press, Oxford 1963, pp. 21–22, emphasizes the importance of sexuality to individuals. The same point can be made about other matters, such as religion, self-expression, and reproductive decisions.
4  William James, *The Varieties of Religious Experience: A Study in Human Nature*, 1st pub. 1902, Penguin, London 1982, pp. 26–52.
5  Frieder Otto Wolf, "A Voice of Disbelief in a Different Key," in Russell Blackford and Udo Schüklenk, eds, *50 Voices of Disbelief: Why We Are Atheists*, Wiley-Blackwell, Oxford 2009, pp. 236–251, p. 250.
6  Robert Wright, *The Evolution of God*, Little, Brown, New York 2009, pp. 17–20.
7  Charles Taylor, *A Secular Age*, Harvard University Press, Cambridge, MA 2007, p. 2.
8  James, *The Varieties of Religious Experience*, p. 31 (emphasis original).
9  James, *The Varieties of Religious Experience*, p. 38.
10  James, *The Varieties of Religious Experience*, p. 53.
11  Taylor, *A Secular Age*, pp. 15–20.
12  James, *The Varieties of Religious Experience*, pp. 38, 53.
13  Jonathan Kirsch, *God against the Gods: The History of the War between Monotheism and Polytheism*, Penguin, New York 2004, pp. 93–94.
14  Kent Greenawalt, *Religion and the Constitution*, vol. 1: *Fairness and Free Exercise*, Princeton University Press, Princeton 2006, p. 372.
15  Greenawalt, *Religion and the Constitution*, vol. 1, pp. 139–140.
16  (1983) 154 CLR 120.
17  (1983) 154 CLR 120, 130.
18  (1983) 154 CLR 120, 133.
19  (1983) 154 CLR 120, 134.

20   (1983) 154 CLR 120, 137.
21   (1983) 154 CLR 120, 150–151.
22   (1983) 154 CLR 120, 174.
23   See Martha C. Nussbaum, *Liberty of Conscience: In Defense of America's Tradition of Religious Equality*, Basic Books, New York 2008, p. 343.

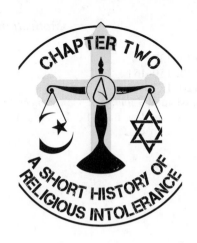

# Introduction

Modern Western ideas of religious freedom had no popular purchase within Christendom before the sixteenth-century Protestant Reformation. This challenged the hegemony of the Roman Catholic Church, and introduced a limited form of theological individualism. The Reformers emphasized the personal relationship between God and the individual Christian – a relationship mediated by the crucified and resurrected Christ – and insisted that the holy scriptures be available in the vernacular for individual study and interpretation. But the Protestant churches could be as zealous as the Catholic Church when it came to persecuting those they regarded as heretics – as the unitarian Michael Servetus painfully discovered when he sought safe passage through John Calvin's Geneva. The authorities moved swiftly to arrest and condemn him, burning him at the stake on October 27, 1553.

Most importantly, the hydra-headed Reformation, in all its forms across Western Europe, led to horrific conflicts that encouraged a rethinking of relations between the Christian churches and the state. By the seventeenth century, philosophers such as Hobbes, Spinoza, and Locke were reconsidering the nature and function of the state, and drawing radical new conclusions. Their thinking then influenced the French Enlightenment and the political leaders of America's founding generation. Modern ideas of freedom of religion owe much to the determination that outrages such as the Thirty Years War must never happen again.

There was a deeper background to these events. Though the ancient pagan religions had been syncretic and largely tolerant, Abrahamic

*Freedom of Religion and the Secular State*, First Edition. Russell Blackford.
© 2012 John Wiley & Sons, Inc. Published 2012 by John Wiley & Sons, Inc.

monotheism had turned out to be far less so. In particular, Christianity became a persecutorial religion during the later centuries of the Roman Empire, continuing through the medieval period, then into early modernity. To the thinkers associated with the seventeenth-century revolution in science and philosophy, and to those of the eighteenth-century Enlightenment, there had to be a better way.

## Pagans and Monotheists, Tolerance and Persecution

Martha Nussbaum laments that, for much of human history, governments have imposed religious conformity on citizens, marginalizing or subordinating those with different beliefs and practices. Just as she says, intolerance has been especially prevalent in the Western tradition.[1] Yet, it didn't have to be like this. The most ancient states were tolerant of many gods and forms of worship.

In ancient Mesopotamia, the tendency was toward syncretism: a pantheon of gods emerged, with the deities of various city states forming an extended family whose members also took part in a rough division of labor. Conquerors were inclined to accommodate the gods of defeated foes, rather than to smash their idols. Sometimes gods from different polities were identified or fused, but one or the other among the gods of conquered peoples generally survived.[2] Ancient multinational empires such as those of Babylon and Persia were willing to respect the religions of their component peoples, so long as those peoples could get along in harmony.[3] Pagan polytheisms did not usually seek to impose themselves on others, because there was always room for another god. Even when new gods arose, the old cults were not necessarily threatened, and the new could be accommodated in the pantheon.[4]

Pagan syncretism dates back as far as civilization itself, and continued for thousands of years. In classical antiquity, the conquering Romans identified the Greek gods with their own – so Zeus became Jupiter, for example, and Aphrodite became Venus. Virgil's *Aeneid* is a kind of Roman sequel to the *Iliad* and the *Odyssey* of Homer, depicting Rome's founding by a Trojan remnant after the destruction of their city. Rome pursued a policy of allowing its subjects to retain their own gods, though there were exceptions. In 186 BCE, an attempt was made to suppress the cult of Bacchus, apparently on grounds relating to public order and safety. Most importantly, Roman leaders expected participation in the traditional rites of the empire – and this led to conflict with both Judaism and Christianity.

That said, tolerance of other gods has always typified syncretic and polytheistic religions. It can be found today in popular forms of Hinduism, much as in the religions of ancient Mesopotamia and Europe. Robert Wright

informs us that Mecca at the time of Muhammad was also a tolerant polytheistic society, accommodating the gods of its trading partners, including
the Byzantine Empire.[5] As Jonathan Kirsch explains, the bright side of polytheism is its tolerance of diverse faiths, while the dark side of monotheism
is its tendency toward religious intolerance:

> At the heart of polytheism is an open-minded and easygoing approach to
> religious belief and practice, a willingness to entertain the idea that there are
> many gods and many ways to worship them. At the heart of monotheism, by
> contrast, is the sure conviction that only a single god exists, a tendency to
> regard one's own rituals and practices as the only proper way to worship the
> one true god.[6]

The Abrahamic religions – Judaism, Christianity, and Islam – rejected
ancient paganism's "easygoing approach." From the beginning, the cult of
Yahweh condemned the worship of any other gods. As Judaism developed
from a monolatrous to a monotheistic religion, it denied other gods any
legitimacy at all: that is, it denied their very existence. In a similar way,
though hundreds of years later, Islam arose as a relentlessly monotheistic,
not merely monolatrous, religion. Muhammad scorned the gods of the
polytheistic Arabian cities and tribes.

The theological purism of Judaism inevitably led to conflict with the
Romans, who allowed worship of the Jewish god along with many others,
but expected all the peoples of the empire to take part in the ceremonies of
the official religion. As mentioned in Chapter 1, the traditional worship was
required by Roman leaders to ensure the gods' blessings on the state. The
official cult invoked transcendent agents to obtain success and prosperity
in *this* world, not to effect the salvation of souls or other spiritual transformations. This clash of pagan and monotheistic viewpoints led to a disastrous rebellion by Jewish zealots in 66 CE. Four years later, Roman forces
destroyed the Temple in Jerusalem; this was followed by mass suicide of
the remaining Jewish rebels in their fortress at Masada.

Like Judaism, Christianity came into conflict with the might of Rome.
The refusal of Christians to conform and to take part in the traditional rites
was principled – to the Christians, the pagan rites were a form of idolatry
– but it was viewed by successive emperors as subversive. The Romans
responded with sporadic persecutions, beginning as early as 64 CE when
the emperor Nero blamed Christians in Rome for a terrible fire in the city.
However, persecution did not reach its peak until the third century, first
under Decius (ruled 249–251) and then Diocletian (ruled 284–305). As
Alister McGrath notes, the persecution under Decius is often attributed to
the emperor's belief that Rome must restore its pagan religion in order to
recover its former imperial glory.[7] This led to repression of any movements,

Christianity prominent among them, that were seen as a threat to traditional Roman values and beliefs. Ironically, however, Christianity emerged as a far more persecutorial religion than Roman paganism, once it obtained secular power.

Meanwhile, brief consideration should be given to the third great Abrahamic monotheism, Islam, which is often praised for having been more tolerant, historically, than Christianity. For example, Nussbaum lauds the millet system of the Ottoman Empire as "a major step toward harmony and respect." As she puts it, "each ethnoreligious community enjoyed considerable autonomy in matters of religion, and was even permitted separate courts and separate taxation."[8] To its credit, moreover, the medieval Islamic civilization did much to preserve the best of the ancient Greek texts and something of the Greeks' spirit of inquiry and disputation.[9]

But was Islamic rule fundamentally more tolerant than Christian rule? In some places, at some points in history, and in some ways, Muslim rulers were more enlightened than their contemporaries within Christendom, but the fact remains that Muhammad himself pursued an aggressive foreign policy, and his successors developed a doctrine that required warring against and subjugating infidels. While military struggle may have been regarded as the "lesser *jihad*," subordinate to the "greater *jihad*" of internal struggle against the self, military conquest was integral to medieval Islam. Under traditional interpretations of Sharia, Muslims lay under a paramount obligation to incorporate new territories. The obligation to convert the world to Islam would remain until the entire world was *dar al-Islam* (the territories of Islam). Once conquered, "People of the Book" (mainly Christians and Jews) were allowed to live as protected communities upon submission to Muslim sovereignty, but not to enjoy equality with Muslims.[10]

The traditional system of *dhimma* classified human beings into three main categories: Muslims, who were the only full members of the political community; People of the Book, who were accepted as having a revealed scripture; and unbelievers. Unbelievers did not qualify for any legal recognition or protection unless granted temporary safe conduct. The term *dhimma* refers to a compact between Muslims and a community of People of the Book whereby the latter were granted security of their persons and property, freedom to practice their religion in private, and autonomy in internal communal affairs – but no right to propagate their own faith. They had to pay a poll tax (*jizya*) and commonly could not exercise authority over Muslims.[11]

Traditionally, Islam worked with a fourth category: "the level of Muslims who either leave the Islamic faith through conversion or choose not to believe (atheists or agnostics)." These were to be punished as unbelievers.[12] Thus Islam allowed no means for a Muslim to change religion. Apostasy applied to any Muslim who denied the existence or a property of God, or a principle based on Islam such as the obligation to pray five times a day and fast during Ramadan, or who declared to be permitted what is manifestly prohibited (*haram*) or prohibited what is manifestly permitted (*halal*). Sharia uses the Arabic term *ridda*, which literally means "to turn back" and a person who turns back, in this sense – someone who has reverted from Islam to unbelief or *kufr* – is despised as *murtad* (apostate).[13] According to Sunni Islam's four legal schools, the punishment for leaving the Muslim community (*umma*), through conversion or renunciation of belief, was a death penalty.

In short, Islamic civilization and the millet system should not be sentimentalized. The concept of dhimmitude implied the inferiority even of other monotheists. As Tibi points out, this would now be viewed as "an expression of discrimination rather than of tolerance."[14]

# The Record of Christianity

In 313 CE, the fortunes of Christianity within the Roman Empire changed dramatically when Constantine and his co-emperor Licinius issued the Edict of Milan, which offered a general liberty to all to follow and practice their own religions throughout the empire. In October the previous year, Constantine had defeated his rival Maxentius at the Battle of the Milvian Bridge, after a dream or vision of the cross. In his dream or vision (the sources differ), he'd been urged to fight under the standard of the chi-rho, representing the Greek word *Christos*. Though still conducting himself in many ways as a pagan emperor, Constantine allied himself with the Christian church, which he saw as a source of political and theological support for his rule.

This led him to take an interest in the church's doctrinal and structural unity, which were, however, threatened by hard-fought theological controversies, partly over the status of Christians who'd given in to the recent persecutions, but increasingly over arcane matters of Christology. What was the position of Christ – the Son – in relation to God the Father? Christian doctrine asserted that Jesus of Nazareth had been, in some sense, divine, while also asserting that God was One. To put it mildly, these claims were difficult to reconcile, no interpretation could easily do them both full justice, and all attempts to resolve the issue met ferocious opposition from one quarter or another. Charismatic leaders arose to defend rival viewpoints, often inciting intolerance and violence.

The Christological problem reached a point of crisis in an ecclesiastical struggle over the ideas of Arius, a priest who denied the equality of Jesus with the Father, whereas his opponents saw the Son as God's eternal Logos, which had been incarnated in human form. As McGrath explains: "The fundamental belief of the Arians was that Jesus was preeminent in rank among beings created by God. Though he was the Logos and the agent of creation of the world, the Logos was itself a creation of God. God existed before the Logos was created."[15]

Troubled by this disunity in the church, Constantine himself convened the Council of Nicaea in 325 CE. Under imperial pressure, a formula was agreed almost unanimously, but this early effort to establish an orthodox version of Christianity by intervention of the power of the state was not successful. Many who were unhappy with the Nicene formula reneged on their agreement to it once they returned to their own congregations, where the pressures on them were very different. Controversy and violence continued to rage.

Disunited or not, however, Christianity prevailed. By the 340s CE, Christian emperors of Rome were issuing anti-pagan edicts. The earliest of these were not vigorously enforced, but Christian intolerance of paganism became more serious with a series of imperial decrees issued by Constantius II in the 350s.[16] Except for a brief period under the rule of Julian the Apostate, who was proclaimed Augustus by his soldiers in 360, the church was triumphant. Julian favored paganism and worked to undermine the influence of Christianity. He was a shrewd, popular leader, but his counter-revolution was doomed to fail. Julian was killed in battle in 363, while on campaign against the Persians, and Christianity soon became the official religion of the Roman Empire.

It obtained that position once and for all under the reign of Theodosius I. In 380 Theodosius issued an edict demanding the universal practice of Christianity, and of Nicene Trinitarian Christianity at that. In this edict, all other views were declared heretical, demented, and insane, worthy of both divine and imperial retribution.[17]

Thereafter, Christian rulers and their followers took more specific – and often brutal – actions to impose their religion on the populace of the empire. Christianity developed from a persecuted faith to an oppressor of rival faiths and outlooks. Jews and Manichaeans were persecuted; pagan statues, shrines, and temples were destroyed, along with Jewish synagogues; and the pagan gods were reinterpreted as evil spirits. The story was not entirely one of a new, militant religion obtaining its hegemony by force: in many cases, pagan festivals were Christianized and pagan gods assimilated to Christian saints. Nonetheless, much in the Greek tradition was crushed, and the classical culture of free thought and philosophical debate was decisively rejected, in a process of forced Christianization that reached even greater heights of ruthlessness under Emperor Justinian in the sixth century.

From the fourth century onward, church leaders sought control of the legislative and executive arms of state power. In his great theological treatise *The City of God* (426 CE), Augustine of Hippo developed a theological position that envisaged the temporal authorities submitting to God's law and the correction of the church. Thereafter, the church gained in worldly power, establishing its own ecclesiastical courts and canon law, and sometimes appointing and deposing emperors. From the eleventh century through to the sixteenth, canonists developed far-reaching legal doctrines to insulate the church, its officials, and its property from the secular and feudal authorities. Their sophisticated jurisdictions defined and enforced many of the rights and duties recognized in medieval and early modern European society – from the rights of family members to the restricted rights of Jews, Muslims, and heretics.[18]

In Britain, William the Conqueror established a system in which common law courts shared authority in criminal matters with the ecclesiastical courts, with the latter applying canon law and exercising jurisdiction over clergy. Papal approval of William's invasion had been conditional, in part, on his promise to set up such a system. In the twelfth century Henry II attempted to alter this, but was opposed by the bishops and failed. His attempts to bring clergy under the same law as others took centuries to work through.

As Marci A. Hamilton explains, there were three main historical privileges in Britain: sanctuary; benefit of clergy; and charitable immunity. From as early as the third century, secular authorities recognized the right for sanctuary from private vengeance for alleged wrongdoing. In the tenth century, this was expanded in the form of chartered sanctuaries that could be quite large in physical extent and had greater scope. But the Crown eventually began to reduce the types and locations of offenses covered by sanctuary. Chartered sanctuary was abolished by 1540, and sanctuary was completely repealed by an act of parliament in 1623, though it continued in relation to service of process until the end of the seventeenth century.[19]

Benefit of clergy was originally a privilege exempting clergymen from criminal process. It was especially beneficial in capital crimes, as the ecclesiastical courts did not have the power to order capital punishment (which was prescribed for all felonies). However, benefit of clergy never covered treason, considered the most heinous of all crimes in the medieval justice system. The thirteenth-century procedure was for the clerk to "plead his clergy" when brought for trial. He was then handed over to the church court for trial (usually by compurgation, an oath supported by those of his chosen oath-helpers). In 1352 the privilege was extended to secular clerks and came to operate as a legal fiction to mitigate the severity of the law. The test was an accused's ability to read the "neck-verse" (Psalm 51:1), which could, of course, be learned by rote. The benefit persisted for centuries before it was finally abolished in 1827.[20]

Organized Christianity did more than seek privileges and immunities. Church leaders zealously guarded its status as the official religion in the Roman Empire and increasingly, after the Western Empire collapsed in the fifth century, in the barbarian kingdoms of Europe. Once it had access to secular power, the church became nakedly persecutorial, as evangelical Christian scholars Rex Ahdar and Ian Leigh emphasize strongly.

Ahdar and Leigh trace the doctrine of two levels of sovereignty, one relating to civil wrongs and the other to spiritual salvation, deep into the Christian tradition, including the writings of Tertullian, around the start of the third century, and the New Testament itself. Tertullian argued that the spiritual concerns of citizens did not fall within the proper remit of the secular authorities, which should not interfere with matters of religion unless there was a breach of the peace. Thus, the idea was originally deployed to ground an argument against religious persecutions. This interpretation changed entirely, however, after Christianity was accepted by Constantine, and especially after it became the official religion of the empire.[21]

During the Middle Ages, it was assumed within Western Christendom that ecclesiastical and temporal authority both depended upon the will of God. In the late medieval period, the church developed this into the two swords theory, according to which Christ had equipped the pope with the swords of both spiritual and temporal power. Although the clergy delegated use of the temporal sword to the civil authorities, it must always be used for the benefit of the church. On this approach, the state's mission is to implement the moral laws given by God and to promulgate God's truth. The temporal sword must serve the spiritual, so sinners are to be punished by the sword of secular power.[22]

All things considered, the moral ethos of Christianity may or may not have been an improvement on what went before. That is a large and controversial question, and involves difficult value judgments that are far beyond the scope of this book. Classical Roman civilization had its own dark side, which the pagan cults did little or nothing to oppose. From a Christian viewpoint, the cults were implicated in such abhorrent practices as gladiatorial combat, crucifixion of rebels and criminals, and neglect of the poor and diseased.

But whatever can be said in Christianity's favor, its obvious downside was its tendency to intolerance, demonization, persecution, and suppression. One of many low points was the Albigensian Crusade, which commenced in 1209 when the church set out to exterminate Cathar heretics in Languedoc. For hundreds of years, Catholic bishops attempted to purge their societies of non-Catholics, mainly Jews (and, in some times and places, Muslims), but also mystics, unorthodox theologians, freethinking philosophers, and anyone else whose views might undermine trust in the orthodox Christian doctrines.

In 1484 the papal bull *Summa Desiderantes* marked the beginning of the European witch hunts, in which thousands of men and women were tortured until they confessed to incredible crimes. Accused witches told of having sexual intercourse with demons, and of traveling through the air for hundreds of miles to participate in parodic and obscene Black Masses devoted to the worship of Satan.[23]

## Reformation and Wars of Religion

The Protestant Reformation of the sixteenth century challenged the pre-dominance of the Catholic Church, but not necessarily the doctrine that temporal power was subservient to the spiritual sword. As we've seen, Calvin's Geneva burned Michael Servetus at the stake in response to his theological teachings, which included his denial of the orthodox doctrine of the Trinity. Indeed, the Reformation was far from the end of religious repression in Europe. Though Martin Luther initially opposed religious persecutions, he gradually moved, under pressure of circumstances, to a far harsher position.[24] Indeed, leaders of the Reformation and the Catholic Counter-Reformation engaged in persecutions with renewed vigor. Throughout the sixteenth century, and much of the seventeenth, Christendom was wracked by religious violence on an unprecedented scale.

In France, for example, Roman Catholics and Calvinist Protestants – the Huguenots – were caught up in a devastating civil struggle, the French Wars of Religion, in which millions died from a combination of causes, including famine and disease. Though both sides had already engaged in provocations and reprisals, the beginning of outright war was marked by the Massacre of Vassy in 1562, when soldiers of the Duke of Guise set fire to a makeshift Protestant church, killing scores of unarmed Huguenots.

The Wars of Religion continued in stages, with a number of truces that stopped hostilities only briefly. They were ended more decisively by the Edict of Nantes, proclaimed by King Henry IV in 1598. This restored the Catholic Church throughout France, and limited the districts where Protestantism could be practiced and taught in public, but it also gave concessions to the Huguenots. It offered them freedom of conscience and private exercise of their religion, along with other defined rights. But even this was not the end of the bloodshed: further conflict between Catholics and Huguenots broke out, and did not end until the Peace of Alais in 1629.

The ruinous Thirty Years War commenced in 1618, and came to involve many of the armies and navies of Europe. The struggle involved the rival aspirations of Catholics, Calvinists, and Lutherans. Though concentrated mainly in the territory of the Holy Roman Empire, it raged from time to time across the continent, inflaming such conflicts as those between the Huguenots and French Catholics. The Peace of Westphalia, which ended the war in 1648, closed an era of extraordinary bloodshed that left many parts of Europe in desolation. Yet many Europeans continued to see religion as worth fighting over. As Nussbaum emphasizes, even the Peace of Westphalia was not reassuring to religious minorities. The controlling principle was *cuius regio, eius religio*, that is the religion established by the local ruler of a region was to prevail. This ended the large-scale warfare, but allowed local rulers to persecute religious minorities within their borders.[25]

Such episodes as the French Wars of Religion and the Thirty Years War cannot be blamed entirely on the Christian churches. Powerful aristocratic dynasties such as the Bourbons and Habsburgs sought to enhance their temporal power, and uninvolved governments intervened as and when they saw opportunities for political or economic advantage. As always, the violence had complex causes, and it is not as if, for example, the parties simply went into battle over the possession of holy relics. But nor should we absolve the churches, whose leaders battled for theological as well as worldly dominance.

In Reformation era Britain, successive rulers engaged in persecution of whatever they regarded as religious dissent. Henry VIII used the Star Chamber and the Court of High Commission to exercise control over religious belief and practice, executing Catholics and heretics. His son, Edward VI, ascended to the throne at the age of nine and died only six years later. During his reign, mighty noblemen ruled in his name while scrabbling for power among themselves. They followed Henry in confiscating church property and promoting the English Reformation. In 1549 the first version of the Book of Common Prayer was completed under the editorship of Bishop Thomas Cranmer. However, the Catholic Queen Mary, who ruled for five years from 1553, responded in her turn by executing many Protestants, among them Cranmer, who was burned at the stake in 1556. Mary was followed by Elizabeth I, who reinstated the Church of England (and was duly declared a heretic by Pope Pius VI).

As Hamilton observes, the British Crown did not adopt a policy of religious pluralism; instead each monarch chose one church and forced subjects to follow. The Tower of London – the Bloody Tower – is a monument to the history of violent religious intolerance in Britain, which was, Hamilton notes, stamped in the mind-set of British subjects, including the pilgrims. It was during the late sixteenth and early seventeenth centuries that the first wave of emigrants left England for the New World, including the *Mayflower* pilgrims in 1620.[26]

Religious bloodshed continued on British soil during the seventeenth century. Civil war broke out in 1642 and continued on and off until 1649. The war was prompted by a power struggle between Charles I and parliament, involving matters of taxation, royal prerogatives, and parliamentary privileges, and as with the French Wars of Religion and the Thirty Years War the blame cannot be assigned solely to religious differences. But once again, religious fervor exacerbated the conflict. Oliver Cromwell, a radical Puritan dissenter who believed he was doing the will of God, ultimately led the parliamentary forces. Once victorious, he invaded Ireland, motivated by theological as well as strategic concerns. In the ensuing war, his men massacred thousands of Irish troops and civilians, and enslaved thousands more. Against this background of war and terror, Thomas Hobbes wrote his masterpiece *Leviathan* (1651), which focused on the requirements for civil peace.

After the restoration of the British monarchy and the return of the exiled Charles II in 1660, religious intolerance took a new turn. The Anglican laity gained control of the English parliament and enacted a series of oppressive statutes, the so-called Clarendon Code, to impose religious conformity on dissenters such as Baptists, Independents, Presbyterians, and Quakers. Parliament favored brutal suppression of religious dissent, though Charles himself took a more tolerant approach. In 1672 he issued the Royal Declaration of Indulgence to suspend penal laws against Catholics and other dissenters. Parliament won the struggle of wills, forced the king to back down and withdraw the declaration, and enacted additional repressive legislation in the form of the Test Acts of 1672 and 1678. In the later 1670s and the early 1680s, however, Charles resisted parliament's attempt to enact the Exclusion Bill, which would have cut James, his brother and heir, from the royal succession because he was a Roman Catholic.

For the last four years of his reign, Charles ruled without parliament. However, he carried out his own acts of repression after an unsuccessful attempt on his life by Protestant conspirators in 1683. During his reign, thousands of Quakers were fined, imprisoned, transported, or executed. Upon his death in 1685, his Catholic brother, James, became James II – and immediately faced the Monmouth Rebellion, led by one of Charles's illegitimate, but Protestant, sons. This was quickly put down, leading to the Bloody Assizes at which some 300 prisoners were condemned to death and over 800 to transportation to the West Indies. James himself was overthrown three years later in the Protestant-initiated Glorious Revolution, which placed William of Orange on the throne and precipitated further warfare.

Mention should also be made of "the Killing Time" – a period in the 1680s when ongoing efforts to crush the Scots Presbyterian Covenanters reached a terrible culmination. Persecutions by the regime of Charles II provoked defiance and rebellion that led, in turn, to a policy of more savage persecution which then continued under James II. This included tortures, deportations, and many thousands of deaths.

On the European continent, meanwhile, religious conflicts and persecutions continued even after the Peace of Westphalia. In most countries, only one religion was tolerated. Despite the Edict of Nantes, King Louis XIV of France adopted a policy of suppressing Protestantism, leading to his revocation of the edict in 1685. Hundreds of thousands of Huguenots were driven out of France, fleeing mainly to other nations in Europe, though some traveled as far as the American colonies.

This was the turbulent background against which John Locke wrote *A Letter concerning Toleration* (1689).

## Conclusion

It is not axiomatic that religions must be mutually persecutorial. On the contrary, the pagan polytheisms of the Near East and Europe generally tolerated one another and tended toward syncretism. While secular governments were closely integrated with local cults and forms of worship, they did not pursue a policy of saving souls or ensuring the "correct" spiritual transformations in their citizens. When they invoked transcendent agents and powers, it was for assistance in collective purposes relating to success and prosperity in this world.

The rulers of ancient Rome saw no need to suppress the strange religions of the territories they conquered, or to correct individual citizens' spiritual strivings. With few exceptions, the ancient cults were welcomed so long as they allowed participation in the official rites. When Jews and Christians suffered persecution, it stemmed from what seemed, from a Roman point of view, their own intolerance: their insistence on worshipping just one deity, and their claim that other gods either did not exist at all or were actually demonic powers. Many cults were permitted, but Rome's tolerance ran out if adherents to a foreign religion refused to participate in the official rites, thus (so it was thought) jeopardizing the empire's worldly prospects.

In our modern world, where major religions such as Christianity and Islam typically resist syncretism, the ancient polytheistic model is not viable, but it does demonstrate one way in which religions could avoid warring with each other over matters of doctrine. As events turned out, however, Abrahamic monotheism took a different historical course. Early Christians such as Tertullian apparently saw religion as a private matter, but Christianity soon became persecutorial. As Ahdar and Leigh acknowledge, neither the Catholic Church nor the Protestant Reformers were exempt from this, and indeed Calvin was especially forthright in maintaining that Christian rulers must employ the temporal sword to enforce the claims of religion.[27]

John Witte, Jr. notes that the right to enter and exit a religion was won in the West only after hundreds of years of cruel experience and stalwart resistance. This came partly from the recovery of earlier patristic concepts of freedom of conscience, partly from new Protestant theologies, and partly from new possibilities of escape from established religion opened up by colonialization and frontier settlement.[28] In the sixteenth and seventeenth centuries, the "cruel experience" that Witte refers to reached an extreme point of mass suffering. Contending armies ravaged Europe, fighting in the name of God; many millions died from accompanying disease and famine; and mighty aristocrats imposed their chosen theologies, burning many dissenters at the stake and sending countless others into exile.

In this setting, bold thinkers such as Hobbes and Locke rethought the entire relationship between religion and the state. Hobbes reversed the medieval two swords model; in his view, religion must be subordinate, once and for all, to the will of the secular ruler. Locke called for what we might call a functional separation of religion and the state. On his account, rulers were responsible solely for their citizens' secular interests – interests in protecting the things of this world. If Locke's views were accepted, the state would have no dominion over otherworldly matters such as the salvation of souls.

Church and state could go their separate ways.

# Notes

1   Martha C. Nussbaum, *Liberty of Conscience: In Defense of America's Tradition of Religious Equality*, Basic Books, New York 2008, pp. 354–355.
2   Robert Wright, *The Evolution of God*, Little, Brown, New York 2009, pp. 79–86.
3   Wright, *The Evolution of God*, p. 205.
4   Karen Armstrong, *A History of God: The 4000-Year Quest of Judaism, Christianity and Islam*, Ballantine, New York 1993, pp. 26, 49.
5   Wright, *The Evolution of God*, p. 336.
6   Jonathan Kirsch, *God against the Gods: The History of the War between Monotheism and Polytheism*, Penguin, New York 2004, p. 2.
7   Alister McGrath, *Heresy: A History of Defending the Truth*, HarperCollins, New York 2009, pp. 136–138.
8   Nussbaum, *Liberty of Conscience*, p. 355.
9   Charles Freeman, *The Closing of the Western Mind: The Rise of Faith and the Fall of Reason*, Vintage Books, New York 2005, p. 325.
10   Abdullahi Ahmed An-Na'im, *Islam and the Secular State: Negotiating the Future of Shari'a*, Harvard University Press, Cambridge, MA 2008, p. 31.
11   An-Na'im, *Islam and the Secular State*, pp. 129–130.
12   Bassam Tibi, *Islam's Predicament with Modernity: Religious Reform and Cultural Change*, Routledge, Oxford 2009, p. 104.
13   An-Na'im, *Islam and the Secular State*, pp. 118–119.
14   Tibi, *Islam's Predicament with Modernity*, p. 104.
15   McGrath, *Heresy*, p. 144.
16   Kirsch, *God against the Gods*, pp. 200–211.
17   Charles Freeman, *A.D. 381: Heretics, Pagans, and the Dawn of the Monotheistic State*, Overlook Press, New York 2008, pp. 25–26; Kirsch, *God against the Gods*, p. 274.

18  John Witte, Jr., *God's Joust, God's Justice: Law and Religion in the Western Tradition*, Wm. B. Eerdmans, Grand Rapids, MI 2006, pp. 11–13, 36–37, 80–81.
19  Marci A. Hamilton, *God vs. the Gavel: Religion and the Rule of Law*, Cambridge University Press, Cambridge 2007, pp. 242–243.
20  By this time, other means had taken over to mitigate the harshness of the law: these included transportation, exercise of the royal prerogative of mercy, and jury findings ascribing fictitiously low values to stolen items. For further discussion, readers might consult any standard legal history text, such as J. H. Baker, *An Introduction to English Legal History*, 4th edn, Butterworths, London 2002.
21  Rex Ahdar and Ian Leigh, *Religious Freedom in the Liberal State*, Oxford University Press, Oxford 2005, pp. 12–15.
22  Isaac Kramnick and R. Laurence Moore, *The Godless Constitution: A Moral Defense of the Secular State*, W. W. Norton, New York 2005, pp. 71–72.
23  Armstrong, *A History of God*, p. 275.
24  A. C. Grayling, *Towards the Light: The Story of the Struggles for Liberty and Rights that Made the Modern West*, Bloomsbury, London 2007, pp. 35–39.
25  Nussbaum, *Liberty of Conscience*, p. 35.
26  See generally Hamilton, *God vs. the Gavel*, pp. 252–254.
27  Ahdar and Leigh, *Religious Freedom in the Liberal State*, pp. 16–20.
28  Witte, *God's Joust, God's Justice*, 104–105.

# Introduction

Can the mere need for civil peace provide an adequate basis for religious freedom? Ahdar and Leigh suggest that this justification may seem self-interested, expedient, and unstable, rather than principled. If it were the only rationale, then freedom of religion might not be required in a nation with a very dominant religion and easily suppressed minorities. Moreover, they add, the opposing idea of a strong state religion has a long historical pedigree as an alternative basis for peace.[1]

Perhaps so, but the need for civil peace motivated much of the reconsideration of church–state relations in the seventeenth and eighteenth centuries. As flagged in the previous chapter, Hobbes and Locke wrote at a time when European civilization was tortured by religious conflict. A century later, the founding generation in the United States of America were intently aware of the suffering caused by religious impositions and persecutions.

Douglas Laycock suggests that three secular propositions suffice to justify a strong commitment to religious liberty, such as that shown by the founding fathers. First, attempts to suppress disapproved religious views had caused vast human suffering in England and Continental Europe, and this had been followed by similar, if smaller-scale, suffering in the American colonies. By the late eighteenth century, when America's constitutional arrangements were settled, hundreds of years of government efforts to establish religious uniformity had failed to produce peace. Second, beliefs about religion are often extraordinarily important to individuals, important enough to fight or die for, and this explained the costly failure of religious

*Freedom of Religion and the Secular State*, First Edition. Russell Blackford.
© 2012 John Wiley & Sons, Inc. Published 2012 by John Wiley & Sons, Inc.

suppression, as well as providing an independent reason to leave religion to the individuals and voluntary associations who cared most about it. Third, beliefs about such matters as theology, liturgy, and church governance were, and are, of little importance to civil government.

These three propositions, Laycock suggests, are not based on theology, but on history and experience. In accepting them, we can be neutral about religious doctrines with the exception of any religious doctrine that the state must or should support religion. If it has any commitment to liberty or even the avoidance of human suffering, a government that accepts these propositions will be rational to leave decisions about religion to individuals and voluntary groups.[2]

By itself, Laycock's approach does not provide a foundation for freedom of religion in any time, place, and circumstance whatsoever. In some circumstances, after all, disapproved religions might be suppressed successfully. So why not aim for the strong state religion mentioned by Ahdar and Leigh? Nonetheless, Laycock identifies compelling features of European Christendom's historical experience. The destructive history of persecution offers plentiful food for thought. That was already so when Hobbes addressed the issue in the middle years of the seventeenth century.

## The Hobbesian Analysis

Although Hobbes's greatest single work, *Leviathan*, consists largely of theological analysis to defend his model of the state, its main line of argument uses entirely secular reasoning. That is, Hobbes analyzes the function and operation of the state in terms of human beings' interests in the things of this world. His real concern is the human situation within the order of nature. In particular, he looks to our common interest in peace and security. The essential idea is the mutual advantage we can each gain by agreeing to live within constraints. To avoid defections from the agreement, its precise terms are set and enforced by an overwhelming sovereign power that we collectively place above ourselves.

The strengths of Hobbes's analysis include, first, its ability to explain the apparent need for the apparatus of the state, primarily as a mechanism to keep the peace within a geographical area. Related to this, it offers a plausible explanation of some main priorities within the criminal and civil law: suppressing violence and serious fraud; establishing a property regime, with some certainty of title; and protecting property from damage or theft. Second, the analysis is consistent with other traditional roles of the state, such as resisting foreign aggression, keeping people to their bargains, and imposing at least some limits on the volatile area of sexual and familial arrangements. Third, it allows room for the elements of economic, social, and sexual competition that seem to exist in all human societies, and for motivations that include biases toward ourselves and loved ones. These sit badly with strongly impartialist moral systems, but they are allowed in everyday moral judgment. In conformity with commonsense morality, Hobbes does not require any of us to act like moral saints or that the state attempt to make us saintly.

Despite all these attractions, the Hobbesian account of the state, and why we need it, has evident flaws. Consider its notoriously bleak picture of human nature and our reasons for establishing the state. As Hobbes tells the story, our mutual distrust and fear, together with our wish for personal glory, tempt us to pre-emptive or aggressive violence. It follows that we are naturally enemies of each other, doomed to undermine each other's positive projects and to lead lives that are "solitary, poore, nasty, brutish, and short."[3] If we were naturally disposed to assist each other and to cooperate, we could produce a better outcome for each individual, but Hobbes sees us as having no natural disposition to cooperate or to abide by agreements to do so. Accordingly, we must establish a power capable of coercing us to cooperate; we need the apparatus of the state as an enforcement mechanism.[4]

There are two sets of problems with all this. First, there are questions about how a social contract of this kind, agreed between self-interested rational maximizers, could even get off the ground. How could such beings begin to form societies? If human societies are the outcome of their attempt to contract out of a war of all against all, how could our predecessors ever have agreed upon, and managed to maintain, an adequate enforcement mechanism?[5] Indeed, Peter Singer asks, why should beings such as Hobbes describes even think of forming societies with each other?[6]

That we have human societies at all is one spur to the conjecture that our species is psychologically predisposed for social life in a way that Hobbes failed to appreciate. That conjecture can be supported by information and reasoning from many fields, including history, myth, and literature; by the observations and speculations of great philosophical writers – from antiquity, through Hume and Rousseau, to the present – who deny that we are merely, or overwhelmingly, self-interested; and, increasingly, by the theoretical knowledge obtained through science.[7] In his *Enquiry concerning the Principles of Morals*, David Hume succinctly illustrates our natural unwillingness to inflict on pain on others. Hume asks rhetorically, "Would any man, who is walking along, tread as willingly on another's gouty toes, whom he has no quarrel with, as on the hard flint and pavement?"[8] Elsewhere in the same book, Hume writes that we find "some particle of the dove kneaded into our frame, along with the elements of the wolf and the serpent."[9] For Hume, then, our nature is not narrowly and entirely self-seeking, but an alloy of selfishness and natural sympathy for others.

Without relying on controversial claims about human nature, based on evolutionary psychology for example, we should conclude that human beings are social animals, through and through. We are practiced in recognizing and relating to each other, primed to show at least some consideration for others' vulnerabilities, and predisposed to engage in various kinds of mutual solidarity and assistance. "Our bodies and minds are not designed for life in the absence of others," as Frans de Waal puts it.[10] Human societies, we may be confident, were never the outcome of prudential calculations, such as described by Hobbes, and never arose from a war of all against all.

Second, we must beware of approaching Hobbes's account as if it could provide the basis for a comprehensive system of morality. Used in that way, it would leave much unexplained about our actual norms of conduct and the feelings accompanying them. It could not, for example, explain the heavily moralized concern that many of us feel for the suffering of non-human animals, not to mention vulnerable or faraway humans who cannot reciprocate our help.[11] Perhaps, however, the theory doesn't need to be so comprehensive. It has a more limited role to play, and it does this with some success.

Though we are naturally responsive to each other, and even, perhaps, to some non-human animals, we are not entirely unselfish. In situations where resources are scarce, we may be tempted to violence and betrayal in pursuit of our individual interests. Even if most of us, most of the time, were inclined to keep the peace and act cooperatively, it takes relatively few people with different inclinations to cause suffering and strife. Worse, those people are not easily identified in advance. All this creates insecurity and encourages acts of pre-emption, even from individuals who might otherwise be inclined to keep the peace. Accordingly, some degree of social conflict is almost inevitable, even though the Hobbesian picture of human nature is, as I've suggested, far too bleak.

Perhaps small societies, such as pre-tribal hunting bands, can live with this problem, enduring a degree of internal violence but relying on social pressure and the personal authority of leaders and elders to contain it. In a small enough society, anti-social acts are difficult to hide or plan. Social prohibitions on such things as violence and stealing are upheld by tradition, local opinion, goodwill toward family members and tribal allies, and the lack of anonymity.[12] This suggests that human societies up to a certain level of size and complexity may be able to function with neither a recognizable state apparatus nor the sort of war of all against all feared by Hobbes. But larger, more complex societies would be impossible without the apparatus of the state, or something recognizably like it: some sort of multi-tiered political structure that keeps public order, and which the population as whole accepts as legitimate.

The larger and more complex the society, the more elaborate and sophisticated the state apparatus must become. Once it exists, the state keeps the peace by such means as establishing a system of property (some resources are taken from the commons and allocated to individuals or groups); sustaining a market for goods and services; and banning most uses of violence to obtain advantage. Some sports and exhibitions may provide limited, regulated scope for prowess in violent acts; otherwise, the expanding state increasingly monopolizes the use of force. In order to carry out these roles, the state must spend revenue on such institutions as police forces and criminal courts, but also systems of registration for major items of property such as allotments of land. In addition, it attempts to deter – and where necessary, to resist – attacks from external enemies, and must spend revenue on military personnel and equipment.

Reconstructed in these terms or something similar, the Hobbesian theory of the state is very plausible. It provides an explanation and justification of the state and its various agencies with no need for a religious foundation. On this account, the state does not provide a comprehensive system of morality; and individual citizens may find sources that they take to be authoritative, in addition to the secular laws, to guide how they act and live. The state aims at limited secular goals, such as peace and security, and the kind of material prosperity that these facilitate. However, it does not claim to know what is right and wrong, all things considered. If there is some higher good or ultimate end beyond ordinary human flourishing, the state knows nothing of it. It should view religious rivalries as just one more threat to peace, without attempting to judge their theological merits.

However, as Lilla explains, Hobbes feared inevitable conflicts between the followers of rival prophets or priests, each offering a distinctive path to salvation and viewing the others as threats. As long as the rival groups think their eternal lives are at stake, there can be no end to religious conflict – so Hobbes thought.[13] While this view of religion may appear cynical, it is understandable how things could appear so in the middle of the seventeenth century. Hobbes responded with an ultra-Constantinian solution: the secular ruler must take total command of religious doctrine and public worship, leaving no rival churches to promote civil strife. The ruler should not make inquisitions into the inner lives of the citizens, attempting to ascertain their true beliefs, but must control all external matters relating to religion.[14]

For Hobbes then, the essential point of the state is secular. It exists to provide peace and security, and all the worldly goods that these make possible. On such an account, however modified to deal with philosophical objections, and with developments since Hobbes's time, the apparatus of the state should be neutral about the truth of this or that religious teaching. Or so it might appear. Nonetheless, Hobbes concluded, the secular ruler cannot be merely indifferent to religious matters. To ensure that the peace is maintained, the ruler must suppress outward expressions of all religions except one. If we follow this argument to the end, secular reasoning shows the need for religious uniformity; no rivalry of religions can be allowed.

## Locke's Alternative

*Leviathan* is a tour de force. It remains inexhaustibly suggestive, and the radical rethinking displayed in its central argument is breathtaking in its scope and insight. Afterward, political philosophy could never be the same. For all that, its approach to religion is not in any sense liberal. For Hobbes, the cure for religious suppression, and the civil strife it causes, is . . . more thorough and effective suppression. He sees no hope for peace without complete outward religious conformity.

However, other thinkers of the seventeenth and eighteenth centuries moved decisively in the direction of modern liberal democracy. Even before *Leviathan* was published, Roger Williams, an English clergyman who had emigrated to America and founded the colony of Rhode Island, had developed a position that anticipated Locke's some 40 years later. In *The Bloody Tenent of Persecution* (published in London in 1644) and other writings, Williams followed a long line of ancient and medieval thinkers in identifying two spheres of human life, to be protected by the state and the church respectively. As usual, one sphere relates to such matters as property entitlements and bodily security, and the other to the soul and its safety. But Williams departs from medieval theorists of the two swords by constraining the role of the churches, as well as that of the state. For Williams, peace is in jeopardy when the churches overreach and attempt to make civil laws or interfere with such things as property, livelihood, and liberty.[15]

As a theorist of church–state relations, Hobbes was followed by Spinoza, Locke, Montesquieu, Hume, and Joseph Priestley. Of these, Locke was enormously influential, far beyond his own time, and was closely studied by American intellectuals of the following century. In *A Letter concerning Toleration*, he accepts the Hobbesian analysis insofar as he defines the role of the state in entirely secular terms. Like Hobbes, Locke thought of the state as the result of a social contract. But he drew totally different practical conclusions.

On Locke's account, men and women enter into social arrangements for mutual assistance and defense – against, for example, rapine, fraud, and foreign invasions. It is the role of the secular government to protect citizens from these things.[16] To this point, his analysis is broadly consistent with that of Hobbes. However, Locke's main line of argument identifies a distinction between the proper aims of government and those of spiritual teaching. For Locke, the apparatus of the state is directed to concern itself with "civil interests," which he defines as "Life, Liberty, Health, and Indolency of the Body; and the possession of outward things such as Money, Lands, Houses, Furniture, and the like." It is the duty of the secular ruler to provide protection for "these things belonging to this Life." The ruler's remit should not "be extended to the Salvation of Souls."[17] Unlike the two swords theory, this contains nothing about the power of the state being accountable to spiritual authority.

Locke reached these conclusions from within Protestant Christianity. His stated reasons for limiting the role of the secular ruler to protecting worldly things are, first, that God has not granted power over religion to the ruler, and the right to seek their own means of salvation is not something that citizens would give up to join in the social contract; second, that the kind of coercive force available to a secular ruler is inadequate to compel belief; and third, that taking on such a task would entail that souls be saved only in countries where the state enforces the correct religion.[18] This is a mix of secular and theological reasoning, but of course the Hobbesian analysis of the state lay in the background, and with it the argument that the essential point of the state is peace and security, and the worldly goods they allow, rather than any spiritual transformation.

By contrast with the state, Locke thought, a church is a free and voluntary society aimed at worship of God and the salvation of those involved.[19] Its only power is of teaching and excommunication, and it has no jurisdiction over those who do not belong to it.[20] Perhaps Locke oversimplifies – for a start, membership in a church or a religious community may not be all that voluntary. Many people are born into a religious community, then socialized into its viewpoint and practices; even if they come to feel estranged, exiting may be far from straightforward. But Locke's main point is the plausible one that religious organizations are focused on otherworldly doctrines and are ill-adapted for the exercise of secular power.

Thus, Locke proposes a functional separation of religion and the state. The state should act for entirely secular reasons, and should be in that sense neutral toward the different religious sects and churches. They, in turn, should not pursue political power or influence in an attempt to impose their doctrines on the people. While Hobbes might have seen this strict division of labor as a recipe for disaster, not trusting religious rivals to keep the peace, Locke thought that a diversity of religious opinion was unavoidable – yet relatively benign. On his account, civil strife does not arise from mere religious diversity or rivalry. Rather, its sources are the persecutorial practices of the state and the jockeying of religious leaders for secular power. Without these, violence and discord could be avoided.

The outcome of Locke's analysis is that violent rivalry between religions can be defused by adopting an independently convincing model of the state (in particular) and the church. On this model, the state exists and acts for reasons that are entirely secular. This much is completely consistent with an analysis such as that of Hobbes. But *pace* Hobbes, secular considerations do not compel the ruler to impose a single religious orthodoxy. Quite the contrary: the various sects will become more moderate if allowed to go about their business without persecution.

History has been kind to Locke. Hobbes had envisaged the rule of a sovereign with absolute power, thinking that any other model was impractical and unstable. For him, the choices were either: (1) a disastrous war of all against all, or (2) a sovereign with almost unlimited political authority. He failed to foresee that the apparatus of the state could be structured internally to allow it to carry out its essential functions, while also being limited in its power to intrude on various private matters such as speech and expression, reproductive rights, and religion. We now have ample experience of governments with important but limited powers – limited by internal structuring of the state apparatus itself, as well as by widely accepted political principles.

Moreover, Hobbes did not foresee that liberal democracies would eventually act in a way that was quite the opposite of what he proposed: limiting the possibilities for religious strife not by imposing a single religious orthodoxy, but by tolerating a vast range of religious viewpoints. To whatever extent the state confines itself to secular reasons for action, it undermines the motivation of the churches and sects to compete for the prize of political authority.

## Arguments for the Lockean Model

All this is fine in theory, and I suggest that the model put forward by Locke is, indeed, plausible, independently of the need for religious rivals to find a temporary *modus vivendi*. It's important to note that Locke is not proposing a mere compromise of rival groups' interests. His arguments are deeper than that, and more principled. However, that is not to say they are rationally compelling for all comers, irrespective of their starting positions.[21] Nor is it to suggest that the detailed views of Locke himself should be treated as sacrosanct and unmodifiable by those of us who basically endorse his model. Indeed, writing in the seventeenth century, Locke sometimes failed to take his own reasoning to its logical conclusion. We can go boldly where he held back.

As we've seen, Locke used a mix of theological and worldly arguments. His first is twofold: from a theological viewpoint, God has not given power over religion to the secular ruler; from the viewpoint of social contract thinking, this power is not one that citizens can be taken as having granted to the ruler in exchange for worldly benefits. Either way, the ruler does not legitimately possess this power. Clearly, the first limb of the argument involves a substantive, potentially controversial, theological claim. What if my starting point were a contrary theological view? I might begin with a collection of religious doctrines that must – according to the doctrines themselves – be promulgated to as many people as possible at all costs and by whatever means are necessary. If, as things seem to me, the stakes are high enough, shouldn't I favor persecutions? If I fear divine punishment in this life or the loss of many souls to eternal damnation, there may be nothing that Locke can say to persuade me to give up my theocratic inclinations without first giving up my theology.

At the same time, I am unlikely to accept the theory of a social contract if I began with a theocratic model of the legitimacy of the state. Even if I accept the legitimacy of the state for purely secular reasons, I may not be rationally compelled to accept social contract theory or Locke's specific version of it. The first line of argument is starting to look very shaky.

Still, Locke does have a powerful point that could be put in a different way: for many people, religious doctrines are so important that commitment to them trumps loyalty to the state. Thus Laycock is correct to highlight their extraordinary importance to adherents. As I pointed out in Chapter 1, religious adherents may feel that too much is at stake if they defect from their sects or churches, so much so that they'd prefer to forgo the benefits provided by the state than abandon their religious beliefs. As Greenawalt puts it, "Many people care deeply about their religious beliefs and practices, and they feel that their religious obligations supersede duties to the state if the two collide."[22]

Accordingly, Rawls makes a compelling point when he imagines us as rational bargainers sorting out sociopolitical arrangements behind a veil of ignorance about ourselves and our beliefs. In such a situation, we would wish to protect a number of basic liberties, including liberty of conscience and freedom of thought.[23] As even Hobbes recognized with the right of self-defense,[24] some areas of freedom are too important for people to surrender them to a sovereign power.

Putting all this in still another way, the state cannot reasonably expect its citizens to accept its theological authority. It certainly cannot expect persecuted religious adherents to accept its legitimacy, or to acknowledge whatever appeals it makes to the common good. For them, freedom to believe and to exercise their religion is a deal-breaker. A smart policy would be one that avoids pushing citizens so far. That's putting the conclusion at its weakest. A stronger conclusion, similar to Locke's, is that this is one area where the state lacks legitimate power and cannot rightly maintain that its citizens are under a political obligation to obey.

Locke's second argument is essentially that attempts at religious suppression are futile, since the coercive power of the state is not able to compel belief. At most, it can compel an appearance of conformity. A Christian theological spin on this would have it that God accepts only sincere belief, not outward shows compelled by torture or fears of punishment. In response, it might be suggested that the state can do at least *something* to alter the spread of beliefs among its citizens: it can, for example, embark on campaigns of propaganda for favored views and censorship of disfavored ones. Moreover, campaigns of suppression are sometimes successful, as John Stuart Mill laments in *On Liberty*:

> To speak only of religious opinions: the Reformation broke out at least twenty times before Luther, and was put down. Arnold of Brescia was put down. Fra Dolcino was put down. Savonarola was put down. The Albigeois were put down. The Vaudois were put down. The Lollards were put down. The Hussites were put down.[25]

Perhaps, then, Locke overstates the case. Nonetheless, successful suppressions have terrible human costs, and historical experience suggests that even the most resolute campaigns of propaganda and censorship, conducted by brutal totalitarian dictatorships such as the USSR under Stalin, have their limits in winning the hearts and minds of citizens. Considering the difficulties in obtaining short-term conversions to or from religion, discussed in Chapter 1, the costs of the game are simply not worth it. Absent some overriding moral imperative, or some compelling reason applicable to specific circumstances, the smart policy for the state is one of avoiding the waste of resources, incalculable costs, and likely futility involved in imposing or suppressing religions.

The third argument put forward by Locke is that state imposition of whichever religion is favored by the secular ruler, accompanied by the suppression of others, will result in souls being saved only in those countries where the correct religion is chosen. Thus, even from a theological viewpoint, it is better if religions can compete freely. That way more souls might be saved (or, we should add, other immensely valuable transformations might be achieved through the involvement of transcendent powers). Again, this may not convince everybody. Imagine you are a secular ruler who favors a particular religion, and believes that the consequences will be severe unless you do your utmost to promulgate it within your territories. Should you stay your hand from attempts at imposing your religion of choice? That might depend very much on the factual circumstances.

Say you are not convinced that religious impositions and suppressions are usually futile. Imagine, too, that the perceived costs of not going ahead – perhaps in large numbers of eternally damned souls – appear to be higher than any foreseeable human costs from a policy of imposition and suppression. Perhaps you should stay your hand if doing so assists the true religion in other countries. For example, you might refrain if you are bound by a multinational treaty that guarantees religious tolerance, and that might collapse if you violate its obligations. After all, you might be confident that the true religion will prevail if it is given a level playing field on which to compete with others. But in many circumstances, perhaps most, what happens in other countries may be little influenced by your own actions. In that case, shouldn't you go ahead? Since these circumstances are common, Locke's third argument has limited appeal.

But there are other arguments in the vicinity, even if they are not rationally compelling for a dyed-in-the-wool theocrat. Again, consider the historical record. Many state-level societies have existed over time, worshipping very many different gods. All of these societies have had some success in protecting the civil order, regardless what god or gods were invoked by their rulers or worshipped by their citizens. Yet, they cannot all have been serving the true religion. It starts to look as if the real point of the state is – as Hobbes and Locke both thought – related to things of this world, such as the provision of social peace and security, the protection of life and property, and so on.

In particular, the Hobbesian analysis of why the state is needed in the first place appears very plausible, once corrected for specific faults such Hobbes's unnecessarily pessimistic conception of human nature. Even from many religious viewpoints, we might draw the conclusion that Hobbes was essentially correct: internal peace and protection of worldly interests are not all there is to human life, but these secular goods are what actually justify the apparatus of the state. To varying extents, they were actually obtained by the many ordered societies in history whose people worshipped false gods, or followed religions with no gods at all. *These* goods are what the state can reasonably provide.

Further consideration of the ancient pagan societies supports this. In those societies, the state apparatus was tolerant of a wide range of beliefs and practices. Any compulsory rites were aimed at pleasing deities who – so it was hoped – would bless the polity with secular rewards. In a sense then, ancient *state* religion, at least, was an adjunct to the state's role in protecting things of this world. Citizens were free to seek spiritual transformation on their own time, as it were, without state interference. In classical antiquity, this might have involved the embrace of one of the many mystery cults. Most notably, however, the worldly success of different societies throughout history has had little to do with what gods were worshipped as part of an official cult. Viewed in this way, it starts to seem that the official religious practices of the pagan societies were an ineffectual and dispensable adjunct to the state's more essential role – that is, a worldly one.

It looks as if the state apparatus can do a reasonably effective job of maintaining order, protecting citizens, and advancing ordinary human flourishing. By contrast, it has no expertise in any otherworldly order of things, in identifying goods that transcend human flourishing, or in assisting with whatever transformations are needed to obtain these transcendent goods. It has no business with the salvation of souls, or anything analogous, because this is simply beyond its competence. Rather than favoring the views of one or other religion, the state should allow them all to pursue their own goals, as long as they don't produce civil harms.

Nor should the state defer to any religion's claimed expertise in how worldly things are best protected. In practice, religions do concern themselves with this-worldly matters such as the plight of the poor, here and now, or the (real or supposed) rights of human embryos or fetuses. While the state may adopt policies relating to these things, it should not simply adopt religious canons of behavior, nor should it base its policies on otherworldly reasoning – such as that certain practices are detrimental to salvation or opposed by a god, or that others are required by an all-wise spiritual source. However, the state is quite able to develop or employ expertise relating to the natural order and human sociability, and to apply that expertise to matters of practical governance. It should make independent decisions about how to play its secular role, uninfluenced by such considerations as the preferred means of salvation, the preferences of a deity, or the wisdom residing in a religious tradition.

Again, I emphasize that these arguments for the state to confine itself to secular considerations will not appeal equally to everyone. To take the clearest example, they will not convince somebody who starts out with a doctrine, supposedly revealed by a god, that the state must impose such and such a religion. When we ask such a person to bracket off her religious commitments, it may be asking too much. Not necessarily too much to *want* from her, but too much to anticipate that she could ever deliver. If we expect the more theocratic sects to soften, to relinquish their pursuit of social and political dominance, we are expecting a transformation. In such a case, as J. Judd Owen puts it: "The political molds the subpolitical."[26]

In practice, it may be impossible to persuade a committed religious adherent to abandon theocratic ambitions without first convincing her to abandon her religion itself – or at least the sect or school of interpretation that she adheres to. That, in turn, may be very difficult, given the previously mentioned problems with disproving otherworldly claims to the satisfaction of a committed believer. Even prior to the establishment of liberal political arrangements, however, many or most people could accept that there is a difference between the goods of this world and those of another world or an afterlife. For that reason, and because of the natural limits of human understanding, civil magistrates are likely to be fallible in regard to heavenly matters.[27] For Locke, most religious believers are not, at heart, religious zealots with theocratic tendencies. Religion is not so important to them as the religious wars seemed to indicate. They are not inclined to revolutionary zeal if their primary needs are met. Owen again:

> All they need is a healthy sense of their own interests – interests that by nature are the most powerful spring of their actions. One need not be an epistemologist in order to know that oneself and one's property are safer in times of peace than in times of war; safer in times of war, when the regime has money and soldiers; and safer in times of peace, when the laws are enforced.[28]

In established liberal democracies, many people – perhaps most – will find some version or extension of Locke's arguments convincing. Such arguments should certainly convince non-religious people: those who believe in the existence only of the natural order. But they should also convince many religious people. Some may be persuaded by Locke's theological claim that God has not granted authority over religion to the secular ruler, and has charged secular rulers solely with worldly tasks. Others may be persuaded by the secular arguments. Weighty and converging considerations lead to a conclusion that the real *point* of the state is to protect things of this world, relying solely upon worldly knowledge. These considerations should convince adherents to any religious viewpoint that does not directly contradict them on a basis such as revelation.

## Implications

Note, however, that the Lockean model does not solve all problems that might involve religious (or anti-religious) views. In this section, I'll explore some of the model's difficulties and potential complexities.

If we follow Locke, the state does not have theological reasons to impose a preferred religion or to persecute dispreferred sects. This enables him to argue for the freedom of other religions, in addition to the Christian churches.[29] Adherents of all religious views, with only a few specific exceptions, should be free to preach, teach, or profess their doctrines. In itself, Locke argues, this could not harm the worldly interests of others. He suggests that persuasion could be used by the secular ruler, but not force,[30] though it might be questioned whether this is consistent with his main line of argument. Both are outside the state's *raison d'être* as Locke portrays it.

If the function of the state is to protect the things of this world, what business does it have even trying to *persuade* the citizens to adopt one or other means of spiritual salvation? While the ruler, as an individual with personal religious views, might have a desire to save souls, Locke is clear that this is not the role of the state apparatus.[31] He does not, however, tease out that distinction. Of course, it's one that can be drawn more readily in twenty-first-century liberal democracies than was possible in seventeenth-century monarchies. Still, an issue remains in current debates: How acceptable is it for the state to give its endorsement to a religious view, without taking coercive action? Arguably, it has no business doing either.

Though the model requires the state to tolerate many religions, it allows for exceptions. It does not rule out the persecution of religion in all circumstances whatsoever, merely persecutions that are based on theological preferences. On Locke's approach, persecutions would need to be justified by sufficiently weighty secular reasons, which might be rare, especially when balanced against the human costs. But they are allowed in principle. Nor, *pace* Locke himself, should the model rule out special accommodations for religion if there are compelling reasons based on the state's worldly purposes. These might also be relatively rare, as they will have costs that must be weighed in the policy balance. But again, they are not entirely ruled out.

In later chapters I will deal more fully with both of these issues. For now, I'll confine my discussion to Locke's own examples. Locke made exceptions to his proposed scheme of toleration, but did not notice that his model should, at least in principle, allow accommodations. First, let us consider the exceptions to toleration.

The point here is that a secular ruler could find good *worldly* reasons to suppress certain viewpoints. It is one thing to refrain from persecutions based on theological motives; it is another to hesitate if persecution appears necessary to protect the citizenry's secular interests. Thus, on Locke's account, the ruler should not tolerate views that are contrary to human society or to morals necessary for the preservation of civil society, such as the view that people need not keep promises, that princes can be dethroned if they differ from the speaker's religion, or that the dominion of all things belongs to the speakers themselves. Likewise, the ruler should not tolerate such views as that faith is not to be kept with heretics or that joining the speaker's religion requires subjection to a foreign power.[32] For Locke, this kind of reasoning justifies persecution of Catholics (for their loyalty to the Vatican) and Muslims (for their supposed loyalty to the Ottoman Empire).

Perhaps most notoriously, Locke argues that atheists must not be tolerated, since atheists have no pretense of a religion to rely upon, and also because, supposedly, they cannot be trusted to keep their promises, covenants, and oaths.[33] As to the first point, however, this is not logical given the scheme of the overall argument: a state apparatus devoted solely to the protection of worldly things would not have a *theological* reason to persecute atheists, and an atheist need not claim any otherworldly beliefs in order to argue against persecution. All she needs to claim is that the state has no secular reason to persecute her. Surely the onus is on the state to provide such a reason, but the atheist can go further and positively argue that she offers no threat to civil society. This, however, leads to Locke's second point, which has some superficial merit. Recall that Locke is assuming that citizens cannot be trusted to keep promises, and so on, unless motivated by fear that successful deceit in this life will be punished in an afterlife. Thus, he assumes a residual role for religion in the sense of bare belief in god or gods, an afterlife, and divine punishment.

Of course, Locke had no experience of a society where atheism is widespread. Indeed, real atheism – atheism as thoughtful disbelief in the existence of any god or gods – was virtually unknown in Europe in 1689. During the seventeenth century, the condemnatory epithet "atheist" was commonly applied to individuals, such as Hobbes, who had unorthodox worldviews by Christian standards, but probably believed in a deity of some kind. If any atheists at all existed in Europe in Locke's day, they certainly were not in such numbers as to allow him to draw robust conclusions about their behavior. In later centuries, however, atheism became a live option, culminating in the current situation when many Europeans disclaim any belief in gods or an afterlife. This has not caused social collapse in European countries or a breakdown in their legal systems. By now, the fair conclusion to draw is that atheists are no more likely than anyone else to renege on promises, covenants, and oaths (or at least solemn affirmations). More generally, no residual role for religion is required in the Lockean model; you can be a perfectly good citizen, by Locke's own standards, without any belief in an afterlife.

As things have turned out, there is no good reason for persecution of atheists. Something similar applies to Catholics and Muslims. Overwhelmingly, loyalty to foreign powers has not undermined the patriotism or good citizenship of either group. I must emphasize, however, that Locke is not being inconsistent or hypocritical in arguing for religious tolerance, and then making exceptions for certain disliked groups. He offers *worldly* reasons why specific groups are a danger to civil society, and why they must be suppressed by the rest of us in self-defense, with the might of the state acting on our behalf. Within the Lockean model, this is a perfectly legitimate move.

The moral, perhaps, is that we should be reluctant to dream up secular reasons for persecutions, however plausible they may seem as a matter of theory. At the same time, there could be circumstances where a sect's actions in this world pose a threat to other citizens' worldly interests. In such circumstances the state needs to weigh up the costs and benefits of taking some kind of hostile action against the sect. There may still be many reasons for it to hold back, given the likelihood of severe human costs and the difficulty of predicting them accurately. A gung-ho, overoptimistic attitude should be avoided, and policy should probably err on the side of toleration. At the end of the day, nonetheless, there may be some compelling reason to act coercively.

In *A Letter concerning Toleration*, Locke offers no room for special accommodations of religion, but his model should not rule them out in principle. Consider the possible effects of non-persecutorial laws of general application. These may be enacted by the state for the purpose of protecting worldly interests, yet also create problems for one or other set of religious adherents. The examples used by Locke himself succinctly illustrate the problem.

According to Locke, the secular ruler may require the washing of children if it is thought to cure or prevent disease but not in order to save their souls, as with infant baptism.[34] So far, so good; this fits the logic of his model. Likewise, he thinks, the ruler may forbid infant sacrifice or religious rites involving sexual promiscuity – the suggestion is that killing infants and engaging in promiscuous orgies are the sorts of things that can be banned for secular reasons.[35] All that is required is that laws against, say, killing infants, or taking part in promiscuous orgies, apply across society generally. But this creates an obvious problem. Exactly what *worldly* reason does the state have for banning promiscuous orgies? Perhaps Locke assumes that strict heterosexual monogamy is necessary for social survival, but of course history suggests otherwise. It looks as if Locke is biased by Christian morality in offering examples of what the state could do for secular reasons. For the moment, I'll set this aside – but I'll need to return to it.

The other aspect of all this is that the state may end up taking actions that seem persecutorial, even though motivated by purely secular reasoning. Consider Locke's example of animal sacrifice. Locke insists that the secular ruler cannot use religious reasons to forbid sacrificing calves. However, the ruler may have perfectly acceptable worldly reasons to ban all slaughter of cattle, which will apply equally to a sect that includes animal sacrifice among its rituals:

> But if peradventure such were the state of things, that the Interest of the Commonwealth required all slaughter of Beasts should be forborn for some while, in order to the increasing of the stock of Cattel, that had been destroyed by some extraordinary Murrain; Who sees not that the Magistrate, in such a case, may forbid all his Subjects to kill any Calves for any use whatsoever? Only 'tis to be observed, that in this case the Law is not made about a Religious, but a Political matter: nor is the Sacrifice, but the Slaughter of Calves thereby prohibited.[36]

The idea is that whatever is generally lawful should also be lawful in church (or other religious meeting places), but whatever is unlawful for good worldly reasons can be made unlawful in church. As long as those requirements are met, no sect can claim that it is being persecuted, and indeed deliberate persecution will be (almost) ruled out. Locke does add that the ruler should always be very careful not to misuse state authority by oppressing a church under pretense of the public good. Thus, he seems to oppose laws that are contrivances, where the secular purpose invoked by the state is a pretense to conceal hostility towards one or other sect.[37] Still, he seems to rule out exemptions for religious adherents from general laws, while encouraging some reluctance, or at least care, before enacting laws that might harm particular religions.

On Locke's model of the state, all this seems reasonable. The state should not impose a preferred religion or, without doing so, persecute religions that it dislikes. But it cannot be accused of either of these things if it merely enacts a law for good secular reasons. As it might be said in modern legalese, neither the purpose nor the primary effect (nor, perhaps we could add, a disproportionate effect) of such an enactment is to persecute a sect or to impose a religious viewpoint. Still, does the state have *no business at all* in assisting religious sects that are adversely affected by its legitimate laws? Consider again the situation where the state needs to take action to replenish the stock of cattle.

While a religious sect that practices the sacrifice of calves cannot plausibly argue that it is being persecuted – harming the sect is neither the state's intention nor the primary effect of its action – enforcement of the law may well *feel like* persecution if you're on the receiving end. Even if the legislators bear no hostility toward the religion concerned, might they not consider the effect of the law on religious practitioners? How difficult would it be to frame the law in such a way that it does not include ritual sacrifices? This might, of course, depend on circumstances: the exemption will have less effect on the state's program for replenishing cattle stock if the number of calves sacrificed is actually very small (perhaps because the sect itself is small, or perhaps because sacrifices are infrequent). On the other hand, the effect on the religious might feel less onerous if their god is prepared to accept sacrifices of some other animal – goats, perhaps, or sheep – instead of calves. Likewise, if sacrifices of calves are not considered mandatory, but are merely optional acts of worship that can be waived in difficult times.

Still, what if these sacrifices are mandatory, and the sect considers them essential for spiritual salvation? If Locke's model of the state is generally acceptable, the secular ruler should not be motivated by any belief in the sect's doctrine or by an intention to impose their religion on others. But again, does it have *no worldly reason at all* to show consideration to the sect's adherents? Might the state not take into account that it is forcing the conscience of a group of its citizens, or placing them in a position where they feel their spiritual salvation is at risk? The state may, in fact, have legitimate reasons to do neither of these lightly. It may be motivated by something as simple as compassion, by the prospect of civil unrest if certain sects feel persecuted (even if wrongly), and perhaps by considerations of fairness or justice if other sects have been given analogous concessions in the past, or if it is well known that they would be in analogous circumstances. If the state offers an exemption for reasons of this kind, it does not necessarily create the appearance of imposing a religion, especially if it shows leniency to different and even opposed religions from time to time.

Still, significant concessions for the sake of conscience or supernatural fears may undermine the efficacy of secular laws enacted for good purposes. Likewise, they may be unfair to others, who will have to bear an additional burden. For example, exemptions to a law forbidding the slaughter of cattle may require that the prohibition be maintained for longer than it would have been otherwise. That may lead to resentment, even justified resentment, from what we'd now call the meat industry – not to mention the wider population.

There is much more to say about such situations, and I'll return to the problem in a later chapter (Chapter 6). At this point, however, it is noteworthy that Locke saw religion and conscience as protected by the relatively narrow remit given to the state.[38] Thus, if the ruler commands a person to embrace a strange religion and join in its ceremonies, Locke held that the person was permitted to refuse. This would be an example of the state exceeding its remit. But what if the ruler determined something to be for the public good, as defined, but an individual disagreed? Here, Locke suggests that the ruler may prevail, but ultimately God will judge who is right.

The general rule is that when the secular ruler gives a command that goes against the individual's conscience, the individual must obey. However, this is unlikely to happen, Locke argues, so long as the government rules for the public good, that is to protect worldly interests, and does not concern itself with matters relating to another order of things. Unfortunately, our current situation is not so straightforward, as I'll discuss in Chapter 6: as the state's functions have expanded, the possible conflicts between secular legislation and religious conscience have multiplied. That is not a reason to return to the medieval doctrine that the state serves religion, which could only make things worse, but it at least requires that the Lockean model be updated to serve contemporary social reality.

# Legacy

The legacy of Hobbes, Locke, and other thinkers of the seventeenth century is a rich tradition of philosophical and political thought pertaining to the functions and limits of state power. Hobbes and Locke thought and wrote against a background of terrible social dislocations: the wars of religion; religion-tinged political struggles between great European dynasties; and the ruinous conflict between the British Crown and parliament. The troubled times, and the personal perils they faced, provided the occasion for fundamentally rethinking the proper relationship between secular political power and the claims of religion.

But the struggles didn't end there. They continued into later centuries, as various parties sought to establish sectarian dominance or to obtain religious freedom. In Britain, a critical confrontation took place during the eighteenth century, involving supporters and opponents of the Test and Corporation Acts, which had been passed during Charles II's reign. Though they were originally directed at Catholics, the main victims of these statutes during the eighteenth century were actually Protestant dissenters. They required military and civil officers under the Crown, and all municipal officers, to receive the sacrament of the Lord's Supper according to the rites of the Anglican Church, and to make a declaration against the Catholic doctrine of transubstantiation.

By the late eighteenth century, high-achieving dissenters were seeking the repeal of the Test and Corporation Acts, closely watched by co-religionists in America. The attempted repeal was opposed successfully by conservatives, most notably Edmund Burke, who saw religion as a solemn responsibility of the secular ruler. The statutes were not finally repealed until 1829. Opposed to Burke and the other conservatives was the great chemist Joseph Priestley, whom we might think of as the Richard Dawkins of his time. Priestley was also an outspoken supporter of the French and American revolutions, and he endured bitter hostility from religious conservatives. In 1791 a rioting mob burned down his house and laboratory, along with the homes of other dissenters. He was eventually forced to emigrate to America, where he lived from 1794 until his death 10 years later.

As Kramnick and Moore point out, Priestley was a close friend and correspondent of Benjamin Franklin and Thomas Jefferson. Along with Locke, he influenced the American conception of a secular state, separated from religious institutions. An important ally of Priestley, and another major influence on Jefferson and others, was James Burgh, a Scottish dissenter and political writer, who advocated the Lockean view that the state merely serve worldly interests.[39] In the event, the framers of the Constitution rejected ideas of state-enforced religious uniformity, and took an approach much closer to that of Locke. They committed the newly created United States of America to an option of "separating religious correctness from public policy."[40]

Such a view is crystallized in the First Amendment to the United States Constitution, but the legal meaning of its words remains disputed, not least among judges of the US Supreme Court. Meanwhile, analogous legal protections have gradually been included in the constitutions of many other nations, and in international legal instruments such as United Nations conventions and the European Convention on Human Rights. In each instance, these protections can be given more or less radical or conservative interpretations, with the result that legal wrangling over freedom of religion continues in many jurisdictions throughout the world.

## Conclusion

As explicated, and somewhat adjusted, in this chapter, the Lockean model is not merely an expedient and unstable *modus vivendi* – rather, it provides a principled case for the functional separation of religion and the apparatus of the state. This model requires the state to act for its own secular reasons, based on knowledge that pertains solely to the order of this world. It should place no reliance on the doctrines of one or another religion. If any religion is to be persecuted, it must be for a good secular reason, and good secular reasons must also be given if religious groups are given special exemptions from the general law (something that Locke himself does not countenance). Those reasons might include the undesirability, other things being equal, of bringing coercive power to bear so as to force a believer's conscience.

The Lockean model tends to defuse the recurrent problem of religious persecution and warfare, while offering an independently attractive explanation of state power. From Locke's own point of view, however, it may actually prove too much. When taken to its logical conclusion, that is, it may have more radical implications than he realized, or would have welcomed. For one thing, it turns out that there is no plausible basis for persecuting atheists, Catholics, or Muslims, though there might be a basis to crack down on a sufficiently fanatical atheist community, Catholic prelature, or Muslim sect, if it became a danger to civil society.

Again, when taken to its logical conclusion the model permits far more in the way of "immoral" behavior than would have been palatable to Locke's opponents or to Locke himself. If he were charged by opponents with permitting sexual immorality, he'd be on shaky ground in denying it. As a matter of logic, that is not fatal to the model; on the contrary, the correct conclusion may simply be that the state should permit promiscuous orgies, whether in church or elsewhere. In principle, Locke could bite the bullet and accept this conclusion. Alternatively, he could attempt to argue that sexual restrictions (to the extent of confining sex to monogamous, heterosexual marriages) are necessary for social stability. After all, human societies have invariably imposed at least some constraints on sexual behavior.

But even if this argument was plausible in Locke's time, it is decidedly less so today, thanks to modern developments in hygiene, medicine, and especially contraception. By appropriate secular standards, relating to the relevant things of this world (such as individual and public health) there might be reasons for the state to take *some* action to encourage certain kinds of sexual behavior rather than others. But the best policy for the purpose might involve sex education in schools, the encouragement of "safe sex," and other relatively non-coercive steps, rather than blanket criminal bans of promiscuity or supposedly illicit sexual behavior – let alone bans on an obscure religious cult's sex rites.

More generally, the Lockean model tends to separate the reasons for state action, not only from religious morality but also from any traditional morality that does not actually assist in the protection of worldly things. Once more, Locke could bite the bullet and accept this point; in strict logic it does not undermine the model. On the contrary, it may be a useful and welcome implication. It is not, however, one that would have been welcomed in 1689 by either Locke or his critics. Nor is it a welcome conclusion to modern-day religious conservatives and legal moralists.

In a sense, therefore, the Lockean model created a ticking bomb: it had radical implications for the role of the state in imposing moral legislation.

# Notes

1   Rex Ahdar and Ian Leigh, *Religious Freedom in the Liberal State*, Oxford University Press, Oxford 2005, pp. 52–54.
2   Douglas Laycock, "Religious Liberty as Liberty," 1st pub. 1996, in *Religious Liberty*, vol. 1: *Overviews and History*, Wm. B. Eerdmans, Grand Rapids, MI 2010, pp. 54–102, pp. 58–61.
3   Thomas Hobbes, *Leviathan*, 1st pub. 1651, Hackett, Indianapolis 1994, p. 76.
4   Hobbes, *Leviathan*, p. 89.
5   J. L. Mackie, *Ethics: Inventing Right and Wrong*, Penguin, London 1977, pp. 120–124.
6   Peter Singer, *The Expanding Circle: Ethics and Sociobiology*, Farrar, Straus & Giroux, New York 1981, p. 24.
7   Howard Kahane, *Contract Ethics: Evolutionary Biology and the Moral Sentiments*, Rowman & Littlefield, Lanham, MD 1995, pp. 8–9.
8   David Hume, *An Enquiry concerning the Principles of Morals*, 1st pub. 1751, Prometheus Books, Amherst, NY 2004, p. 61.
9   Hume, *An Enquiry concerning the Principles of Morals*, p. 109.
10  Frans de Waal, "Morally Evolved: Primate Social Instincts, Human Morality, and the Rise and Fall of 'Veneer Theory,'" in Frans de Waal et al., *Primates and Philosophers: How Morality Evolved*, Princeton University Press, Princeton 2006, pp. 1–80, p. 5.
11  Peter Singer, *Practical Ethics*, 2nd edn, Cambridge University Press, Cambridge 1993, pp. 80–81.
12  Robert Wright, *The Evolution of God*, Little, Brown, New York 2009, pp. 20–26.
13  Mark Lilla, *The Stillborn God*, Alfred A. Knopf, New York 2007, pp. 83–85.
14  Lilla, *The Stillborn God*, pp. 86–90.

15 For detailed discussion of Williams, see Martha C. Nussbaum, *Liberty of Conscience: In Defense of America's Tradition of Religious Equality*, Basic Books, New York 2008, pp. 34–71.
16 John Locke, *A Letter concerning Toleration*, 1st pub. 1689, Hackett, Indianapolis 1983, pp. 47–48.
17 Locke, *A Letter concerning Toleration*, p. 26.
18 Locke, *A Letter concerning Toleration*, pp. 26–28.
19 Locke, *A Letter concerning Toleration*, p. 28.
20 Locke, *A Letter concerning Toleration*, pp. 30–31.
21 Kent Greenawalt, *Religion and the Constitution*, vol. 2: *Establishment and Fairness*, Princeton University Press, Princeton 2008, pp. 442–443.
22 Kent Greenawalt, *Religion and the Constitution*, vol. 1: *Fairness and Free Exercise*, Princeton University Press, Princeton 2006, p. 3.
23 John Rawls, *A Theory of Justice*, 1st edn, Harvard University Press, Cambridge, MA 1971, pp. 60–65; rev. edn 1999, pp. 52–56.
24 Hobbes, *Leviathan*, p. 87.
25 J. S. Mill, *On Liberty*, 1st pub. 1859, Penguin, London 1974, p. 89.
26 J. Judd Owen, *Religion and the Demise of Liberal Rationalism: The Foundational Crisis of the Separation of Church and State*, University of Chicago Press, Chicago 2001, p. 126.
27 Owen, *Religion and the Demise of Liberal Rationalism*, pp. 157–158.
28 Owen, *Religion and the Demise of Liberal Rationalism*, p. 29.
29 Locke, *A Letter concerning Toleration*, pp. 42–54.
30 Locke, *A Letter concerning Toleration*, pp. 46–47.
31 But see Greenawalt, *Religion and the Constitution*, vol. 2, p. 21. Greenawalt thinks it clear that Locke is countenancing the highest officials expressing support for particular religions in their official capacity. However, he adds that this "lies in tension with the limited role [Locke] ascribes to government."
32 Locke, *A Letter concerning Toleration*, pp. 49–51.
33 Locke, *A Letter concerning Toleration*, p. 51.
34 Locke, *A Letter concerning Toleration*, pp. 39–40.
35 Locke, *A Letter concerning Toleration*, pp. 41–42.
36 Locke, *A Letter concerning Toleration*, p. 42.
37 Locke, *A Letter concerning Toleration*, p. 42.
38 Locke, *A Letter concerning Toleration*, pp. 48–49.
39 Isaac Kramnick and R. Laurence Moore, *The Godless Constitution: A Moral Defense of the Secular State*, W. W. Norton, New York 2005, pp. 78–83.
40 Kramnick and Moore, *The Godless Constitution*, p. 177.

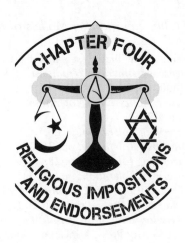

CHAPTER FOUR

RELIGIOUS IMPOSITIONS AND ENDORSEMENTS

## Introduction

If we follow the Lockean model, religion and the state should go their separate ways, and the state should act only for secular reasons, not to support or oppose doctrines relating to another world or to supernatural agents and powers. That, of course, leaves much detail to be filled in. In this chapter, I'll consider such questions as whether the state should endorse religion in any way and how it should deal with historically established religions such as the Church of England. In Chapter 5 I'll turn to whether it should enforce religious morality.

Related to all these issues is the question of how far the state's powers should be held in check by constitutional provisions, as opposed to unwritten political principles that are widely recognized by citizens and honored by legislatures. Constitutional protections relating to religious freedom, such as those in the First Amendment, may not be sufficient to guarantee a functional separation of church and state, but this does not mean that they are simply useless. Such provisions may be successful in stopping many oppressive laws. Other laws may be stopped by different constitutional provisions, while still others may be blocked by the political culture and principles of a liberal democracy.

I don't propose in the following chapters to enter into complex questions of how constitutional provisions should be drafted – for example, whether the US Bill of Rights is in some sense better or worse as a legal instrument than the Canadian Charter of Rights and Freedoms or the European Convention on Human Rights. All of these documents, and others with similar purposes, may have their share of merits and flaws. Moreover, each must be interpreted in accordance with its actual wording, its historical context, and, at least to some extent, its accumulated body of associated case law. I do, however, propose to discuss more general considerations that affect the interpretation of such documents.

A good place to begin is with religious establishments. Here we find the most blatant impositions of religion by the state, but even here there is no absolute rule requiring urgent disestablishment.

## Religious Establishment

A secular state is not one that is hostile or persecutory toward religion, merely one that acts for secular or worldly reasons (bracketing off the things of another world). As Locke puts it, the secular state aims at protecting "these things belonging to this Life."[1] It appears obvious that a secular state has no business in declaring any particular religion to be correct, or in promoting its doctrines, and that it certainly has no business establishing an official religion within its jurisdiction. The state does not need to separate itself from religion entirely: for example, churches and mosques should have the same legal right as secular organizations to assistance from publicly funded police and emergency services. However, the state does not exist to promote doctrines aimed at rightness with God, salvation of souls, escape from the round of *samsara*, or other such benefits.

Perhaps, however, we shouldn't move so quickly. Might not a modern government, in its attempt to achieve secular objectives, adopt a policy of judiciously assisting some religions and hindering others? Legislators and other officials need have no actual belief or disbelief in any religious doctrines, merely a calculated pursuit of worldly outcomes. What is wrong with this approach?

For a start, such an attitude could undermine much of what makes the secular state so attractive in the first place, namely its promise of religious peace. Still, it might be pressed, the state could adopt a policy of refraining from persecutions except in carefully chosen cases, combining a general environment of religious toleration with astutely selected exceptions that advance secular interests. Indeed, there is a sense in which this argument is unanswerable – there *may* be a case for one-off exceptions to almost any political principle if the need is sufficiently compelling. Nonetheless, secular officials should not be too Machiavellian. They should be mindful of the good worldly reasons for ongoing official neutrality about religion. As history demonstrates abundantly, state intolerance of any particular religion, of religion in general, or of all religions except one that is favored, can lead to terrible results. Intervention to enforce an official preference (adopted for whatever reasons) might have endless and perhaps catastrophic ramifications, such as social division, stigma and misery, and violent civil conflict.[2]

I submit, therefore, that the secular state should fulfill its promise of religious peace by avoiding any promotion of one or another religion as the official doctrine within its territory. Moreover, given the long history of favored religions persecuting others through the power of the state, any positive act to establish a religion, even in the weak sense of promoting its doctrines, carries an element of menace. This increases the more a religion becomes integrated into the state's activities and deliberations. Establishment all too easily leads to imposition, which results in persecutions. Thus, constitutional rules forbidding the establishment of any religion can be useful in two respects. First, they discourage governments and electorates that might be inclined to impose their favored religious views, in violation of the whole idea of a secular state. Second, they discourage the standing temptation to cunning political rulers to employ the judicious encouragement of one or other religion, not for its own sake but as an arm of secular policy.

Once again, I cannot rule this out in all possible circumstances – no matter how extraordinary and compelling. After all, I've conceded that there could even be cases where the state has secular reasons to suppress a sufficiently fanatical and dangerous sect. That much granted, perhaps the state could also respond more subtly, undermining the sect by promoting a more moderate rival. My point is a weaker one, that such actions may be all too tempting, despite their potential dangers. It is all to the good, then, if religious establishments are forbidden by constitutional provisions. Even where these provisions don't exist, religious establishments should be considered almost unthinkable as a matter of political principle.

Nonetheless, Ahdar and Leigh offer a limited defense of established churches, such as those of Denmark, Finland, Norway, Iceland, Greece, and the United Kingdom (the Church of England and Church of Scotland). More generally they conclude that a "mild or weak form of establishment," one "where the state does not coerce or compel religious practice or observance," is compatible with freedom of religion.[3] Once again, there's a sense in which this is unanswerable. If freedom of religion is thought of, as I suggest it should be, primarily as freedom from *persecution*, it is surely obvious that no one is actually being persecuted if the state's promotion or special acknowledgment of a religion involves no element of coercion or compulsion. Conversely, a state that did little or nothing to promote any particular religion might nonetheless persecute particularly despised or feared religions from time to time.

Ahdar and Leigh also make the legitimate point that countries such as the United Kingdom do not start with a clean slate. Because church establishment antedates attempts to establish a secular and liberal state apparatus, the issue is about positive moves, whether comprehensive or incremental, to *dis*establish.[4] Even from a secular viewpoint, this may have a different impact from merely refusing to establish a religion or church in the first place. In many cases, the dislocation and ill-will that disestablishment would generate might make it more trouble than it's worth. After all, the countries with formally established religions include some of the most secular and liberal in the world. In these countries, establishment is not generating persecutions. Nor, apparently, is it seriously distorting the state's processes of policy deliberation. Denmark and the rest are far from being theocracies.

Thus, positive and total disestablishment may often be a low priority – at least for now, and into the indefinite future. Still, current establishments take a variety of forms: for example, the Church of Scotland is quite separate from the state and thus plays a different role from the Church of England's. There is an obvious problem if the secular state includes decision-makers with a formal remit to consider issues on other-worldly grounds. Accordingly, church leaders, in their official capacities as such, should not wield any part of the power of the state. Consider the Church of England, then. All things considered, it may be acceptable, even desirable, to permit its ongoing establishment, including its involvement in such ceremonial functions as coronation of the monarch. However, steps should be taken to remove formal political power from churches or sects. Like Denmark, the United Kingdom is not a theocracy, but the entitlement for certain bishops of the Church of England to sit in the House of Lords cannot be defended. Unlike disestablishment itself, removal of this privilege should be a political priority in the UK.

In a context where religious establishment does not already exist, any steps by the state to promote a religion or its doctrines should be avoided for all the reasons discussed so far. According to the Lockean model, the state's fundamental purpose is secular; thus, it should not be claiming otherworldly knowledge or judging the truth of religious causes. Moreover, state favor toward one religion often leads to persecution, or at least disparagement, of others, and citizens who do not adhere to a religion that the state is promoting have every reason to feel alienated, excluded, and fearful.

## Religious Endorsement

Accordingly, where a constitutional provision such as the First Amendment forbids establishment of religion, this should be read broadly to include any endorsement of a religion by the state. Where possible, similarly broad meanings should be given to instruments that declare a fundamental freedom of "conscience and religion" (as in section 2 of the Canadian Charter of Rights and Freedoms) or a "freedom of thought, conscience, and religion" (as in Article 9 of the European Convention on Human Rights). However, such instruments need to be interpreted according their wording and context.

For example, it is unsurprising that the European Convention on Human Rights has not been used to strike down long-standing formal establishments, such as that of the Church of England. Indeed, the European Court of Human Rights refused to find a breach of Article 9 when a challenge was made to Italy's provisions requiring the display of crucifixes in public schools. The court made clear that it would require something considerably more dramatic in the way of religious indoctrination, or alternatively persecution of non-Christian students, than what it saw as the passive display of a religious symbol.[5] We might well doubt what secular purpose is served by the display of religious symbols in state-run classrooms; however, the European Court of Human Rights has little choice but to accommodate some kinds of governmental favoritism toward particular religions or churches. It tends to allow governments a fairly wide margin of appreciation in such matters, leaving any tighter restrictions to the respective constitutions of the countries covered by the European convention.

Impermissible state endorsements of religion need not involve something as a specific as the advocacy of a particular Christian denomination. Rather, the state has no business giving its endorsement to any otherworldly doctrine, however generic. It should not, for example, endorse the doctrine that a particular god exists, that there is an afterlife for human beings, or that we undergo a process of death and rebirth. The starting point is that the state knows nothing about such things. Nor, prima facie, does it know that there is only the one world – this world – and that these doctrines are incorrect.

*In one sense*, however, the state must act as if all religions are false. That is, its starting point should be a general policy of religion-blindness, of acting just as it would if none of these religions existed. Note that a starting point need not be the finishing point. In the real world, where the various religions do exist, the state should not hold them to be false, or persecute them, for religious or anti-religious reasons of its own. It should not, for example, take the attitude that Zeusism is a false worldview and that its adherents are wasting their lives on a delusion. That sort of claim is not for the state's secular officials, acting in their official capacities, to judge one way or the other. Wherever it can, the state should adopt a neutral or agnostic attitude to the diversity of otherworldly claims made by the religions that are practiced within its territory. Its ideal should be to disparage none and endorse none.

Eisgruber and Sager make the key point about endorsement very clearly with their example of an imaginary town, "Fineville." They explain how a prominent, highway-spanning sign might say either "Fineville – A Nuclear-Free Community" or "Fineville – A Christian Community." While the first might be irksome for supporters of nuclear energy, it is not pernicious in the same way as the second. The difference depends on the way religions function as relatively comprehensive belief systems that include some people, exclude others, and typically attach spiritually momentous consequences (e.g., the difference between salvation and damnation) to inclusion or exclusion. Official endorsements of one religious viewpoint or another inevitably come with highly charged messages of disparagement for those who do not share the endorsed religious view.[6]

In effect, the state sends to those who lack the preferred religious identity a message that they are second-class citizens (or something even less). Of course, the same would apply if the sign said: "Fineville – An Atheist Community." The state should not be making judgments about otherworldly things, including the judgment that they do not exist. It follows that freedom of religion provisions should, where possible, be read as excluding state promotion of disbelief, or of anything like philosophical naturalism or materialism, along with state promotion of one or other form of religious belief. That has, in fact, been the direction taken by the American courts in interpreting the First Amendment.

Unfortunately, concerns about religious endorsements can lead to seemingly absurd outcomes. The state does many things that could potentially be interpreted as promotion of disbelief or, more usually, as promotion of one or other form of belief. Promotional messages may be inexplicit, more or less subtle, and sometimes in the eye of the beholder. One action might lie very close to the borderline, with the effect that an embarrassingly similar one might be assessed as falling on the other side. In the United States, the Supreme Court allowed the display of a Christmas nativity scene in one case where the context was thought to detract from any religious message,[7] but disallowed the display of a nativity scene in another case where it was presented more baldly.[8] In the latter case, however, the court allowed a display that combined a Christmas tree, a Jewish menorah, and a plaque inscribed with a salute to liberty. This composite display was not held to express any endorsement of Judaism or Christianity.

Cases such as these have become an important, but unsatisfactory, area of American constitutional disputation. The courts are often forced back on their own interpretations of what message is communicated by a particular government action, even if they present this in terms of the likely perceptions of a reasonable bystander. As this area of jurisprudence develops over time, the line between acceptable and unacceptable speech often has to be drawn on a case-by-case basis. Accordingly, the decided outcomes can appear unprincipled and the ultimate disposition of any new case is unpredictable.

The waters are muddied further by the Supreme Court's evident (and perhaps prudent) unwillingness to disallow each and every expression of religiosity in the processes of government. Indeed, some expressions of religiosity appear relatively innocuous for similar reasons to those applying to long-established religions in Europe. They may date back to earlier times when the secular state was in its infancy, the full implications of the Lockean model were far from obvious, and the language or conduct concerned was more or less ceremonial. In these circumstances, such customary activities as a call for God's blessing on a court may not seem very menacing, even to non-believers. They are holdovers from the past rather than precursors of more blatant or comprehensive religious establishment. Greenawalt formulates the argument like this, without wholeheartedly endorsing it:

> Certain practices have a long historical pedigree; and purists about constitutional principle should not insist on uprooting them. Perhaps these practices should never have been started; or perhaps they were entirely appropriate for the country at the time they began. In either event, they are now moderately out of joint with the principles that should guide the behavior of the state. But long historical customary practice underlies an argument for continuance. Governments and societies are not entirely rational in their applications of valid first principles. The development of public institutions is messier than that. Continuity and stability matter in social life, and history has its claims.[9]

I have a degree of sympathy for this, but some actions by the state seem calculated to send a deliberate religious message, and even to disparage those who find they cannot agree. During the Cold War period, in particular, the US government took a number of steps to differentiate American society from the "Godless Communism" of the Soviet Union. In 1956 it changed the official US motto from *E Pluribus Unum* ("One from Many") to the zealously religious "In God We Trust." This was not far from proclaiming: "The United States of America – A Theistic Country." The courts have, however, been unwilling to declare it unconstitutional. Even as I was revising this chapter for publication, the US Supreme Court refused, on March 7, 2011, to hear an appeal from a finding by the United States Court of Appeals, Ninth Circuit,[10] that the words "In God We Trust" are merely patriotic or ceremonial. While this outcome may be socially expedient, I submit that the alteration of the motto should never have taken place.

Likewise, the Pledge of Allegiance was amended in 1954 to alter the words "one Nation indivisible, with liberty and justice for all" by inserting after the words "one Nation" the further words "under God." Such actions are perniciously divisive: they suggest that citizens who disagree are somehow second-class or unwelcome. They should not be taken by the ostensibly secular governments of modern liberal democracies.

But some symbols that originally had religious meanings have taken on more secular meanings – at least arguably, at least to some extent, and at least in some contexts. For example, *Salazar, Secretary of the Interior v. Buono*[11] is one of a number of American cases in which the courts have been asked to rule whether a Latin cross, when erected on public property as a war memorial, amounts to a government endorsement of Christianity. Cases such as this can be difficult to decide and may turn on their precise, sometimes complex, facts. In *Salazar*, the original cross (which was later replaced many times) was erected in the Mojave Desert by war veterans in memory of the dead in all wars. Over the years, its local message was arguably established as a secular one, even though the cross is obviously a Christian symbol. In other circumstances involving the same symbol, however, government endorsement of Christianity might be clearer.

More cases of alleged religious endorsement are likely to find their way through the American court system, and it is not my intention to arbitrate their individual merits in advance. Given the broad range of issues that can arise, it would be foolish to propose detailed guidelines; something would always be left out. From one viewpoint, alas, these cases can seem like a waste of resources. They often turn on their own particular facts, sometimes lead the courts to make strained distinctions, and seldom involve absolutely unequivocal endorsement of any religion by the state. It would, however, be wrong to regard the litigation cynically or to wish it were not pursued. For better or worse, many actions taken by the state fall within a gray zone where reasonable people may differ about what messages are sent.

In some situations, the public officials responsible may have acted for genuinely secular reasons. Many of the cases that arise involve peculiar circumstances and depend on their own facts – perhaps on matters of local history and shared understandings. We should not insist, in a spirit of hostility, that the spaces and processes of the state be purged by the courts of every image or text that could possibly have a religious connection. In all the circumstances before a court, it may be a close thing trying to decide whether or not, on the occasion concerned, the state endorsed religious beliefs. On some occasions, however, there may be a deliberate, or even defiant, effort to expand the envelope of how much government-endorsed religious speech is allowable. In this complex political environment, ongoing vigilance is warranted.

## Religious Endorsements in Education

The education of children is a major responsibility taken on by the modern state over the past one to two centuries: "Most modern democratic states introduced compulsory education in the nineteenth century in recognition of the state's responsibility to ensure at least a minimum level of education in the population as a whole."[12]

Once the state plays this role, it inevitably creates controversy, since there are many conflicting views as to what children should be taught. Should education be solely about the natural or immanent order, or should it extend to (alleged) truths about another order of things? What, exactly, should the secular content be? Should teaching concentrate on facts and skills, or should it include morality? If the latter, whose morality should be taught? Not surprisingly, different religions have differing views on all these issues. In Chapter 8 I'll discuss a range of issues that arise with children, particularly in the context of public education. For now, I'll focus on religion's endorsement – or absence of endorsement – in the school setting.

Ahdar and Leigh complain that the prohibition, or mere absence, of religion in schools "promotes a powerful but contestable message about the inappropriateness or irrelevance of religion – a message that some believers may find biased and oppressive." They add that "even a short act of worship may serve as a reminder that knowledge has a broader spiritual context."[13] But what is the secular state to do when it takes responsibility for teaching children? It professes no knowledge of otherworldly matters, so it can hardly offer a "reminder" that knowledge has a "spiritual context." How can it claim to know that? It is a controversial opinion, based on religious views. It may be the private belief of some, or many, government officials that knowledge has a "spiritual context," but the state exists to protect the things of this world, not to endorse such opinions. A "short act of worship" in a state school conflicts entirely with the Lockean model of the state.

Besides, what sort of worship should the state introduce? In practice, the only tenable possibilities would seem to be worship of the following: the god or gods of the region's majority religion; the god or gods of its *established* religion, where applicable; or some generic, ambiguous god with little in the way of a specified character. In all cases, somebody may be offended – not only non-believers but also believers in different gods, or in more specific gods, or in an otherworldly order with spirits or powers but nothing in the way of a god. All of these could complain that the state is endorsing a religion that is foreign to them, and offering it to children with a seal of official approval. Why is this any of the state's business? What is the secular reason for it?

Though Ahdar and Leigh complain that mere absence of worship in public schools sends an undesirable message, there is no other choice. The presence of worship requires a choice as to *which* worship, and the message that a particular form of religion is approved over others (and over non-belief). In any event, a quite different message is communicated by the refusal of state schools to include religious worship or endorsement. The message is simply that the state is neutral between belief and non-belief and between the many different forms of belief. These are not matters on which it claims expertise. Arguably, that is a *good* message to send to children – good in that it serves worldly aims such as social peace.

If believers in a particular religion find such neutrality "biased and oppressive," that is unfortunate – yet there is no alternative. Forthright opponents of religion may likewise feel that the state is biased in not debunking "obviously false" beliefs: in principle, hard-line atheists could take the attitude that state schools must purvey anti-clerical propaganda, or otherwise they'll feel oppressed. Within reasonable limits, of course, it remains open to parents to send children elsewhere for teaching on religious matters. For Christian parents, this might involve Sunday school and other church activities. Other parents might have other options – doubtless there are places where children can be taught secular humanist ideas if their parents so desire. But none of this falls within the proper goals of the state.

Accordingly, the American courts have acted quite properly in successive cases that forbid teachers in state schools from leading students in prayer.[14] This practice necessarily gives state endorsement to religion, perhaps rising to the level of imposition. Situations vary, no doubt, but there is a power differential between teachers and the pupils over whom they exercise authority. If a teacher leads a class in prayer, children may, quite reasonably, feel pressured to take part. The state, through its employees such as teachers, should not be endorsing or imposing any form of religion, and nor should officials try to test the envelope on a fundamental point such as this, seeing how much ambiguous endorsement they can get away with in the constitutional courts.[15]

## Conclusion

This brings me to a key issue that is often given short shrift in discussions of religious freedom: state imposition of specifically religious morality. This issue is often neglected, or quickly dismissed, even by passionate advocates of religious freedom such as Douglas Laycock. By contrast, I'll give it its due.

Examples could include the prohibition of homosexual acts or the contraceptive pill because they are deemed by the Catholic Church to be immoral. Another example would be a prohibition, intended to please a Muslim constituency, of eating pork or drinking alcohol. An obvious problem here is that clear-cut examples are difficult to find: there is usually some secular rationale, even if far-fetched, that can be given for such prohibitions. But it doesn't follow that nothing can be said against them, based on the Lockean model for the secular state. For a start, electors and officials can be asked to consider, in good faith, whether they really have sufficiently strong reasons for action – reasons that outweigh contrary considerations and are based solely on the need to protect or promote secular interests.

While that is a start, there is far more to be said. In particular, there are good reasons for a secular state apparatus to evolve into a liberal state apparatus, administering a liberal democracy that allows much in the way of social pluralism and individual liberty. In the following chapter, therefore, I discuss how a secular state logically develops into a liberal one.

# Notes

1   John Locke, *A Letter concerning Toleration*, 1st pub. 1689, Hackett, Indianapolis 1983, p. 26.
2   Compare Susan Mendus, *Toleration and the Limits of Liberalism*, Macmillan, Basingstoke 1989, p. 34.
3   Rex Ahdar and Ian Leigh, *Religious Freedom in the Liberal State*, Oxford University Press, Oxford 2005, p. 154.
4   Ahdar and Leigh, *Religious Freedom in the Liberal State*, pp. 82–83.
5   *Lautsi v. Italy*, Mar. 18, 2011, §§71–76.
6   Christopher L. Eisgruber and Lawrence G. Sager, *Religious Freedom and the Constitution*, Harvard University Press, Cambridge, MA 2007, pp. 124–127.
7   *Lynch v. Donnelly*, 465 US 668 (1984).
8   *County of Allegheny v. ACLU*, 492 US 573 (1989).
9   Kent Greenawalt, *Religion and the Constitution*, vol. 2: *Establishment and Fairness*, Princeton University Press, Princeton 2008, p. 92.
10  *Newdow v. Lefevre*, 598 F 3d 638 (9th Cir. 2010).
11  559 US ___ (2010) (Docket No. 08-472).
12  Ahdar and Leigh, *Religious Freedom in the Liberal State*, p. 255.
13  Ahdar and Leigh, *Religious Freedom in the Liberal State*, p. 236.
14  See particularly *Engel v. Vitale*, 370 US 421 (1962).
15  Again, contrast the outcome in *Lautsi v. Italy*, Mar. 18, 2011, in which the Grand Chamber of the European Court of Human Rights was unwilling to order the removal of crucifixes from public school classrooms.

CHAPTER FIVE

RELIGION-BASED MORALITY AND THE SECULAR STATE

*what is non-religion based morality?*

# Introduction

Is it legitimate for the secular state to impose a religion-based morality on its citizens? Expressed in this way, the answer seems apparent: it is no business of the state to enforce religious canons of conduct. That, however, is far from the most common approach adopted by jurists and legal scholars, many of whom dismiss the idea that there is a problem. Describing any contrary viewpoint as "nonsense," Laycock asserts that the Establishment Clause separates from government only questions of theology, worship, and ritual. It does not separate questions of morality, right conduct, or proper treatment of others, which he sees as "questions to which both church and state have historically spoken." He adds: "They are questions within the jurisdiction of both [church and state]. In a democratic society, the state will ultimately decide these questions at least to the extent of deciding what conduct will be subject to legal sanctions. But these are also questions on which churches are absolutely entitled to speak."[1]

However, Kent Greenawalt dissents from this view: "I believe," he writes, "that requiring people to comply with the moral code of a religion, absent any belief about ordinary harm to entities deserving protection, is a kind of imposition of that religious view on others." Theoretically, therefore, "enactment of a religious morality could violate the Establishment Clause, even if the religion, as a set of beliefs and religious practices, is not promoted or endorsed in a more straightforward sense."[2]

I submit that Laycock's approach is simplistic and that Greenawalt's should be preferred. First, it is misleadingly ambiguous to say that the

---

*Freedom of Religion and the Secular State*, First Edition. Russell Blackford.
© 2012 John Wiley & Sons, Inc. Published 2012 by John Wiley & Sons, Inc.

churches have an entitlement to speak about certain issues. In societies with freedom of speech, they most certainly have a legal entitlement to do so. It does not follow that the churches' speech should actually be heeded by government officials; that their arguments, on any particular occasion, are consistent with good political principles; or that their views are beyond criticism. Many ideas that have little merit should nonetheless not be censored in a liberal democracy that values free speech.

Second, and even more fundamentally, how can Laycock distinguish questions of theology so neatly from questions of morality? The moral views of churches and sects may be based on the contents of holy books; the reasoning of ancient or medieval theologians, who may have assumed a divine purpose behind the operations of nature; the direct commands of a god, supposedly received via leaders or prophets; or, more generally, claims about otherworldly principles and entities. Certain forms of conduct may be prescribed because they conduce to spiritual salvation, rightness with a deity, or escape from worldly attachments and achievement of a spiritual condition or state such as *moksa* or nirvana. If claims about how we should conduct ourselves are based on considerations such as these, they can hardly be contrasted with "theological" matters.

There is no doubt that many people *feel* as if real-world moral legislation is imposing theological views on them, as evidenced by the frequent complaints to that effect, and they are not merely indulging in "nonsense." Often the campaigns in favor of moral legislation are, indeed, motivated by recognizably theological considerations. The difficulty is not that legislation on such matters as reproductive rights and homosexual conduct is inherently non-theological. Rather, it is that a mixture of theological and secular reasons may be operating in any particular case. Thus, in the American context, it may be difficult to rely specifically and solely on the Establishment Clause to oppose moral legislation. In any particular situation considered by the courts, the state may be able to offer some kind of secular justification for its actions.

In principle, however, the Establishment Clause should be dispositive if the courts are confronted with a sufficiently clear-cut case where the main purpose of a statute is to enforce religious morality. Even if no sufficiently clear-cut case finds its way to the American courts, the more general issue goes far beyond the United States and beyond situations that are justiciable.

## From Secularism to Liberalism

If the power of the state is deployed only for worldly reasons, and not for spiritual ones such as rightness with God or salvation of souls, what are the practical implications for government decision-making? It follows from the previous chapters that the state should never promote religious doctrines for their own sake, and should be most reluctant to do so as a Machiavellian means to secular ends. The state's officials should not, furthermore, promote the morality of a particular religion for its own sake or attempt to enforce what they believe, *all* things considered, to be the "correct" system of morality.

Recall the problem confronted by Locke, that his account of the dramatically different functions of church and state could, when taken to its logical conclusion require that the state permit a great deal in the way of "immoral" behavior. For example, it would allow a religious sect to engage in seemingly scandalous behavior such as promiscuous orgies within its congregations. Locke responded that these could be made illegal in church as long as they were also illegal outside of church – no religious organization could claim to be persecuted if it were simply required to obey the general law applying to everybody else. This, however, was not as good an answer as it seemed to Locke. He depicted the state as existing only to protect the things of this world, such as life, health, and worldly possessions, but there was a deeper question that he left unanswered: why did the protection of these things necessitate bans on promiscuous orgies either in church or elsewhere?

In Chapter 3 I suggested that Locke could have argued that sexual restrictions – confining sexual contact to monogamous, heterosexual marriages – were justified on the secular ground that they were required for social stability. However, this no longer seems plausible. Furthermore, the problem can be generalized. If we accept that the point of the state is to protect worldly goods, we will separate the state not only from religion but also from religious morality – and, what is more, from any traditional morality that does not actually assist in protection of worldly things.

Thus, the legislators and other officials of a secular state are on weak ground if they propose to enforce traditional morality for its own sake. They need to show how their laws actually protect the worldly interests of citizens, irrespective of whether they track a traditional moral code that has operated in their society. Moreover, we can start at a different end and question why legislators and other officials would ever enact laws that enforce a specifically religious morality. How is this *not*, contrary to ideas of religious freedom, imposing a religion (or at least its canons of conduct) on people who may not accept it?

It should be clear enough that secular rulers or leaders cannot invoke religious grounds for banning homosexual acts (or specific acts such as male–male anal sex), eating of pork, consumption of alcohol, the contraceptive pill, or anything else. The state has no more justification for such religion-based prohibitions than it would have if its officials wished to suppress the wording of the Catholic mass or to compel attendance at a Muslim mosque. In principle, *any* of the above could be done by the legislature if some dramatically compelling secular reason presented itself, but the state's purpose should not be the imposition of religious views. For example, it should not ban homosexual acts on the ground that they are forbidden in the biblical book of Leviticus. Nor should it impose such a ban because, having examined the teachings of various religions and considered numerous other matters, it believes that homosexual conduct is immoral, all things considered. "*All* things" would include such things as the existence of certain gods or other transcendent agents or powers, but the state has no official knowledge of these agents, or powers, or of any otherworldly matters.

A better reason to ban homosexual acts might be that they somehow undermine the social order, but this claim now seems absurdly implausible. Still better would be some harm to others' civil interests caused by homosexual acts, though this will be more impressive if the others do not consent to the harm or the risk that it might eventuate. After all, why should I want the state to protect me from a risk that I am prepared to take? Even if homosexual acts caused harms to others' civil interests, the state's officials would need to consider the effect of their own actions. In this case, a criminal ban would produce harms of its own, impeding the liberty of citizens to engage in conduct that large numbers of them find enjoyable.

That, in fact, is putting it very mildly. Our central projects can vary a great deal from person to person, but sexuality and erotic love are extraordinarily important in most people's lives. Attempts by the state to control an area such as this are likely to cause deep suffering, which must be weighed against any secular benefits that might be obtained. Thus, Hart recognizes the special misery of laws enforcing sexual norms,[3] and Nagel states that a prohibition of homosexuality puts at stake the affected individuals' "deepest and most acutely personal desires."[4] Moreover, sexuality and erotic love affect motivations so powerful that they may override individual citizens' commitments to abide by their society's laws and conventions. Attempting to suppress sexual conduct has some of the same dangers, viewed from a secular viewpoint, as attempting to persecute religion. In short, there are powerful secular reasons for the state to adopt a permissive attitude to sexual conduct. It would take something quite compelling to override these reasons, for example if the conduct were not consensual or involved the exploitation of individuals too young to give properly informed consent.

Religion and sexual conduct are not the only areas where the state should be reluctant to issue prohibitions even in pursuit of its secular goals. John Harris is on strong ground when he observes that, if the state were allowed to override choices about family formation, this would restrict the ability of people to confront the most fundamental questions about the meaning and value of their own lives.[5] Another obvious area where the state should exercise its power with great reluctance is freedom of speech, which I shall come to in Chapter 9. Indeed, such considerations apply whenever important and deeply personal interests are at stake. As Kymlicka puts it, civil and political liberties are important because "they allow us to have control over the central projects in our lives."[6] Nagel comments that we need negative rights against the state to make its otherwise enormous power tolerable to all.[7]

Once religious reasons for action are out of the picture, and the state's reasons for conduct are examined from a purely worldly viewpoint, it becomes clear that the state should often defer to the choices of its citizens. The balance of *worldly* reasons favors barriers to overreaching by state officials. These might include constitutional provisions and/or widely accepted political principles against, say, government intrusion in sexual intimacy, reproductive liberty, and freedom of speech.

Can we go even further, to put some sort of onus on the state to justify all its actions, or at least those that are coercive? In *On Liberty*, John Stuart Mill famously argues that only the prevention of harm to others can justify the exercise of power over an individual in a civilized community.[8] As elaborated by Mill, this rules out the use of social power (including, but not limited to, legal sanctions) to intrude on actions that directly affect only the individual concerned and any consenting parties. It is not sufficient, in Mill's view, that others might be affected, and perhaps harmed, indirectly.[9] This is the famous harm principle, and though it has certain difficulties, it also has obvious strengths. They are apparent even in writings by thoughtful authors who would not support Mill's views in their full generality.

Consider the views of James Fitzjames Stephen, who was no friend of Mill's overall defense of liberty. He concluded that there are many cases in which the criminal law is inappropriate for suppressing "vice." On Stephen's account, crimes need to be acts capable of specific definition and clear proof. They also need to be acts of such a character as to justify the infliction of great harms on those who commit them. In that regard, he sees the harshness of the criminal law as a last resort. Moreover, the enforcement of criminal legislation must not lead to vague attempts at proof, unnecessary, inordinate expense, or the widespread invasion of privacy. Finally, Stephen suggests, the criminal law is largely futile as a means of suppressing actions that do not violate the agent's own conscience or cause direct harm to others.[10]

Even Michael J. Perry, who argues for the legitimacy of criminalizing or otherwise disadvantaging conduct on purely religious grounds, identifies powerful considerations against coercive action by the state.[11] One is the recognition of our own fallibility, which provides a reason to avoid paternalism: we should be reluctant to think that we know better than others what is good for them. Another is social pluralism, which can act as a brake on the tendency to condemn and prohibit different choices, behavior, and ways of life. Still another is self-interest, which can help us if the winds change and we cease to be part of the politically dominant coalition. Again, Perry is recognizing powerful *worldly* reasons to support a limited role for the state.

Other relevant values identified by Perry include compassion and friendship (in the sense of fellowship among citizens). To coerce someone to make a choice that she does not want to make is to cause her to suffer. To coerce a member of one's own political community to make a choice that she does not wish to make will provoke resentment, which is corrosive of the community. If the coercion is extreme, forcing an individual to do something that she believes to be morally forbidden to her or destructive of her well-being, the suffering will be extreme, and likewise the accompanying resentment. This can cause alienation, lack of respect for the law, political instability, even rebellion and civil war.

All of this suggests, Perry says, that we should be wary of using a coercive political strategy unless fundamental interests are at stake – especially the interests of those who are relatively incapable of protecting themselves – or we need to protect basic social institutions such as the courts. In much the same spirit as James Fitzjames Stephen, he worries about laws that are difficult to enforce and likely to be enforced patchily or inequitably, laws that are likely to produce evils such as blackmail, and laws punishing people for things that they largely cannot help. He concludes that all these considerations call for a strong reluctance, or "discriminating wariness," when we consider using coercive political strategies.

Finally, I must add that liberal societies have been relatively successful in accommodating a vast range of cultural and individual differences, including conflicting worldviews; divergent life plans and styles of personal presentation; and a baffling range of obsessions and self-definitions. Sitting in our armchairs, we might expect this diversity to put social harmony under strain, but the tendency has been to accommodate differences in the belief that greater strain would be produced by attempts at suppression. Generally speaking, this approach has succeeded. In addition, many of us enjoy the overall diversity of societies where many personal styles, ways of life, and socially mediated experiences are available. We may value the sheer variety, the wide smorgasbord of possibilities, on offer. Even if, like Mill, we don't value diversity for its own sake, we may welcome it as a sign that we live in societies where people are free to develop their individuality.[12]

All these considerations suggest that the logical direction of a secular state is toward liberalism. Once the state ceases to act for religious reasons, imposing the views of one religion or another, it can concentrate on protecting the things of this world. At that stage, it is left with no real reason to impose a traditional morality for its own sake. Moreover, it has positive reasons to embrace social pluralism and restrain its own interference in people's lives.

The secular state can permit many ways of life, as long as their participants are willing to tolerate those who disagree. In short, once the state backs away from supporting its preferred religion, there is a logic to increased liberality. Secularism easily segues into the broader liberal ideal of a society where individual citizens are permitted to develop their own potentials as they see fit, and to pursue their own values or visions of the good.

## Personal Freedom and the Harm Principle

*[handwritten margin note: secular reason against as it harms people and others rights whether accepted or rejected by religion.]*

For all these reasons, the secular state should not simply enforce whatever moral beliefs have been accepted in its territory as a matter of tradition. It should, moreover, display great reluctance to interfere in certain areas of individuals' lives: not only their religious beliefs and practices, but also their consenting sexual conduct, their reproductive choices, and their self-expression. This has been a tendency in the United States, where developments in constitutional law now protect a sphere of personal freedom that goes well beyond the enumerated rights in the Constitution. Such is the outcome of a line of Supreme Court cases culminating in *Lawrence v. Texas*.[13]

In *Lawrence*, the Supreme Court struck down an anti-sodomy law under which two gay men were convicted after the police caught them having sex. The majority of the judges clearly affirmed a principle that "Liberty presumes an autonomy of self that includes freedom of thought, belief, expression, and certain intimate conduct."[14] This was elaborated to cover much private and consensual sexual conduct between adults, as well as much in the way of family formation and child-rearing. Whether or not this somewhat vague idea is easily captured in constitutional provisions, it merits widespread acceptance as a political principle to guide decision-making in a liberal democracy.

Moving from the specific to the general, Mill's harm principle would require the state to exercise caution even outside the areas referred to in *Lawrence*. Mill argues that state coercion is not justified merely because others might ultimately be affected by our conduct – and perhaps harmed – through an indirect process.[15] In this respect, his thought is notably more liberal than that of Locke, who believed that the state should suppress dangerous ideas with a potential to undermine the social order.[16] Though history has been kind to Locke, it has been kinder to Mill in this regard; it now seems possible to tolerate (without necessarily approving) a wide range of beliefs and activities that produce no harm directly, though they may do so indirectly. *[handwritten: secular concerns]*

In Mill's spirit, I suggest that the secular authorities should be reluctant to introduce coercive measures unless confronted with serious harms relating to worldly things, such as life, health, liberty, and property, rather than to such as things as traditional morals, spiritual salvation, holiness or purity from sin, or the gratification of a deity. The harms should also be direct, but it must be recognized that directness is a matter of a degree. Perhaps what really matter are such things as the urgency of a situation, the likelihood of harm eventuating, or the futility of attempts to avert the risk by relatively non-coercive means, such as education or persuasion. This does not reflect Mill's own language, but it does explain his famous example of an angry mob gathered in front of a corn dealer's house. According to Mill, it is permissible to punish words that might rouse the mob to immediate violence, such as a demagogue's claim that corn dealers are starvers of the poor.[17] Mill accepts the possibility of punishment in such a case even though the words by themselves do not harm the corn dealer. In all, it is perhaps better to think in terms of an urgent risk, or a clear and present danger, than to make an inflexible distinction between direct and indirect harms.

Another important issue here is that the harm principle is aimed only at wrongful harms, not at those that are somehow deserved, consented to, or otherwise considered legitimate. This notion of legitimacy is, again, difficult to define in such a way that a clear line can be drawn. Briefly, however, advocates of the harm principle generally argue that not all adverse outcomes from involvement in social or economic competition should be cognizable as harms by the law.

Mill's own discussion excludes the harm suffered from lack of success in a competitive examination or an overcrowded profession, unless the means involved have included fraud, treachery, or force.[18] Similarly, Feinberg is at pains to confine his conception of harm to those setbacks to interest that are also wrongs.[19] On Feinberg's account, it is not wrongful to defeat a rival for a beloved's heart, or for a desirable job, unless the methods involve some kind of indefensible attack on the rival's interests (such as a kick in the groin to a rival in love).[20] In a similar spirit, J. L. Mackie suggests that society should not try to suppress competition and conflict – as opposed to regulating and attempting to accommodate them.[21] This is an important point, for the conceptions of the state developed by Hobbes and Locke never proposed that all competition and conflict be abolished, merely that they be constrained sufficiently for the benefits of human society to be possible.

Feinberg's four-volume *magnum opus*, *The Moral Limits of the Criminal Law*, explores the ramifications of the harm principle in intricate and (I suggest) generally persuasive detail.[22] In addition to the harm principle, Feinberg adopts a qualified version of the offense principle, accepting offense to others as a legitimate basis for criminalization in some limited circumstances.[23] On this approach, the relevant considerations for public policy include the intensity and durability of the experienced repugnance, the extent to which it could have been anticipated to affect people who are not especially susceptible, the ease with which it could be avoided by those who experience it, and the extent to which the latter have assumed the risk of being offended, through their curiosity or anticipation of pleasure. Feinberg also emphasizes that the interests of those giving the offense must be given due consideration when a policy response is formulated.

Wherever a liberal democracy might draw the line, it cannot accept that serious offense – sufficiently serious to justify political coercion – follows merely from knowledge that a deeply disliked activity is taking place in private.[24] On the contrary, it should provide strong protections even to public displays. Feinberg comments that a principle relating to offense must be formulated with precision and fenced in by "mediating maxims." This is partly because of the propensity of people to take offense at many useful, or even necessary, activities, and partly because of the history of offense-taking by mere bigots, who would, for example, have forbidden the public expression of love between interracial couples.[25]

One aspect of this should be qualified, however. Should the state, as Feinberg seems to think, discount certain emotional responses because they are unpalatable or morally repugnant? This has its own dangers, since intuitions about moral repugnance can vary immensely, and they are, indeed, partly shaped by religion. In one generation, love between inter-racial couples may be regarded by many people as repugnant. In another, *this attitude may itself cause repugnance* – I certainly feel it, and I hope my readers share the feeling. How, then, should the state respond?

At this point, it is worth emphasizing that I do not propose to defend the political thinking of Mill or Feinberg in its entirety. Nor do I seek to defend any comprehensive moral system. Even if it were desirable, either of these projects would require a separate study. The thesis of this chapter is somewhat weaker: if we accept, as I argued in Chapter 3, that the real point of the state is to protect the things of this world, relying solely upon worldly knowledge, this leads in the direction of liberalism, and to a political philosophy similar to Mill's and Feinberg's. If the role of the state is to maintain order, protect citizens, and advance ordinary human flourishing, it should not impose the canons of conduct of one religious group or another on those who don't accept them. We can also learn from historical experience that pandering to such things as racial prejudice, or to various forms of oversensitivity, does more harm than good. If we consider the issue from a worldly point of view, it is wisest to lean against the prohibition of mere offense, and to concentrate on more clear-cut harms than "harms" to particular sensibilities.

This brings me to the question of self-inflicted harms. Like Feinberg, Hart and Raz accept a limited role for the state in protecting citizens against harms that they bring on themselves.[26] How far should we accept such paternalism? That depends, I suggest on a number of factors. It is clearly more acceptable where those who are protected from themselves are children, young teenagers, or others who may not appear competent to make their own decisions, though even here there is a danger of offensively condescending treatment of mature minors. Paternalism is less acceptable where it overrides the decisions of adults at the height of their deliberative powers. As a general proposition, competent adults have good reason to trust their own decisions about how they live their own lives, and to distrust the efforts of the state to make decisions on their behalf.

However, paternalistic laws may be more acceptable when they impose only trivial burdens, or in those areas where something more than ordinary adult competence in understanding and deliberation is required to make a sound decision. The scientific study of medical drugs, for example, is highly complex, and few people who are not specifically trained can seriously claim the expertise to treat themselves with the vast and complex pharmacopoeia of drugs that are legally available. Hence, it is not an insult to our competence or a serious violation of our autonomy if the government sets up bodies and standards to regulate the availability and prescription of drugs. But paternalistic laws relating to medical drugs might become unacceptable if taken to an extreme that prevents adults from making simple decisions that fall within their own competence.

This brief discussion of harm to others, offense to others, and paternalism is not intended to be exhaustive, but it strongly suggests that the use of political coercion is most likely to be justified when direct, secular harms to others are involved. If coercion can be justified in respect of some indirect harms, it is to the extent that they resemble more direct ones in the need for an urgent response; if it can be justified in respect of some kinds of "mere offense," it is to the extent that the impact of offense merges with that of unequivocal harm; if it can be justified in respect of some self-inflicted harms, it is largely to the extent that we have good reason not to trust our own judgment in areas requiring sophisticated technical competence.

## Objections

Still, the harm principle as I've elaborated it has difficulties that ought to be considered. Importantly, some "harms" are more controversial than others. Consider, for example, an individual who is living a life in which all her preferences are satisfied, but only because she has adapted to a subordinate position in her society, or perhaps to some loss of her cognitive or physical capacities. Sher discusses women who are raised in traditional ways that socialize them to have preferences within a narrow range (involving marriage, children, and traditional careers).[27] Have they been harmed? Perhaps so, if we think in terms of opportunities denied to them, but some secular thinkers such as utilitarians may find it difficult to explain why this is *harm*.

Accordingly, it may not be possible to obtain full agreement on what amounts to "harm," even if it is restricted to worldly interests. To some extent, this must remain a matter for political debate and decision-making. That, however, should not lead us to the extreme sort of skepticism expressed by Steven D. Smith. Smith claims that the harm principle is vague, even vacuous, and endlessly manipulable, since almost anything can be said to "harm" someone by some standard or another – perhaps, for example, because certain conduct causes psychic distress to somebody (even from its mere contemplation!), or perhaps because of indirect effects on the social environment. In the limit, so this argument goes, I can claim that almost anything is "harmful" to me if it somehow frustrates my preferences.[28] In Smith's view, attempts to narrow the concept of harm, such as those of Mill and Feinberg, become overly complex and technical, fail to track ordinary usage, have no principled basis, lend themselves to equivocation, and ultimately rely on circular arguments.[29] In particular, Smith claims that many things cause harm in what he thinks of as the ordinary sense of the word, even if not in the narrower senses defined by liberal philosophers such as Mill and Feinberg.[30]

I disagree. I submit that the sort of reasoning exemplified in the previous section was not at all arbitrary. It progresses naturally from acceptance of the Lockean model of the state. Nor is it arbitrary to exclude psychic distress from the state's calculations. It is one thing for the state to provide us with some protection from high-impact offenses that we cannot easily avoid, such as nauseating odors or shocking images in public places. It's quite another to introduce such a tyranny of the sensitive that actions can be prohibited merely because some citizens strongly disapprove of them.

Perhaps there is more merit to Smith's concern about effects on the social environment. Let us consider it. One way to express the argument is to say that liberalism confronts some people with the prospect of living in a society in which they tend to feel alien. Though they may be free to live as they please, they don't wish this for others; rather, they wish to live in a society that gives exclusive support to their particular way of life and conception of the good. Certain changes may deprive them of the benefit of living in the kind of society that they wish for, and in which they feel most comfortable. That, however, is not something that a secular and liberal state should even attempt to provide.

The argument is best interpreted as a variation on a familiar class of illiberal arguments discussed by Feinberg: it is a kind of impure moral conservatism based on alleged harms to interests.[31] It suffers the problems of all such arguments, in that it advocates an attempt to freeze social change, and it values the interest in controlling what kind of society one lives in above others' interests in living in accordance with their own values. There is, of course, always the possibility that a future society will be dramatically different from our own, and there may be some limit to how quickly individuals can adapt to truly rapid and sweeping social changes. If enough changes happen at a sufficiently great pace, some people may merit our compassion as they come to feel like strangers in a strange land.[32]

But only draconian, highly illiberal actions by the state could prevent this or even hinder it. Any decision to do so – or to try – must be made with great reluctance. Unless they are truly rapid and sweeping, as with invasion by a technologically superior civilization, changes that alter the social environment and the exact cultural meanings of practices can be absorbed, psychologically, as they take place. They need not make anyone's life seem pointless or worthless. Conversely, an attempt to freeze certain aspects of society would severely restrict how many people choose to live their lives.

In a liberal democracy, the fear of change must be faced constantly, social innovation by social innovation, but this steady process is all to the good. Acceptance of the inevitability of change allows many kinds of people, with a wide range of values and interests, to flourish together peacefully. As Feinberg argues, it is not reasonable to analogize gradual changes, even to ways of life, to acts of invasion or genocide, to the violent suppression and obliteration of a religious faith, or to the abrupt extinction of an animal species by catastrophe or overhunting. Where change is incremental and unforced, it is fairer to compare it to the development of languages over time, or to the evolution of biological species. Those at the end of the process will have no legitimate grievance against those who produced the changes along the way.[33]

Smith's skepticism (or even cynicism) notwithstanding, it can be productive to engage in rational discussion of secular harms and benefits. As Neil Levy points out and elaborates, there is a powerful psychological pressure on participants in such discussions to justify practices, or their prohibition, with reasons that relate to harms and benefits of widely recognizable kinds.[34] Other things being equal, we are at least likely to recognize someone as having been harmed if she is prevented from living the life that she deeply wants to live, even if we do not share her particular values. This is a good reason, in many cases, for the state's officials to defer to individuals' wishes.

At the same time, those who control the apparatus of the state, with its vast power to help or harm individuals, have their own ideals about how human lives ought to be led. If we do not want that power to control our own lives, we have a good reason to constrain the activities of Leviathan.

## Perry's Arguments

Notwithstanding the considerations that favor social pluralism and individual liberty – considerations that he himself has identified and elaborated

– Perry defends the propriety of governments enforcing what he calls religiously grounded moral beliefs. He argues that legislators and citizens may legitimately support government action that they would *not* support if they relied purely on non-religious grounds. His concept of a religiously grounded moral belief is relativized to individuals, in the sense that some people might hold the same belief for non-religious reasons. For Perry, a belief is partly or wholly religiously grounded if, for the person concerned, it is wholly or partly rooted in one or more of the following three ideas: (1) the idea of a God-inspired text or texts such as the Bible which contains, if not all moral truth, at least all that is needed to be saved; (2) the idea of a God-anointed figure or figures, such as the pope, believed to teach moral truth; (3) the idea of an order created or maintained by God (particularly a God-fashioned human nature) believed to provide a fundamental criterion for moral truth.[35]

This concept of religious grounding could be tidied up, since it is not clear why Perry imagines that the relevant holy text, anointed individual, or order of things must receive authority from any particular god, Christian or otherwise, or from only one god. Nor is it clear why the idea of religious grounding does not include knowledge of an otherworldly order that is not created or maintained by any particular deities, but nonetheless provides us with criteria for moral truth. In principle, the concept could be extended to any moral claims that are grounded in (alleged) truths about an otherworldly order. Still, the force of Perry's arguments does not depend on this distinction. While it is well to see that his concept of religious grounding is too narrow (distorted by a focus on Christianity), the arguments will go through if a broader concept of religion is used – if they go through at all.

Perry does suggest that Christians should be reluctant to support or enact laws disfavoring a practice, based on biblical authority, if two conditions pertain: (1) contemporary human experience does not support the proposition that the practice is hostile to human well-being (properly understood); and (2) there is widespread controversy even among Christians that the Bible teaches what is attributed to it.[36] He suggests that these criteria can be applied to oppose laws against homosexual relationships.[37] Nonetheless, the overall direction of his argument is that it's legitimate for the state to enact coercive laws solely to enforce religious morality.

This is a startling conclusion, particularly given the many powerful considerations that Perry himself has adduced, pointing in the other direction (discussed in some detail earlier in this chapter). If Perry is correct, there is little that stands in the way of modern Western states establishing what would look very like theocracies. It's no use arguing that a parade of horribles would not arise in practice, on the basis that electors and officials would show restraint or common sense.[38] Even if highly repressive laws are currently unlikely, it hardly follows that enacting them would be legitimate if circumstances changed. Constitutional protections are meant to last for all time, or at least indefinitely, whereas the community's political and moral sentiments may change quite suddenly (particularly if pressured by large-scale events such as war, environmental disaster, or economic ruin). Despite Perry's expression of scorn, it is easy enough to imagine a future USA in which only the constitution and the courts stand between individual liberty and the enforcement of oppressive laws.

Perry's main argument is based on a narrow reading of the Establishment Clause. He believes that it prevents government action from favoring membership in a particular church or a particular prayer, liturgical rite, or religious observance.[39] That, however, is all. With due respect, I submit that this is an astonishingly incomplete list. It omits the most important aspects of almost anything that we would regard as a religion: its doctrines relating to another world and otherworldly powers; its concepts of personal transformation, aided by otherworldly powers or agents; and its canons of conduct, based on access to otherworldly knowledge. It appears, then, that Perry must see nothing wrong with the state promoting belief in a particular god or supernatural principle, a particular path to salvation, or a particular canon of conduct based on (for example) divine revelation or mystical experience.

Admittedly, he thinks that the state cannot legitimately interfere with actual church membership or forms of worship, but nothing in his analysis of the Establishment Clause prevents it from issuing propaganda in favor of its preferred doctrine of salvation or from promulgating such views as that eating pork or shellfish is a sin. Perry's conception of the Establishment Clause gives the state a broad scope to proselytize for a very wide range of religious viewpoints.

Perhaps Perry can complain that I'm misrepresenting his position. He could, I suppose, claim that the state is prevented from promulgating the doctrine of salvation through faith in Jesus Christ because this would interfere with membership in churches or sects that don't hold this doctrine. For similar reasons, he might say, it cannot promulgate the Hindu doctrine of transmigration of souls. If the government promotes a particular doctrine of salvation or life after death, it is thereby favoring churches that support this doctrine, rites that accompany the doctrine, and liturgies that express it. Thus, Perry might argue, government support for such doctrines is precluded by a kind of back door. But of course the same applies to religious canons of conduct. If the government promulgates the doctrine that using contraception is a sin, that modest clothing of a certain kind is required by God, or that homosexual acts violate the divine order, it thereby favors churches or sects that support these doctrines.

Put bluntly, the state favors a religion if it favors the religion's distinctive moral code. *Pace* Perry, legislation that disfavors certain conduct on religious grounds clearly bestows legal favor on the relevant churches or sects.[40]

It greatly assists the credibility, and perhaps the social goals, of the religion concerned. It's bad enough, I dare say, if the state declares that eating pork is a sin. It's so much worse if it takes an extra step and prohibits the eating of pork. If it prohibits eating pork on the ground that it is forbidden in the Qur'an, how is that *not* bestowing legal favor on Islam? If it bans the contraceptive pill on the basis that it's forbidden in the Vatican's 1968 encyclical *Humanae Vitae*, how is this *not* bestowing legal favor on the Roman Catholic Church?

Of course, the state might have its own secular reasons to ban the eating of pork (perhaps if all available pork supplies were contaminated with an infectious disease) or the use of the contraceptive pill (perhaps if its use were contaminating the environment with dangerous chemicals). In those cases, it would be acting to protect civil interests. In some circumstances, it might be difficult to show that the purpose – or perhaps a disproportionate effect – of a legal prohibition is to support religion. That, however, is merely a practical issue of proof in the courts. A course of conduct does not become legitimate merely because the circumstances create problems of proof. The important point here is that acceptance of the Lockean model entails that the state cannot act on the basis of essentially untestable otherworldly claims, such as the claim that eating pork or using contraception violates the will of God or the operation of a divinely appointed order. A constitutional provision such as the Establishment Clause should be read broadly enough to forbid this kind of state action.

Perry's confusion on these issues becomes apparent when he asserts: "the claim that conduct is immoral is typically an important part of the argument that the law ought to ban, or otherwise disfavor, the conduct."[41] In a similar vein, Stephen L. Carter claims that the state makes moral decisions all the time,[42] as if there's nothing wrong with this, or with basing political judgments on otherworldly knowledge claims. In one sense, of course, there's an element of truth here. Governments and political parties often engage in blatant moralizing. When the crunch comes, however, and policy must be made and implemented, the state seldom attempts to discover the true morality applying in all the circumstances. A moment's thought shows that this would be an untenable role for it to play: it would need to inspect all the holy books, establish which, if any, contains the genuine word of one or more gods, examine such philosophical questions as whether the commands of a god are morally binding in any event . . . and the gods only know what else.

Such a process could be interminable if conducted with any degree of rigor. It would inevitably alienate the disfavored religions and the non-religious, who would be coerced into following canons of conduct from a tradition that is foreign to them, and to which they might well have strong objections. In practice, fortunately, the government reports and inquiries that precede legislation seldom read as if this had been the task. Some legislation is driven by an urge to enforce morality for its own sake, but it makes up an increasingly small proportion of the statute books. More commonly, governments support their legislative programs with analyses of this-worldly considerations, weighing up secular costs and benefits. The so-called "moral decisions" that Carter offers as examples fall into such familiar areas as the core criminal law, anti-discrimination legislation, taxes, and the regulation of capital and trade practices. All of these are readily explicable as attempts by the state to protect or promote citizens' interests in the things of this world. None relies on any form of otherworldly knowledge, or even upon a supposed imperative to enforce traditional morals.

On the Lockean model of the secular state, it is no business of the state's officials to inquire into what is morally right or good, all things – including otherworldly things – considered. When the state acts to protect our civil interests, it accepts the risk of forbidding practices that, if otherworldly things were considered, might turn out to be morally permitted or even required. More often, perhaps, it risks allowing practices that, if otherworldly things were considered, might be morally forbidden.

It would be convenient if religious doctrine in its generality could be separated from religious *moral* doctrine, but that is impossible. As long as moral doctrines are based on otherworldly considerations, the state should make no attempt to decide their correctness, one way or another, any more than it should claim to settle the existence of Allah, Vishnu, or Aphrodite. What it *can* do, of course, is consider any claim, from any source at all, that some practice or other will have effects (positive or negative) on civil interests. For example, the adherents of a religion that forbids alcohol might trust that their god disallowed it for essentially secular reasons, perhaps to prevent harms caused by intoxication. Nothing stops them from identifying those harms and putting evidence forward in political debates.

If, however, they can identify no worldly basis to support their preferred policies, they have a choice. One option is obvious enough: they can simply reject the Lockean model. After all, the arguments for the model are not of a kind that must rationally convince all comers, regardless of their starting point. Compare Brian Barry, underlining the practical limits of arguments for liberal principles: "if the parties want peace enough to make the concessions that are needed to reduce their demands so that they become compatible, liberalism proposes a formula for doing so." But, Barry warns, not everyone will be convinced: some will regard peace and equity as less important than "winning."[43]

In contemporary circumstances, a group that rejects the Lockean model, perhaps in favor of an attempt at "winning," will pay a price. It will find itself advocating policies that violate widely accepted political principles such as the harm principle or the principle of sexual privacy. If it takes this path, religious conflict is in the offing, since it can hardly use the Lockean model

– which it has rejected – to argue against persecutions or lesser consequences. That is not to suggest that the state should persecute such religious groups: on the contrary, the balance of secular considerations will almost certainly not favor this. For one thing, persecutions cause suffering that we all must shy away from. Nonetheless, when a religious group within a liberal democracy rejects the Lockean model, it creates a quandary for all concerned.

The least that should be expected by any religious group that rejects the Lockean model is severe criticism from its religious and secular opponents. Indeed, these opponents may come to regard the religious group as a danger to their civil interests. In self-defense, and defense of individual liberty, they may attempt to discredit the group by attacking its doctrines directly (freedom of speech allows them to do this). They may take other lawful actions to undermine the group's appearance of moral authority, and may even go further, by calling for political measures to weaken its influence. These might, for example, include calls for the government to marginalize the group by shutting it out of official consultative processes.

More generally, a climate of mutual resentment and anger is likely to develop. "How far," the group's opponents may ask, "must we tolerate the intolerant?" This question is neither unexpected nor unfair. The outcome, however, is likely to be a culture war with endless ramifications and unforeseeable results.

The less dangerous option all round is acceptance of the logic of the Lockean model. In that case, any particular group can distinguish between its specifically religious morality, binding in conscience on the faithful, and public policy that relates to the things of this world. Once again, nothing prevents a religious group from identifying whatever worldly reasons are available to support its favored policy outcomes. If, however, those reasons are not strong, the group's best recourse is to accept that its moral norms or canons of conduct will not be reflected in the secular law.

## Justiciability

Much of Perry's discussion relates to the difficulty of demonstrating that any particular law breaches the Establishment Clause unless it deals with such matters as liturgy and church membership. The underlying point here is that a law imposing a religion's canons of conduct on the general population can almost always be supported by *some* allegedly secular ground. For example, Perry says, secular reasons may be put forward to think that abortion is immoral.[44] That may be so, but it misses the point to some extent. The question for the secular state is not whether abortion is *immoral* but whether it is necessary to ban or regulate it in order to protect civil interests. That then becomes a complex issue: I don't propose to settle the abortion question, which has its own vast and complex literature, but, for a start, it is difficult to see how a fetus can even have any civil interests, at least until it reaches a point of development when it can experience pain.[45] Even then, its interests may be outweighed by those of a pregnant woman who does not wish to be a mother. Nor is it clear how abortions are sufficiently harmful to the civil interests of anybody else for the state to have a reason to enact prohibitions.[46]

Furthermore, Perry misses an essential point about the imposition of religious morality in modern liberal democracies. The first line of defense against this is not a provision such as the Establishment Clause in the US Constitution (or another country's constitutional guarantee of freedom of religion). Rather, it is the widespread commitment to liberal political principles, such as freedom of speech, reproductive liberty, sexual privacy, and the harm principle. Attempts to impose religious canons of conduct will be criticized and opposed, quite rightly, whenever they violate such principles.

The harm principle itself is not apt for constitutionalization. Any attempt to write such a broad, and somewhat vague, principle into a constitutional instrument would create difficulties that appear insurmountable. Courts would need to explore such gray areas as just where acute offense begins to shade into harm, where a degree of paternalism might be acceptable in the circumstances, the urgency of dealing with merely indirect harms through outright prohibitions, and so on. Though clear enough to be useful as a political standard, the harm principle defies precise definition, and is certainly too fuzzy to be applied predictably by the courts. Any attempt to write it into a constitutional instrument would give judges a very broad, unstructured area of discretion. It would be too much like handing legislative power to judges, whose expertise and access to information is quite different from that of legislators.

Nonetheless, the harm principle can be invoked in political debates, where the purpose is not to determine, as a matter of law, that the state has overstepped a line. Rather, the purpose is to show that a proposal enters dangerous territory where conduct is being forbidden, and liberties curtailed, without convincing secular reasons. Pointed questions can be asked about what worldly harm a proposed law is aimed at deterring, whether alleged indirect harms are provable or merely speculative, whether the latter could be ameliorated by means that have a lesser impact on individual liberty, and so on. The outcome might be the withdrawal of a legislative proposal, but it might also be its replacement by narrower, more specific, less draconian regulation.

Like the harm principle, principles relating to such matters as free speech, reproductive liberty, and sexual privacy are always available to be raised in political debate. They are more apt than the harm principle for constitutionalization, since it is reasonably clear what intrudes on, say, sexual privacy and what does not. Where principles such as these are given constitutional backing, laws that restrict free speech, reproductive liberty, or sexual privacy can then be scrutinized by the courts. These will ask such questions, depending on the jurisdiction and legal tradition concerned, as whether the law is supported by a compelling state interest, whether it is crafted narrowly to achieve no more than required, and whether its effects are in proportion to the mischief it addresses. At this stage of the process, a state that is constitutionally disqualified from establishing religion will not be able to rely on specifically religious arguments. This leaves the courts to assess the strength of whatever secular reasons are advanced, and whether they show a sufficiently compelling state interest (or whatever the equivalent test might be). In such a process, the state will need to rely on something more concrete than an assertion that that it has banned something it considers "immoral."

To be fair to Perry, it is true that a provision such as the Establishment Clause provides a relatively weak barrier, taken by itself, to impositions of religious canons of conduct. This is exemplified in a US case, *Harris v. McRae*,[47] where the Supreme Court narrowly upheld restrictions on public funding for abortions. Among the arguments dealt with by the court was the claim that these restrictions violated the Establishment Clause, since they supported the religious morality of the Catholic Church. This point was properly rejected, since the proposition "Statute X is supported by, or coincides with, the moral teachings of Church Y" never entails "Statute X is supported *only* by the moral teachings of Church Y." But the court did not hold that a law could be valid if it really was supported only by religious morality. On the contrary, it cited authority requiring a secular purpose. Unfortunately, it countenanced a very low standard of what might amount to a secular purpose, observing that restrictions on abortion funding were as much a reflection of traditionalist values toward abortion as a specifically religious morality.[48]

As a further complication, some moral theories that are traditionally associated with religion are now represented in public debate by proponents who deny that they are religious. Thus, contemporary proponents of natural law theories deny that their theories are inherently religious, and claim, instead, that they are based on "natural reason."[49] An obvious difficulty, however, is that natural law theories have typically relied on a teleological vision of the universe in which all things incline to fulfill their "true purposes," "rational natures," or "essential natures." This way of thinking often relies crucially on a concept of God as underpinning the teleological system concerned.

Even if God is not mentioned, the idea of the state acting in such a way as to facilitate things realizing their "essential natures" goes far beyond the concept of protecting civil interests such as those in life and health. When a moral theory is cast in terms of pursuing highly abstract values such as "life" – and this is interpreted in a far more esoteric sense than protecting the lives of citizens – we are moving outside the role of the state discussed in earlier chapters. Thus a law against masturbation (if anyone imagined that this could be enforceable or otherwise useful) would need to rely on a moral theory that values "life" in a more esoteric sense than our civil interest in not being killed.

It might, nonetheless, be almost impossible to prevent the imposition of religious morality by relying solely on a provision such as the United States' Establishment Clause. Where an alleged establishment of religion can be interpreted as "merely" the enforcement of traditional values or morals, the US courts are unlikely to adopt an approach of "strict scrutiny." This is because they seem prepared to consider the enforcement of traditional values or morals to be a sufficiently secular purpose rather than an imposition of religion, whether or not the traditional standards really function to protect civil interests. Where strict scrutiny applies, a law must promote a compelling government interest – and in the least restrictive way. Legislation subject only to ordinary scrutiny, by contrast, need show only a "rational" basis for the law, such that almost any alleged justification suffices in practice.

However, a provision such as the Establishment Clause can combine with other constitutional provisions and with liberal political principles. Let us assume that the secular case for a proposed law is weak. That is, the law does not appear to protect our civil interests such as Locke described. Perhaps it does no more than impose certain traditional values or enforce the requirements of an esoteric moral system. If so, this can be pointed out in the course of political debate. Reference can be made to the harm principle, supplemented by pointed questions as to how the imposition of traditional values or the enforcement of esoteric moral principles operates to protect our interests in worldly things. If it is clear that the impetus for a proposed law derives mainly from religious concerns, that is also a legitimate point to make in public debate.

The lack of any strong secular case for the law may be all-important if, once enacted, it violates a constitutional protection of, say, sexual privacy. If this becomes an issue in the course of litigation, the state will, indeed, need to identify some compelling reason why the law should be upheld. If the jurisdiction has a provision such as the Establishment Clause, that reason cannot be a religious one, and it will need to have more substance than a wish to embody traditional values in the law, or to give legal effect to an esoteric and highly contestable system of morality. Those sorts of reasons are unlikely to be regarded by the courts as *compelling*. Thus, a provision such as the Establishment Clause can offer a powerful protection when combined with other constitutional protections.

Furthermore, we cannot rule out the possibility of very pure or clear-cut cases where a specifically religious morality is imposed. In a sufficiently clear case, the Establishment Clause may yet provide a shield against the operation of some laws. Such a case might be one where legislators were demonstrably motivated to impose a particular religion's canons of conduct on the general population. It might be tempting to reject the very idea of such cases, based on skepticism about provable group intent (the group in this case being the members of legislature). But this kind of skepticism should be kept within bounds. As Greenawalt points out, the US Constitution bears on the conduct of the legislators, forbidding them to act to achieve impermissible objectives. If many have done so, it is a short (and reasonable) step to saying that the legislature has done so. Moreover, we can readily attribute a purpose to a legislature if it is stated in the law itself, and we can easily speak of the intent of a group if we know the intent of most members. Even a subset of members less than the majority can steer a group in a particular direction.

Nor are the courts without evidence of legislative intent: views expressed by individual legislators may explain what the legislature has done, including whether it has acted on improper grounds. Courts might, quite properly, show some leaning to attribute benign purposes to a legislature, but in discerning legislative objectives they should be able to rely on legislative history and what is said during the process by leading legislators.[50] Indeed, courts draw inferences about legislative intent every day, and would be hamstrung in their work if this were forbidden.

Greenawalt also answers the argument that legislators could simply enact or re-enact laws while hiding their true aims:

> First, legislators often are not careful, and, further, certain legislators now discern political advantage in coming out foursquare in favor of promoting religion. The remote possibility that down the road a court may rely on what they said to find an improper purpose may not affect their candor. Second, were legislators to believe that they could not divulge a purpose to promote religion, they might become more restrained about promoting religion. Third, the values of nonestablishment are undermined to a degree if aims at odds with these values are spread upon the public record and widely reported. Thus, legislative veiling of purposes itself could be of some benefit.[51]

Thus, we can imagine cases in which a court would quite properly conclude that the sole, main, or real purpose of a legislative provision was to impose specifically religious morality. Imaginary examples are, however, likely to be somewhat far-fetched. We might imagine, for example, a total ban on eating bananas, advocated by a religious cult that considers bananas taboo and has somehow (perhaps in the distant future) become popular in the jurisdiction concerned. Indeed, we can imagine many such science-fictional scenarios, but they have little to do with contemporary reality in the world's liberal democracies.

In the end, the American case law does not stand against the proposition that a law enacted simply to impose religious morality would be unconstitutional. It merely suggests that the US courts will resist making such a finding in actual cases before them. In practice, there are unlikely to be cases that are sufficiently clear for moral legislation to be struck down solely on Establishment Clause grounds.[52] Rightly or not, the US courts are prone to accept dubious "secular" purposes such as upholding traditional morals or values. This conclusion could doubtless be extended to various other jurisdictions whose constitutional provisions forbid religious establishment. In Australia, for example, section 116 of the Constitution applies only at federal level and has been read very narrowly, perhaps forbidding only formal establishments such as that of the Church of England.[53]

But the courts in some jurisdictions may be more willing to strike down legislation with a religious moral purpose. For example, in *R. v. Big M Drug Mart* the Supreme Court of Canada invalidated a statute preventing large businesses from opening on Sundays.[54] Big M Drug Mart had been charged with the crime of selling goods on a Sunday contrary to the *Lord's Day Act*, which imposed Sunday as a weekly holiday on religious grounds. This was clearly religiously based legislation, as shown by its history and the very title of the statute. No doubt some similar-looking requirements with secular purposes, such as protecting employees from being worked for unreasonable weekly hours, could be imposed within a liberal democracy by legislative action or through the progressive development of workplace standards (e.g., via union/employer negotiations). That, however, could not save blatantly religious legislation such as the *Lord's Day Act*. I submit that the court was correct to invalidate this act for its repugnance to the guarantee of religious freedom in the Canadian Charter of Rights.

In any event, we must not be fixated on likely outcomes in the courts. In political debates within a liberal democracy, it is sometimes cogent and legitimate to draw an inference that opponents are motivated, in substance, by a desire to impose religious morality – and that their secular arguments are mainly a smokescreen. The evidence for this may be strong, especially if the supposedly secular arguments appear weak or contrived, or if much of the publicly expressed support is couched in religious terms or emanates from religious lobbies. The legitimacy of such criticism in the robust give and take of political debate is not removed by the possibility or likelihood that the courts would hesitate to reach such a damning conclusion. Once a statute is actually enacted, and possibly enforced, courts of law should probably display a degree of respect for other branches of government, and so lean against finding any constitutionally improper purposes. The rest of us, however, need not be so deferential.

In short, we should not make too much of the fact that a particular law, once enacted, may be difficult to overturn in the relevant country's courts.

Instead, this makes it all the more important for electors, lobby groups, and legislators to act in good faith to support or enact only those laws which have good secular justifications. It is not cogent to argue, as Perry sometimes appears to do, that the *practical difficulty of demonstrating* that the substantial purpose behind a law is religious entails that there's *nothing wrong* with that purpose being religious. There is very much wrong with it, and it is fair and proper to make that point as and when appropriate.

## Humanitarian Catastrophe

This brings me to the most impressive argument that I know of in favor of a strong role for churches and sects within the political life of a liberal democracy. This is the argument from humanitarian catastrophe, and it is often raised in defense of the Christian churches' moral advocacy within the sphere of political debate. For example, Carter emphasizes the use of religious rhetoric in the American civil rights movement, as part of a mass struggle fought on many fronts.[55] The argument has some force, but it also has important limits.

In some historical circumstances, even democracies may fail to protect the civil interests of citizens and others within their territorial jurisdiction. Dramatic examples are provided by the horrors of chattel slavery in the United States and the obnoxious Jim Crow laws by which African Americans were oppressed long after slavery was abolished. The campaign against slavery happened at a time when *both* sides used religious arguments and religious rhetoric, and liberal thought was in its infancy. There was no realistic prospect of opposing slavery with purely secular arguments. However, the struggle against racial segregation was much more recent. The civil rights campaign reached its height as recently as the 1960s. This example, in particular, shows how a democratic nation with many liberal trappings might nonetheless be tyrannical toward minorities.

In strict logic, evils such as slavery and segregation could, and perhaps should, be opposed with entirely secular arguments. I don't doubt, however, that urgent political mobilization in the face of humanitarian catastrophe can be assisted – even dramatically – by the intervention of charismatic religious leaders speaking without inhibition about their deity and their faith. What should we make of this?

First, I'm in no way opposing the churches' freedom of speech. There should be no question of suppressing their speech, on these issues or others, but how far should their speech be positively welcomed? As to that, the Lockean model of the state does not trump all other values. It would be churlish to demand that strict adherence to it must override the urgent need to mobilize populations against large-scale suffering. At some tumultuous historical moments, such as the mobilization against racial segregation in the US, this need must take priority. It does not follow, however, that the Lockean model should be set aside as irrelevant or unimportant.

Martin Luther King's rhetoric, or something of the kind, might be required at critical points in history, but not all religious leaders can be Martin Luther King. Furthermore, King did not set out to impose specifically religious canons of conduct on non-believers. The struggle for civil rights in the United States involved powerful secular considerations, and the outcomes are easily justified in secular terms (without resort to pseudo-secular reasons such as enforcing traditional values or morals).

In the upshot, there is no hypocrisy or inconsistency in welcoming King's intervention. He did not advocate the enforcement of a specifically religious morality, and even if he encouraged law-making on a religious basis – contrary to the Lockean model of the state – we can accept that some values are even more important than upholding the Lockean model. That is quite consistent with defending the model in all but the most extraordinary circumstances. Even in extraordinary circumstances, opponents of religious activists are entitled to ask whether the position being put could also be defended on secular grounds or whether it relies entirely on religious doctrine of some kind. At the end of the day, the state has no business in taking action that can be justified *only* on otherworldly grounds of some kind.

Some religious leaders might claim that their particular favored political issues of the day are just as extraordinary as the evils of chattel slavery or racial segregation. In some cases they may have a point – surely this is a matter of judgment – but in many others they will be plainly wrong. For example, a political campaign to ban stem-cell research on religious grounds (perhaps because early embryos destroyed in such research are ensouled or because they are precious to a deity) does not invoke any humanitarian catastrophe. It clearly does not involve catastrophic circumstances of a kind that is obvious from a purely worldly viewpoint. An early embryo is not the kind of thing that can experience suffering, and indeed the humanitarian balance goes in the other direction: stem-cell research offers at least some prospect of *reducing* the world's load of suffering, if it leads to new medical therapies.

In cases such as these, there is every reason to regard religious interventions with suspicion.

## Conclusion

According to the Lockean model, religious bodies and the state have separate functions. That does not mean they can never come in contact, for the state should treat churches and sects much like other organizations for such purposes as police and fire protection. But the state should not try to save souls, lead its citizens to nirvana, or impose religious canons of conduct. Instead, it should act for secular reasons, advancing its citizens' interests in worldly things such as life, liberty, and property. Once it goes down this path it is likely to transform from a secular state to a truly liberal state, accepting a wide range of social pluralism and individual liberty, and restraining itself in accordance with liberal political principles such as the Millian harm principle.

Inevitably, some citizens reject these liberal principles, or the Lockean model itself, but others may criticize them for this, even to the extent of seeking that their voices be marginalized. Nothing about the Lockean model forbids such a reaction, though attempts at marginalization should not normally go so far as outright persecution or restrictions on freedom of speech. If individuals or groups put forward essentially illiberal proposals, seeking that their religiously based views be imposed on the general population by force of law, they are open to cogent and deserved criticism.

However, a different set of questions arises if religious commitments come into conflict with public policies that are genuinely based on worldly imperatives. What should happen if I am required by a legitimately secular law to act in some manner that is contrary to my conscience and the teachings of my religion? How far should religious beliefs be accommodated in a secular society, where public decision-making is detached, as far as possible, from religious teachings? Questions such as these form the subject matter of the following chapter.

## Notes

1   Douglas Laycock, "The Benefits of the Establishment Clause," 1st pub. 1992, in *Religious Liberty*, vol. 1: *Overviews and History*, Wm. B. Eerdmans, Grand Rapids, MI 2010, pp. 33–53, p. 41.

2   Kent Greenawalt, *Religion and the Constitution*, vol. 2: *Establishment and Fairness*, Princeton University Press, Princeton 2008, p. 533.

3   H. L. A. Hart, *Law, Liberty, and Morality*, Oxford University Press, Oxford 1963, p. 22.

4   Thomas Nagel, *Equality and Partiality*, Oxford University Press, Oxford 1991, p. 147.

5   John Harris, *On Cloning*, Routledge, London 2004, pp. 58–66.

6   Will Kymlicka, *Contemporary Political Philosophy: An Introduction*, 2nd edn, Oxford University Press, Oxford 2002, p. 144.

7   Nagel, *Equality and Partiality*, p. 149.

8   J. S. Mill, *On Liberty*, 1st pub. 1859, Penguin, London 1974, pp. 68–69.

9   Mill, *On Liberty*, p. 71.

10  James Fitzjames Stephen, *Liberty, Equality, Fraternity*, 1st pub. 1874, 2nd edn, Liberty Classics, Indianapolis 1993, pp. 97–98.

11   Michael J. Perry, *Under God? Religious Faith and Liberal Democracy*, Cambridge University Press, Cambridge 2003, pp. 81–84.
12   Mill, *On Liberty*, pp. 129–132.
13   539 US 558 (2003).
14   539 US 558, 562 (2003).
15   Mill, *On Liberty*, p. 71.
16   John Locke, *A Letter concerning Toleration*, 1st pub. 1689, Hackett, Indianapolis 1983, pp. 49–51.
17   Mill, *On Liberty*, p. 119.
18   Mill, *On Liberty*, pp. 163–164.
19   Joel Feinberg, *Harm to Others*, Oxford University Press, New York 1984, pp. 35–36.
20   Feinberg, *Harm to Others*, pp. 113–114.
21   J. L. Mackie, *Ethics: Inventing Right and Wrong*, Penguin, London 1977, pp. 232–237.
22   The four volumes are: *Harm to Others*, Oxford University Press, New York 1984; *Offense to Others*, Oxford University Press, New York 1985; *Harm to Self*, Oxford University Press, New York 1986; and *Harmless Wrongdoing*, Oxford University Press, New York 1988.
23   Feinberg, *Offense to Others*, p. 26.
24   Hart, *Law Liberty, and Morality*, pp. 46–47.
25   Feinberg, *Offense to Others*, pp. 25–26.
26   Hart, *Law, Liberty, and Morality*, pp. 30–34; Joseph Raz, *The Morality of Freedom*, Clarendon Press, Oxford; Oxford University Press, New York 1986, pp. 22–23.
27   George Sher, *Approximate Justice: Studies in Non-Ideal Theory*, Rowman & Littlefield, Lanham, MD 1997, pp. 112–113.
28   Steven D. Smith, *The Disenchantment of Secular Discourse*, Harvard University Press, Cambridge, MA 2010, pp. 77–87.
29   Smith, *The Disenchantment of Secular Discourse*, pp. 87–98.
30   Smith, *The Disenchantment of Secular Discourse*, pp. 98–104.
31   Feinberg, *Harmless Wrongdoing*, pp. 55–63.
32   Feinberg, *Harmless Wrongdoing*, pp. 48–49.
33   Feinberg, *Harmless Wrongdoing*, pp. 68–82.
34   Neil Levy, *Moral Relativism: A Short Introduction*, Oneworld, Oxford 2002, pp. 191–192.
35   Perry, *Under God?* p. 22.
36   Perry, *Under God?* pp. 64–69, 79–80.
37   Perry, *Under God?* pp. 69–74.
38   Perry, *Under God?* p. 33.
39   Perry, *Under God?* p. 7.
40   Perry, *Under God?* pp. 24–25.
41   Perry, *Under God?* p. 22.
42   Stephen L. Carter, *The Culture of Disbelief: How American Law and Politics Trivialize Religious Devotion*, Anchor, New York 1994, pp. 256–257.
43   Brian Barry, *Culture and Equality: An Egalitarian Critique of Multiculturalism*, Polity Press, Cambridge 2001, p. 25.

44  Perry, *Under God?* pp. 25–26.
45  I explore some of the issues elsewhere, in the context of stem-cell research rather than abortion. See Russell Blackford, "Stem Cell Research on Other Worlds, or Why Embryos Do Not Have a Right to Life," *Journal of Medical Ethics*, 32, 2006, pp. 177–180. As to abortion, see Russell Blackford, "The Supposed Rights of the Fetus," *Quadrant*, 389, Sept. 2002, pp. 11–17.
46  However, the state may well have legitimate secular reasons to regulate abortion clinics to ensure that they meet certain standards of safety, competence, and so on.
47  448 US 297 (1980).
48  448 US 297, 318–320 (1980).
49  Greenawalt, *Religion and the Constitution*, vol. 2, pp. 513–516.
50  Greenawalt, *Religion and the Constitution*, vol. 2, pp. 170–173.
51  Greenawalt, *Religion and the Constitution*, vol. 2, p. 173.
52  However, Perry himself contemplates that there might be only one respectable (as he sees it) argument that could be put against government recognition of same-sex unions as marriages. That is, the argument that a large number of Americans affirm the view that same-sex sexual relationships are contrary to the will of God (Michael J. Perry, *Toward a Theory of Human Rights: Religion, Law, Courts*, Cambridge University Press, Cambridge 2007, pp. 136–138). If that really is the only available "respectable" argument against recognizing same-sex marriages, then same-sex marriages should be recognized.
53  See *Attorney-General (Vict.); Ex Rel. Black v. The Commonwealth* (1981) 146 CLR 559.
54  [1985] 1 SCR 295.
55  Carter, *The Culture of Disbelief*, pp. 227–228.

# Introduction

As a rule, everyone must obey the general law. Even religious organizations are bound by laws of general effect that are enacted for legitimate secular reasons, rather than for the purpose, or with a principal or disproportionate effect, of suppressing a religion. If "religion-blind" laws are otherwise justified (when assessed against the harm principle, for example), they are not illegitimate merely because they have an incidental effect of hindering the practice of a religion's rituals or adherence to its canons of conduct. To repeat Locke's extreme example, the secular authorities may not, in support of their favored religious doctrine or its wish to suppress a rival religion, forbid the sacrifice of calves. They may, however, forbid the slaughter of all cattle if there is some independent secular reason.[1]

In practice, far more mundane issues have occupied much of the sitting time of contemporary courts: issues such as the applicability of zoning regulations to church buildings. Taken at face value, such matters have nothing to do with freedom of religion, understood as freedom from religious persecution. They involve no more than compliance with the ordinary secular law. If we followed Locke faithfully, that would be the end of the story, and much litigation could be avoided. We should, however, acknowledge the problems that arise for religious practice from the complexity of modern social regulation, much of it driven by vastly increased population densities since Locke's time, some stemming from an ongoing reassessment of the position of formerly despised or disadvantaged groups, and much of it aimed at establishing a social and economic safety net.

*Freedom of Religion and the Secular State*, First Edition. Russell Blackford.
© 2012 John Wiley & Sons, Inc. Published 2012 by John Wiley & Sons, Inc.

The upshot of all these developments is that the citizens of modern liberal democracies live within an extraordinarily complex web of social regulation, even as liberal principles such as the harm principle give them unprecedented freedom in certain aspects of their personal lives. The state clearly exercises a broad discretion in fashioning the detail of all this regulation, and the system can allow a degree of flexibility. So, should some discretion be exercised to accommodate sincere and otherwise law-abiding people who would be adversely affected by demands for strict compliance? Yes, I suggest, to a limited degree. That is the theme of this chapter.

## Laws of General Application

It is clear enough that the state should not impose its preferred religion or persecute religions that it dislikes. But as I suggested in Chapter 3, it cannot be accused of either of these things if it merely enacts a law for good secular reasons, that is to protect interests in worldly things. Nor should churches have any claim to special privileges such as they enjoyed in medieval times and the early modern period: the historical tendency has been to eliminate such advantages as sanctuary, benefit of clergy, and charitable immunity. These cannot be justified once the state moves to a position of neutrality about religious claims and the otherworldly goods that religions may or may not provide. Speaking in general, churches and sects cannot complain if they are hindered by the effects of neutral, generally applicable laws.

Such laws can, of course, have collateral effects on religious organizations and adherents: perhaps preventing them from doing something their faith demands, or at least encourages, perhaps requiring them to do something it forbids. Locke thought that there would be few problems in practice: "if Government be faithfully administered, and the Counsel of the Magistrate be indeed directed to the publick Good, this will seldom happen."[2] But is Locke right on this?

The Lockean model of the state rules out deliberate religious persecutions, thus giving various churches and sects some confidence that they will not be crushed by state power. Because it reduces the goals of government action to protection of civil interests, the model also offers confidence that even those actions which merely *feel like* persecution will be relatively rare; if all goes well, few laws will have unwanted incidental effects on the practice of a religion. Indeed, the unfolding logic of the Lockean model should lead to even fewer examples arising than Locke imagined: as the state comes to adopt liberal political principles, it will have increasingly little reason to enact laws that interfere with individuals' religiously motivated conduct.

Collectively, these considerations should go far toward defusing the problem of religious persecutions and counter-persecutions. If the state authorities act in good faith to protect civil interests, paying no heed to otherworldly doctrines, the various religions can live in harmony. Or so the theory goes.

In at least some cases that actually arise in the courts, the problem is not with the theory. It stems from neither the Lockean model itself nor liberal principles such as the harm principle. Instead, blame attaches to the unwillingness of contemporary liberal democracies to apply their own principles with any real commitment. The prime example of this is the leading American case on accommodation of religion, *Employment Division v. Smith*.[3] In this case, the Supreme Court was asked to find that peyote, a banned drug, could be used lawfully in Native American religious ceremonies. The opinion of the court has been much maligned, but it was, I submit, correct as a matter both of law and of political principle. The problem did not lie with the Supreme Court judges, whose analysis could have come straight from Locke, but with the Oregon legislature's sweeping anti-drug laws and the governmental policy throughout the US of a "war on drugs."

The litigation had a complex history, arriving twice at the Supreme Court. However, its essentials were as follows. Two men were fired from a private drug rehabilitation clinic for ingesting peyote during their participation in ceremonies of the Native American Church. Subsequently, they were denied state unemployment benefits on the basis that their dismissal had been for misconduct. In defending this decision, the Oregon government argued that denial of benefits was lawful since the conduct was a crime. The US Supreme Court was required to determine this point by considering whether sacramental ingestion of peyote was exempted from Oregon's general prohibition of the drug. The constitutional issue was whether such an accommodation of religious practices was required by the Free Exercise Clause, which prevents governments from "prohibiting the free exercise" of religion. In one sense, the case provided a perfect occasion to subject Locke's philosophical views to legal scrutiny. Did the Free Exercise clause go further than Locke argued for, or was it consistent with his approach to neutral laws of general application?

As it happened, a strong majority of the judges sided with the Oregon government, holding, exactly as Locke would have advocated, that religious belief could not ground a constitutional exemption from neutral laws of general application. Here, the same law that applied inside the church applied equally outside it, and this was crucial to the court's reasoning. The opinion of the court, delivered by Justice Scalia, was fully in line with Locke's views in *A Letter concerning Toleration*. Moreover, its reasoning is defensible as a matter of law and policy. While the secular state may not, without some (very) compelling secular reason, establish, endorse, persecute, or disparage religions, it does none of these things if it simply gives religious individuals and groups the same benefits (such as police protection) as anyone else. The same applies if it subjects them to the same burdens, such as taxes of various kinds and the generality of the criminal law.

But the case shows the wisdom of the Lockean model in another regard. The harsh outcome for the two dismissed employees could have been avoided if the state had not adopted an illiberal policy toward drugs such as peyote. Prima facie, the prohibition of such a drug violates the Millian harm principle, as any risk of harm is consented to by the user. Nor is this an obvious situation where paternalism is justified – why prevent adult users from ingesting a drug whose effects are reasonably well known, and after due deliberation about what they are doing? Paternalistic laws should always be viewed with suspicion, and even if some are justified this one is not a clear example. For the sake of argument, however, let us stipulate that some paternalistic regulation of peyote is justified. Even so, why make it so sweeping as to criminalize the drug's ingestion during the religious ceremony discussed in *Smith*? A government devoted to promotion of civil interests, and not, for example, to enforcement of morals, could take a narrower approach – for example, it could exempt small doses, require licensing, or restrict availability to minors.

Public policy in this area should weigh any paternalistic considerations against loss of liberty and other possible harms from over-criminalization. Not least, the latter can include wasted public resources, possible police corruption, perverse effects in strengthening the power of organized crime, and other perverse effects if criminalization leads to the sale of adulterated (possibly more dangerous) products. As far as peyote is concerned, such a balancing exercise might have led to much narrower legislation, with far less ambitious aims than total suppression of the drug. In that case, the Native American ceremonies involved in *Smith* may not have been unlawful in the first instance, and no exemption would have been needed.

The best lesson to draw from *Smith* is not that constitutional provisions such as the Free Exercise Clause should be read expansively or bolstered by legislation to achieve the same result. It is, rather, that a government devoted to its citizens' civil interests should honor the Millian harm principle, or at least move in that direction. This would protect individual liberty to take part in many self-regarding activities, including religious ones.

Greenawalt claims that the approach in *Smith* emasculates free exercise and sacrifices a constitutional guarantee.[4] But *Smith* does not allow the persecution of a religion, or of individual adherents, on religious grounds; it simply does not give them the right, on religious grounds, to be exempted from laws that are of general application and not motivated by disfavor toward any religion (or favor toward a rival religion). This may not give religious adherents everything they'd prefer, but the constitutional guarantees in the Bill of Rights continue to rule out the state persecution of disfavored religion that was such a blight on Western history for many centuries. To say that free exercise of religion is emasculated is to assume, rather than to demonstrate, that religious adherents are entitled to something more than that from a document such as the Bill of Rights. It is begging the question to claim, as Greenawalt does, that *Smith* involves "blatant inattention to the fundamental political rights of citizens."[5]

## Religious Persecutions

But does this leave a danger that ostensibly neutral laws will be enacted to discourage the exercise of an unpopular religion?[6] This issue arose in the US in a case that involved Locke's own example of laws forbidding animal sacrifice. *Church of the Lukumi Babulu v. City of Hialeah*[7] provides a rare case where the American courts struck down legislation aimed at suppressing a religion. Perhaps if the legislators had paid more attention to Locke's *Letter concerning Toleration* they could have avoided this particular debacle.

The case concerned Santeria, a syncretic religion that contains elements of Roman Catholicism mixed with traditional African spirituality. Santeria involves the worship of spiritual beings known as *orishas*, who can assist individual adherents to obtain their divinely appointed destinies. Though powerful, these beings are not immortal and depend on animal sacrifices for their survival. A variety of birds, mammals, and reptiles are killed in Santeria rituals, by means of cutting the carotid arteries. In the late 1980s members of a Santeria church sought and obtained appropriate permits for a house of worship in Hialeah, Florida. In response, the city council took a series of actions to prevent animal sacrifice within the city boundaries. These culminated in a series of ordinances specifically prohibiting animal sacrifice, defined in such a way that the ordinances' primary effect was to prevent the kinds of killings practiced in Santeria.

In the circumstances, it was unlikely that any other killings were captured by the ordinances, which contained various exemptions, including for kosher killings. Santeria was not mentioned by name, and the wording of the ordinances applied to anyone conducting relevantly identical sacrifices. Nonetheless, the objective was clear: to make it impossible to practice Santeria within the boundaries of Hialeah. There was no real pretense that the ordinances were about something other than sacrifices to the *orishas*; thus they were remote from Locke's example of a (permissible) law forbidding all slaughter of cattle in a jurisdiction to allow stocks to recover after a plague.[8] But even if there'd been more pretense, this was a transparent example of contrived law-making whose real object was to suppress the activities of a disfavored sect.

Despite the ordinances' superficially neutral and general language, the Supreme Court had no difficulty finding that their object was to suppress the Santeria religion, and that they breached the Free Exercise Clause. Coming in the wake of *Smith*, the outcome surprised some commentators, but the Lockean model makes good sense of both. In retrospect, it's surprising that the Santeria church had to fight such a blatant case of persecution all the way to the Supreme Court.

I submit that, like *Smith*, *Lukumi Babalu* was correctly decided – not only as a matter of law but also as one of policy. Taken together these cases show how courts can distinguish, at least on occasion, between genuinely neutral and generally applicable laws, aimed at conduct that would be unacceptable no matter who engaged in it, and laws aimed suppressing a particular church or sect. There might be borderline examples, but that is a problem for the courts in every area of the law. If these two cases were taken in isolation, they would suggest that all is well with Locke's analysis in 1689. All that's required to supplement it is a strong commitment to liberal political principles.

Other considerations, however, suggest that there should be more scope than this for religious accommodations in modern liberal democracies. This arises from the extensive activities of the modern state.

## Religion, the Individual, and the Modern State

As Witte points out, "the modern welfare state, for better or worse, reaches deeply into virtually all aspects of modern life – through its network of education, charity, welfare, child care, health care, construction, zoning, workplace, taxation, and sundry other regulations." In Locke's time, or early in the life of the United States of America, the state could fairly easily avoid interfering with religion. It could confine itself to the preservation of public order and protections of legal rights from the trespasses of others. However, as Witte concludes, "this traditional understanding of a minimal state role in the life of society in general, and of religious bodies in particular – however alluring it may be in theory – is no longer realistic in practice."[9]

Many social tendencies over the past few hundred years, and especially since the mid-1800s, have led to the state's conduct of increasingly broad functions. While gradual acceptance of the Millian harm principle has reduced some of the burden of the criminal law, for example in respect of homosexual conduct, governments now conduct a vast array of programs. The state takes considerable, even prime, responsibility for education, public health, and many forms of physical and social infrastructure, while regulating many of the transactions between corporate entities and the public. Dense urban populations require planning and coordination, while the potentially harsh outcomes of industrial capitalism have led to an increased emphasis on economic welfare. This involves the tuning of macro-economic settings, encouragement of specific industries, and provision of a social safety net.

In the upshot, any modern jurisdiction's total body of written law is far larger than ever. Increasingly, it becomes misleading to adopt the formula that the state (merely) *protects* interests in things of this world. While the secular state may confine itself to worldly interests, it is expected to do much more to *promote* the interests of citizens, such as by providing educational and cultural opportunities.

I don't regret this tendency, and it's notable that modern liberals in the tradition of Mill are not usually opposed to the welfare state.[10] Mill himself accepted that individual citizens could have responsibilities to contribute positively to the social good. These could include giving evidence in the law courts, making a contribution to national defense or other "joint work" needed for society's interests, and such actions as saving another's life or interposing to protect the weak against "ill usage" by the strong. Failure to do these things counted, for Mill, as harming others by omission.[11] Thus, whatever Mill's views might have been on any particular government program, the Millian tradition is not committed to a Libertarian view that taxation is theft, or that government spending (beyond a few core areas) is illegitimate. Developments relating to the state's expanding social role have been tied closely to the civil interests of citizens, and they are, in general, reasonably necessary in the social and economic circumstances emerging since Locke's time.

While there are ongoing debates about the size of government, Western electorates and major political parties expect the state to play this extended role. Accordingly, very large amounts of revenue must be raised through the imposition of taxes on (for example) income, profits, and certain private spending. The revenue is then distributed to the ever growing array of government programs.

Where the tax transfer system works efficiently, it has a considerable impact in redistributing wealth from the rich to the poor, overcoming market failures, ameliorating many of the harsher aspects of contemporary life, and providing citizens with diverse opportunities. One inevitable outcome is that most individuals will be opposed to at least some programs that receive government support. Still, as Thomas Nagel points out, this is worse when the state acts on our behalf in a way that violates our deepest convictions about the meaning of life than when it merely promotes, say, controversial aesthetic values.[12]

It is, I submit, usually acceptable for the state to spend taxpayers' money even on contentious projects, provided there is some rationally understandable secular purpose. What it must not do is suppress the personal activities of individuals who disagree. Wherever possible, room must remain for citizens to live in accordance with their own priorities and values. For example, Norwegian citizens should accept that their country spends revenue in an effort to develop elite athletes in preparation for the Olympic Games, even if this is not every citizen's preference. But they should *not* accept laws that involve the infliction of punishment or stigma on those who depart from the values that the state thus promotes, for example if they prefer professional wrestling to the Olympics. The latter course of action would impose the values of the state, or the electoral majority, far more obtrusively.

Fortunately, public funds spent on subsidizing Olympic Games preparations in no way inhibit the enjoyment of professional wrestling and may not even diminish the latter's success in the commercial marketplace. That is partly because there are practical limits to how much overall taxation can be levied. As Braithwaite and Pettit express the point, "the exigencies of fiscal politics first lead to the setting of a target budget deficit or surplus and then different spending programs compete for the scarce resources available under the expenditure ceiling."[13] Most probably, the money expended by the state would otherwise have been spent by it somewhere else. Realistically, it should not be regarded as an additional amount coerced from the unwilling especially for the purpose of this particular subsidy.

Acute questions arise when the state proposes to give funds to religious (or anti-religious) organizations or to programs that some religions consider immoral. Generally speaking, the latter should be accepted. For example, it is legitimate for the state to fund abortions, not as an expression of anti-religious sentiment but simply for health and other secular benefits to women: the state would likely act in the same way if religion did not exist at all. A funding decision such as this can, therefore, be religion-blind and non-persecutory. However, the issues become more difficult if the state provides funds to religious organizations, or avowedly anti-religious ones, to carry out some of its programs.

Even this should not be ruled out entirely. Concern is likely to arise if the funding is spent in such a way as to provide state assistance or endorsement to a religious or anti-religious viewpoint. Thus, it might be acceptable for an atheist organization to tender successfully for a contract to deliver social services – but not if some of the money is spent on attempts at persuading clients to give up religion. There may, of course, be difficult judgments of circumstance and degree, and not all may be readily decidable in the courts. As a first line of defense, however, we can ask that state officials act in good faith to avoid assisting religion or irreligion in their struggles of ideas. Where, for example, a religious organization wins a contract to deliver government services for a fee, it may be best to impose strict conditions to ensure that the services will be delivered without proselytizing.

## Accommodation of Religion

Many other commentators have noted the changing role of the state and its impact on religious practice in contemporary liberal democracies. For example, Carter states correctly that none of the modern welfare state type of laws existed in 1791, when the Free Exercise Clause was written into the US Constitution.[14] Indeed, the roles of organized churches have also ramified and evolved. Kramnick and Moore observe:

> Today government and organized religions do many things that they did not do in the seventeenth century. Churches then did not build hospitals or own fishing fleets. Government then did not provide church-founded universities with money to carry on scientific research.[15]

In objecting to the idea of a literal separation of church and state, Eisgruber and Sager also emphasize that churches do many things that cannot be literally separated from state activities:

> Churches buy and sell property, build buildings, run schools, maintain staffs of paid employees, need roads for access, and are vulnerable to the same risks of fire and theft as every other entity. Church members drive cars, pay taxes, interact in countless ways with their fellow citizens, and vote in public elections. The state, for its part, maintains the regime of private law upon which contract and property rights depend, promulgates building codes, regulates the use of land, protects its citizens from unfair and discriminatory employment practices, builds roads, and acts as the default provider of police and fire protection.[16]

As a consequence many laws of general application can affect the activities of churches and sects:

> Religion . . . assumes many forms and comprises many beliefs. Not surprisingly, in America, which is home to a diverse range of religious beliefs and practices, it is not uncommon for persons in the grip of their religious commitments to discover that those commitments are at odds with public regulations.[17]

In previous chapters, I emphasized that secular authorities should not be motivated by any belief in, or favor toward, the doctrines of a church or sect. But there remains an issue of whether the authorities might have worldly reasons to show solicitude to a sect's adherents when they fall foul of the extensive provisions of modern regulation. In principle, the state could act for its own reasons to exempt certain religious adherents even from aspects of the general law. Without accepting the *truth* of a religious doctrine, it might acknowledge that adherents to it feel bound in conscience to honor it by their conduct. Note, once again, that no principled distinction can be made between religious morality and other religious doctrines: adherents will feel just as bound to follow a religious canon of conduct, such as not conducting abortions, as they are to accept the claims that certain gods exist or that the afterlife takes a particular form.

Thus, the state might have worldly reasons to exempt religious organizations and individuals from certain laws that are of general application. It might be reluctant to force citizens to act against their conscience, bearing in mind James Fitzjames Stephen's warning that the criminal law is largely futile as a means of suppressing actions that do not violate the agent's own conscience or cause direct harm to others.[18] Out of compassion, it might not wish to place citizens in a position where they believe their spiritual salvation is at risk. Pragmatically, it might wish to avoid civil unrest if its laws placed a particular religion in an untenable position. Moreover, it might be concerned not to play favorites: once it gives accommodations to some religions for these sorts of reasons, it might wish to be reasonably consistent in the way it treats others, even if they have less political clout.

If it is clear that the state is acting for purposes such as these – and that a variety of religions are receiving accommodations from time to time – it cannot reasonably be accused of endorsing one religion or another. However, three critical points should be emphasized. First, these kinds of considerations do not apply only to religion. There may be *many* circumstances where the state has good reasons to craft exemptions from neutral and generally applicable laws. For example, people who are not religious could have strong conscientious reasons to disobey certain laws. An obvious example is military conscription. If the state is unwilling to force the consciences of its citizens, it should take this consideration into account, whether or not a particular citizen is religious.

Second, situations will vary widely. At one extreme, compliance with a certain law may bring about the destruction of an entire religion or it may force individuals to act in a way that (as they see the world) guarantees their eternal damnation. In these circumstances, the state should be reluctant to insist. The outcome if it did so would be much suffering, alienation, and possibly civil strife. At the other extreme, the state's action may involve nothing that provokes such anguish, though it may cause a religious group expense and inconvenience, or it may hinder the group's members in carrying out religious activities that are not compulsory within its canons of conduct.

Third, any accommodation granted to a religious group is likely to place a burden on somebody else – whether it be the agencies of the state (and ultimately the taxpayers) or other individuals and groups in society. To return to Locke's example, imagine that a legitimate law against slaughtering cattle is enacted in order to increase stocks after an extraordinary plague. Perhaps a religious group that practices animal sacrifices for the forgiveness of sins could be given an exemption, but this will create a burden for others. State officials need to weigh this burden against the benefits of granting the exemption. If they do go ahead and grant it, they may have good reason to grant it in only the most limited practical terms. For example, sacrifice of cattle may be compulsory twice a year, within the teachings of the religion concerned, and merely encouraged on a weekly basis. In those circumstances, the state may wish to craft the exemption to allow the religious group to sacrifice twice a year but no more.

Defenders of accommodations for religion often write as if all religious accommodations involve laws that produce the highest level of personal anguish and as if the interests of others who are affected count for little. That, however, is an unfair assumption. Consider the relatively common situation where large-scale, multi-purpose church buildings are planned for residential neighborhoods. Problems with obtaining permits may cause frustration for church officials with ambitious objectives, but they do not involve the use of state power to force believers' consciences; nor is the fate of a religious group at stake if it has difficulty finding an ideal location. Instead, the difficulty is the same as any organization might face if it aimed to establish intense, large-scale, and disruptive operations among suburban homes.

Conversely, homeowners are entitled to ask that their civil interests be protected. Zoning or land-use laws have that secular purpose, and any exceptions to them have real effects on individuals and families. The effect can be financial, as housing values plummet, or "merely" on safety, comfort, aesthetic values, and local tradition.[19] It is by no means obvious that religious organizations should prevail when their interests clash so directly with the welfare of citizens. Nor is this a matter that can be settled according to a clear principle: conflicting values must be weighed, and different decision-makers might reasonably come to different conclusions. Decisions like these are best left to legislatures, or at least to local tribunals with the legislature's delegated power, rather than being settled by the courts as matters of constitutional law.

More generally, there are doubtlessly circumstances where the strict rule proposed by Locke should be relaxed, and even neutral laws of general application should have exceptions. The state has much discretion in framing the content of its voluminous legislation, and much of it would meet its purposes without strict compliance being required of all parties in all circumstances. There is certainly room to make exceptions where the impact on churches, sects, or their adherents would be disproportional to the secular gains obtained from universal compliance. In suitable circumstances, accommodation of religion should not be viewed as religious *establishment* or *endorsement*. These are, however, the sorts of issues to be weighed by legislatures, which have access to advice and information far beyond what is available to the courts, as well as being democratically accountable for their discretionary judgments.

Religious organizations and communities cannot be allowed to choose for themselves what laws they propose to obey, but sometimes the state should be flexible. One judgment of the Constitutional Court of South Africa expresses this well: "believers cannot claim an automatic right to be exempted by their beliefs from the laws of the land." Where possible, however, the state should "seek to avoid putting believers to extremely painful and intensely burdensome choices of either being true to their faith or else respectful of the law."[20]

## Barry's Fork

Brian Barry is critical of the practice of granting legislative exemptions from neutral laws of general application, and I believe that he somewhat over-states his position. Nonetheless, he is on strong ground when he argues that many laws should either have no exemptions or should not be enacted in the first place. We might refer to this argument as "Barry's Fork."

Barry acknowledges that a law may bear on some people with special harshness, and that this "is at least a reason for examining it to see if it might be modified so as to accommodate those who are affected by it in some special way." Such an examination might be prompted by considerations of prudence or generosity.[21] It is well to add that there could be issues of fairness or justice. Consider Greenawalt's argument from the experience with Prohibition in the US – a time when alcohol was prohibited, but an exemption was given for communion wine in Christian church services. For Greenawalt, this shows an "obvious point": "allowing people to participate in acts of worship that are at the center of their religious practice is a very strong reason to create an exemption."[22] The issue of justice is this: if the state is prepared, even counterfactually, to tailor its laws to provide for the religious requirements of large Christian denominations such as Roman Catholicism, why not also for the followers of Native American religions?

Of course, there is something to this argument. As I've already suggested, the state has good secular reasons to avoid acts that suppress religions, even if that is not the intention or the principal legislative effect. Moreover, it has good reasons to act fairly, treating analogous cases in ways that are relevantly similar. But here's where Barry's Fork becomes relevant. Surely the most obvious point that emerges from reflection on the Prohibition era is the foolishness of sweeping bans on activities that give people pleasure and are not directly harmful to others. While carefully tailored regulation of alcohol consumption may well be justified (I have no desire to argue against it), the Prohibition experiment was disastrous. Once again, the crucial point to be gleaned is not that religious exemptions from sweeping laws may sometimes be a good idea, even though that is true; rather, it is that governments should pay more attention to the harm principle. That would result in some laws not being enacted in anything like their actual form.

Barry suggests that we can always ask whether it is better to find a less restrictive version of the law that would satisfy everyone and avoid invidious distinctions among the rights of citizens, rather than retain the law, unchanged, while exempting a group from it. In practice, he suggests, the rule-and-exemption approach is followed as a way of buying off the most articulate objectors while gaining most of what was sought. Although he does not rule out this approach in all cases, he suggests that there will usually be two possibilities: either the case for the law is sufficiently strong to rule out exemptions *or* the case for exemptions will be strong enough to suggest that the law should not exist in its current (or proposed) form at all.[23]

Surely there's a point here: governments should not lightly enact laws that are not really needed, and once they enact laws that really *are* needed they should not lightly make exceptions. In developing his approach, Barry shows little sympathy for the idea that somebody's religious freedom is abridged if, for example, all meat must be slaughtered in ways that don't match Jewish ritual requirements, or if all motorcyclists are required to wear helmets (preventing male Sikhs from wearing turbans when they ride motorbikes). No one's religious practices are being *prevented* in these cases, since no one is required by religion to eat meat or to take up motorcycling. These laws simply alter the nature of the activities concerned in such ways that Jew and Sikhs, respectively, no longer prefer them.[24] In such circumstances, Barry says, there is no need to provide for exemptions.

That is not to say that Barry himself would apply Barry's Fork in all cases. Imagine that motorcycles were needed to get obtain jobs in a particular locality or that riding a motorcycle was a requirement for joining the police force (arguably, it is important to have representatives of minorities in the force). Again, what if the argument shifted to wearing hard hats in the building trade, where many Sikhs traditionally obtain work? In cases such as this, Barry suggests, there may be a public interest in having both the general law and the exemption to serve the special interest in allowing Sikhs, or at least those already in the industry, to participate.[25] Another example where a rule-and-exemption policy might be justified on Barry's approach is if a school has a policy, perhaps supported by good reasons, of requiring a uniform, but a Sikh boy seeks an exemption from it in order to wear his turban. This may be justified, according to Barry's analysis, but only because it meets precise conditions:

It must be important to have a rule generally prohibiting conduct of a certain kind because, if this is not so, the way in which to accommodate minorities is simply not having a rule at all. At the same time, though, having a rule must not be so important as to preclude allowing exceptions to it. We are left with cases in which uniformity is a value but not a great enough one to over-ride the case for exemptions.[26]

In short, Barry argues that the rule and exemption sort of approach has a role to play, but only in a very restricted range of cases. His point is that these cases are genuinely exceptional: they involve something that approaches a social or personal necessity, such as that in getting a job or attending school, rather than a mere matter of preference or convenience. No one *has* to ride a motorcycle as recreation, or to eat meat when healthy vegetarian diets are available. Or so the argument goes. So if people's preferences for these things clash with a certain religious prescription, they can abandon the relevant preferences.

Barry also considers a pragmatic argument against removing an exemption once it's in place. Repealing the law entirely – as if exempting everybody – will mean that its purpose is no longer fulfilled, but simply removing an exemption that has hitherto been enjoyed may increase social tensions, cause alienation, and give encouragement to bigots. Better, perhaps, to compromise and leave the exemption alone. Even so, he suggests, such well-entrenched exemptions cannot act as precedents for new ones.[27]

The general effect of Barry's Fork is that some laws should not be enacted at all. Others do not require exemptions, since they do no more than make certain activities less attractive to people who can no longer (1) engage in them legally while (2) also complying with their religious canons of conduct. They can resolve the problem by opting not to engage in the activity.

## Considering Exemptions

Barry's Fork is supposed to leave few legitimate exemptions, but it certainly does not rule out all cases whatsoever. Part of the effect of the argument is to emphasize that there is a spectrum of effects that a neutral, generally applicable law might have on religious conduct. At one extreme, it might have the effect of banning a compulsory rite, such as animal sacrifices in a religion that demands these for spiritual purposes. Or it might prevent specifically religious conduct that is not compulsory for purposes such as salvation, for example if animal sacrifices are only one approved way to please the gods.

In other cases, the law will prevent an individual from engaging in activities that are pretty much necessary for a decent life in contemporary societies (such as attending work or school). She will be prevented as long as she's unwilling to violate her religion's precepts. There are also cases where the individual will be prevented from engaging in less important activities, and there are cases where the effect is to prevent business enterprises that might be owned by a religious organization or adherent from being run as the owner desires. Here, the effect is to make running the business less attractive, but not to prevent anyone obtaining a livelihood in other ways, such as through paid employment. Nor, in such a case, is anyone's enjoyment of her private life affected, as with the examples of meat-eating and riding a motorcycle.

As I'll discuss in the next chapter, business owners exercise a form of private power that the state may have an interest in restraining. Generally speaking, the case for business enterprises with religious connections to be exempt from, say, anti-discrimination laws is weak.

Even in what may seem like the less draconian cases, a secular government may have good reasons to provide exemptions: this will depend on such issues as how important it considers full compliance and how important it might be to keep certain activities open to people of many religious convictions. The case for an exemption seems stronger if the collateral effect of the law is to ban a religious practice, even a non-compulsory one, than if it merely makes a non-religious practice more difficult for some people. But there is an undoubted benefit in having conscience-clear access to such worldly goods as eating meat or riding a motorcycle, and I don't see why, at the level of principle, the state might not weigh up such benefits when it enacts legislation, including exemptions.

These two examples, used by Barry, actually raise an interesting issue. Some people oppose eating meat and riding motorcycles, and may even wish they could be banned. Reasons for this include the effects of eating meat on factory-farmed animals, moral scruples about taking the lives of sentient creatures, and the environmental effects of farming or herding animals for meat. In the case of motorcycles, opponents might claim (plausibly or otherwise) that they decrease overall road safety. In both cases, opponents may be glad (perhaps secretly) if some people are prevented from taking part in the disliked activities. Though Barry does not rely on any such argument, he uses these as examples where the state should *not* usually show leniency. Part of the attraction of his examples for that purpose might lie in the sneaking suspicion that these activities are, in any event, morally dubious or contrary to enlightened public policy. It might even be suggested that people who are prevented from enjoying these particular activities are receiving a net benefit, since both activities involve personal hazards.

If these considerations are made overt, I suggest that they be resisted. The suggestion I am considering is that legislators could take advantage of people's religious convictions to obtain, indirectly, part of what they cannot gain, or are unwilling to gain, directly. For example, they could reduce the consumption of meat or the number of motorcycles on the roads. The purpose behind this would be, to a degree, paternalistic. However, it is especially offensive if the state claims to know the interests of a group of people better than they know them themselves, and refuses to grant an exemption on paternalistic grounds that apply equally to the general population. It would be most unfortunate if these kinds of reasoning began to be used in policy deliberations.

This is not to suggest that, for example, Sikhs should automatically get an exemption from wearing motorbike helmets. Here I agree with Barry. In a circumstance such as this, exemption from the general law should be seen more as a privilege than as a right. Once the state considers granting such a privilege, the safety effect of riding without a helmet is one thing for it to consider in the policy process. It should not, however, take into account the opportunity to reduce the overall occurrence of an activity that it disapproves of but cannot expediently ban. That is an opportunistic use of people's religious beliefs to achieve an ulterior end. Though done for a secular reason, it is divisive and offensive.

Once the state begins to accommodate religion-based needs and desires, it will need to work through complex issues of how and how much. While it might be best to acknowledge the consciences of the faithful, showing some flexibility and leniency, there is an obvious risk, in a large class of cases, of burdening others. It follows that religious accommodation, in the form of exemptions from neutral, generally applicable laws, is not a straightforward matter for the secular state. In any particular case where exemptions from a law are sought, the legislators will have much to weigh up during the deliberation process – and this is a proper matter for them rather than for disposition by the courts.

## Conscientious Objection

With these considerations in mind, I turn to a vexed issue in many areas of employment, mainly but not solely in the broad area of health care. This is the refusal of individuals or organizations to provide certain services on conscientious grounds, usually based in religion. Speaking of the US – though much of his analysis would extend to other liberal democracies – Ronald A. Lindsay notes that, prior to the 1970s, conscientious objection applied only to individuals who were compelled to join certain groups with the effect that they would then have to perform actions that were against their strong religious objections. Examples included Quakers objecting to being drafted into the military and Jehovah's Witnesses being required to attend school.[28]

Now, however, many health-care workers make conscientious objections in a range of situations, and many jurisdictions provide them with statutory exemptions. The most obvious cases involve assistance in carrying out abortions – proscribed by the Catholic Church and other religious organizations – but there are many others. These include refusal to prescribe or supply contraceptives to unmarried women, refusal to supply emergency contraception, and refusal to cease life support. Outside the area of health care, issues can arise with registration of same-sex marriages or providing same-sex partners with counseling. In contemporary societies, with many religious views and citizens engaged in a vast, diverse range of activities, numerous and varied circumstances arise where individuals or organizations may be motivated by religious scruples not to provide their services.

Viewed in another way, however, the circumstances fall into two main categories: the state may require certain activities for the benefit of the public, but these may be objected to by employers (such as pharmacies, medical practices, or hospitals); or an employer may require certain activities to be carried out, only to have its employees object. Obviously, there are mixed situations. Examples are when an employer *and* its employees object to the activities requested by the state, or when the employees are public servants and their duties are intended to advance government programs.

Where the state itself wants the duties to be performed, and is met with non-compliance, it needs to balance the effect of exemption on citizens' civil interests against any harsh outcomes if it insists. In other situations, somewhat different issues must be considered. On one hand, the various business enterprises within the jurisdiction are entitled to operate and seek profits. On the other hand, there may be a public benefit in ensuring that religious beliefs do not provide too great an impediment to employment in the mainstream economy. Accordingly, the state may establish a regime of anti-discrimination law broad enough to proscribe discrimination in employment on the ground of religion. Obviously this will require at least some exceptions, such as where religious organizations themselves genuinely need to employ someone of their particular faith – perhaps in a leadership or advocacy role. The question is how far such protections should extend.

I'll deal with anti-discrimination law in more detail in Chapter 7. For now, let us note that employers have a strong case to base personnel decisions on relative efficiency or effectiveness, not just on ability to carry out essential functions. We should, however, also take note of the problem that some people entered their professions at a time when they could not conceive of being required to carry out duties that troubled their consciences:

> When the rules of appropriate behavior change radically, as with the status of most abortions, one especially cannot expect people to abandon a vocation with the onset of a novel conflict between general expectations about its practice and individual moral standards.[29]

For example, a supermarket may introduce Sunday opening after decades of opening six days a week, scientific advances may create entirely unforeseen ethical problems, a sex education or equality policy may be introduced, and so on. Why should the onus then be on the religious employee to seek alternative work?[30]

Well, one reason might be that we now live in a changing world, and no employer can guarantee that the work it is offering in return for wages or salary will always meet the employee's requirements. Jobs do change over time, and employers cannot be expected to retain workers who refuse to do whatever they are being paid for. For example, an employee who has voluntarily entered a shift-work environment should be on notice that her individual rostering preferences may not be met forever.

In other situations, however, changing duties or a changing work environment may create real unfairness. Sometimes it may be possible to insulate an individual employee from particularly burdensome changes, but business efficiency won't always allow this. In other cases, it may be best to think of the situation as a redundancy – where, in effect, one job has been abolished and replaced with something different. It may, at least, be more like a redundancy than poor performance or misconduct. In many jurisdictions, termination for redundancy carries relatively generous benefits, which may provide room for compromises and settlements, case by case.

The fact remains that employers are entitled to structure their businesses for economic efficiency. It is not religious persecution if your employer no longer wants your services because, for whatever reason, you are simply not prepared to carry out the duties that the employer wants.

## Services Required by the State

Additional considerations apply where services of one kind or another are required by the state itself. These situations may apply to the state's own agencies, to other organizations to which it has "contracted out" service provision, or to other organizations or individuals whose activities are regulated for reasons of public interest. Duties required by the state may also include jury service, providing evidence in court (perhaps under subpoena), and many small acts of cooperation with the official bureaucracy. Controversy can arise over something as simple as having a photo taken for a passport or a driver's license. I will focus on the duties of workers (whether or not they are technically employees), but much could be written about other situations.

Services provided or required by the state occur in many areas that are crucial to citizens' life planning, and hence to important civil interests. Once the state decides to promote its citizens' interests in a particular way, it should be reluctant to introduce exceptions that shift burdens back to citizens. Some of the most controversial issues arise in the health-care context, where the state imposes extensive obligations, even on private clinics. In many cases, the interactions of doctors and patients are matters of life and death. Patients may suffer pain, distress, and confusion about what is happening. They are psychologically vulnerable, and are often required to deal with providers who have an effective monopoly. They should not, as Ronald Lindsay puts it, be expected "to navigate among Catholic nurses, Muslim pharmacists, Wiccan nurses' aides, and Hindu dieticians, and so on, all of whom claim the right to refuse medical care."[31]

Lindsay suggests several factors that should weigh for or against granting conscientious objector status: first, whether or not the conflict between the obligation to take an action and the opposed obligation of conscience was generated by the person herself. Thus, an individual who is drafted into the military has a better claim than another who volunteered. Second, whether the person is prepared to take some other action that might ameliorate the harm of not providing the service (as well as showing sincerity). Third, whether any exemption can be tailored narrowly to limit the harm to others from her not providing the service. Fourth, whether the cost of forcing someone to perform the action would be outweighed by the harm of allowing an exemption. In a military context, for example, there may be disproportionate cost in jailing someone for refusing to use a rifle that they were unlikely to fire in combat, when others may be readily available to perform the service.[32]

According to Lindsay, most of these factors weigh against allowing conscientious objections for health-care workers – at least in the majority of cases. Far from being conscripted, Lindsay points out, health-care workers have usually entered voluntarily into professions that have fought for, and obtained, monopolistic privileges. Would-be conscientious objectors typically seek to avoid any costs to themselves or to do anything to mitigate the harm to others' interests. Rather than compromise on a narrowly tailored exemption, they often refuse to assist patients even in locating an alternative provider. In a minority of cases, however, pragmatic considerations might weigh in favor of exemption, since nobody wants a physician who is adamantly opposed to abortion performing an abortion on her – or a doctor who is opposed to IVF overseeing her IVF program. In other circumstances, these latter considerations won't be so strong. In the majority of situations, health-care workers will have a weak case for accommodation of their religious scruples.[33]

Lindsay acknowledges that the balance may be different for physicians. In addition to the obvious pragmatic considerations, physicians have traditionally had the right to limit their practices, as well as some shared responsibility with patients for making health-care decisions. Moreover, there may be more scope to find an alternative doctor than to find an alternative nurse or pharmacist. But even if physicians are given some right to limit their practices or the procedures that they are prepared to carry out, they should notify patients at early stage of any such limitations in the services they offer. If they fail to do so, and the patient needs (say) an abortion, they should provide the patient with a prompt referral.[34] Finally, Lindsay suggests that there is nothing wrong with religious bodies owning and running health-care institutions, but they should not receive public support, such as funding and tax exemptions, unless they provide the public with the full range of legal medical services.[35]

Against all this, we might repeat that there's value in avoiding dilemmas for religious believers, or for others with strong moral commitments. Where practicable, the state should not require them to make the hard choice between complying with their faith, or their moral commitments, and complying with the law. Indeed, as Greenawalt states in a discussion of military exemptions, it is not wise from any point of view to force people to take part in conduct that they oppose:

> People who are fervently opposed to military missions do not make ideal soldiers. . . . [F]orcing people to choose between violating their most deeply felt conscientious convictions and going to jail (or leaving the country) is not wise. Selective objectors should not be drafted, and volunteer army personnel should be able to refuse to go to a theater of war where service would be repugnant to conscience.[36]

Where services to the public are actually required by the state, for example if it demands that doctors carry out certain abortions, then, prima facie, the public interest does require that the services be provided. Still, there might sometimes be room for compromise, for an element of give and take. If the situation is not an emergency, perhaps another doctor can be sought and found quickly enough to avoid extra risk to a patient's life or health. Accommodation does not mean having things entirely your own way, and any conscientious exemptions should be contingent upon some cooperation with the secular purpose of the law, even if the doctor finds this distasteful. For example, a Catholic doctor might, in non-emergency situations, at least be required to provide a referral to a colleague with no similar scruples.

An approach along these lines was adopted in the state of Victoria (Australia) when abortion law was reformed in 2008. As a result, registered health practitioners, such as doctors and registered nurses, are under an absolute obligation to perform or assist in an abortion only in an emergency situation where the woman's life is in danger. In other situations where advice or assistance is sought with an abortion, the practitioner may state a conscientious objection and refer the patient to a colleague.[37]

This provides health practitioners who have religious or moral scruples with a considerable area of exemption from the requirements of the general law. Unfortunately, many participants in the debate surrounding the law reform process characterized the lack of more sweeping exemptions as a breach of religious freedom. That is a flawed analysis: the real question was how far those with religious or moral scruples should be given a privilege not to abide by the secular law applying to everyone else. The mere failure to give a complete exemption from generally applicable provisions crafted for religiously neutral secular purposes is not religious persecution.

As with any employment, there are situations in the health sector where some sympathetic regard should be given to the fact that work requirements have altered over time. And there are also, of course, good reasons against driving entire religious groups out of certain professions such as medicine and nursing. Those reasons relate both to social cohesion and to the goal of any society to gain the benefits of its citizens' natural talents (at least to the extent that this can be done non-coercively). Ahdar and Leigh are right to comment that "the economy and society will suffer if whole occupations become closed (on grounds of conscience) to religious people who are otherwise well-qualified."[38] Similarly, the state may sometimes, as a matter of fiscal practicality, need to provide services through such organizations as religious hospitals, which are partly funded from private sources. It may have little choice but to compromise on the delivery of certain services.

None of this, however, should blur the essential point, which is that the state should determine on secular grounds precisely what services it wants delivered to the public. Those services should be aimed at protecting and promoting civil interests, rather than such things as spiritual salvation. Depending on the circumstances, the state may or may not make some room for conscientious objections, but not at the cost of compromising its secular goals. This may require a degree of mutual compromise. Individuals who will not compromise, even when the possibility is offered, are entitled to their beliefs. But they may need to find work in other professions.

## Conclusion

The logic of the Lockean model suggests that the state must not establish, impose, endorse, or persecute religion in general or any particular religion. More accurately, it must not do these things without some adequately compelling secular reason. In liberal democracies, outright religious persecution very seldom occurs and could almost never be justified. *Lukumi*

How is ~ talking about the state?

*Babalu* was a rare case, and the US Supreme Court rightly protected Florida's followers of the unpopular Santeria religion. In principle, however, sufficiently extreme religious sects can pose a real and immediate threat to citizens' civil interests. In extraordinary circumstances, the state could treat such a sect much like any criminal organization. That is an issue for the next chapter.

While the state should avoid outright persecutions, it cannot give religious groups their own way on all things. It acts for its own worldly reasons, often enacting laws that apply to all. In one sense only, this process is agnostic or atheistic. More accurately, it is religion-blind: the secular state does not exist to suppress religion, but nor should it seek to promote religion. Its starting point in policy deliberations is a purely worldly one. Indeed, state officials should adopt broadly similar policies regardless of which religions, if any, operate within their jurisdictions. Whichever gods are worshipped in my country or yours, both of us need protection against violence, theft, poverty, and sickness.

That, however, cannot be the finishing point for all political deliberation, especially not in modern societies where the state's role is greatly enlarged. The state's expanded role leads to many government programs that we cannot all, individually, endorse, but this is a situation that we must tolerate. Some difficulties arise because certain of the state's requirements' impact on religion. Though reflecting no policy of hostility, various laws can frustrate the plans of religious organizations and restrict the options of adherents. This is an extra factor to weigh when secular policy is made. Prima facie, then, the state should be blind to religion, but it should then consider the impact of its actions on belief and conscience.

Where practicable, citizens should not need to choose between their religion and the law. Nonetheless, the state cannot guarantee that no one will ever have to compromise. It cannot guarantee that all religious projects will go ahead unhindered, or that everyone will find a job whose duties conform to their beliefs. These are matters to be weighed in the policy process, and in many cases, reasonable minds may differ.

# Notes

1   John Locke, *A Letter concerning Toleration*, 1st pub. 1689, Hackett, Indianapolis 1983, p. 42.
2   Locke, *A Letter concerning Toleration*, p. 48.
3   494 US 872 (1990).
4   Kent Greenawalt, *Religion and the Constitution*, vol. 2: *Establishment and Fairness*, Princeton University Press, Princeton 2008, p. 331.
5   Greenawalt, *Religion and the Constitution*, vol. 2, p. 333.

6  Greenawalt, Kent, *Religion and the Constitution*, vol. 1: *Fairness and Free Exercise*, Princeton University Press, Princeton, pp. 81–82.

7  508 US 520 (1993).

8  Locke, *A Letter concerning Toleration*, p. 42.

9  John Witte, Jr., *God's Joust, God's Justice: Law and Religion in the Western Tradition*, Wm. B. Eerdmans, Grand Rapids, MI 2006, p. 241; see also p. 260.

10  In the US, it is often the Christian Right that promotes and reinforces laissez-faire capitalism, seeking to dismantle welfare programs while promoting military and corporate interests.

11  J. S. Mill, *On Liberty*, 1st pub. 1859, Penguin, London 1974, p. 70.

12  Thomas Nagel, *Equality and Partiality*, Oxford University Press, Oxford 1991, p. 167.

13  John Braithwaite and Philip Pettit, *Not Just Deserts: A Republican Theory of Criminal Justice*, Oxford University Press, New York 1990, p. 108.

14  Stephen L. Carter, *The Culture of Disbelief: How American Law and Politics Trivialize Religious Devotion*, Anchor, New York 1994, p. 133.

15  Isaac Kramnick and R. Laurence Moore, *The Godless Constitution: A Moral Defense of the Secular State*, W. W. Norton, New York 2005, p. 59.

16  Christopher L. Eisgruber and Lawrence G. Sager, *Religious Freedom and the Constitution*, Harvard University Press, Cambridge, MA 2007, p. 6.

17  Eisgruber and Sager, *Religious Freedom and the Constitution*, p. 79.

18  See Chapter 5.

19  For detailed discussion of such disputes between suburban neighborhoods and large religious organizations, see Marci A. Hamilton, *God vs. the Gavel: Religion and the Rule of Law*, Cambridge University Press, Cambridge 2007, pp. 78–110.

20  *Christian Education South Africa v. Minister of Education* (2000) Case CCT 4/00, para. 35.

21  Barry Brian, *Culture and Equality: An Egalitarian Critique of Multiculturalism*, Polity Press, Cambridge 2001, p. 38–39.

22  Greenawalt, *Religion and the Constitution*, vol. 1, p. 71.

23  Barry, *Culture and Equality*, p. 39.

24  Barry, *Culture and Equality*, pp. 40–46.

25  Barry, *Culture and Equality*, pp. 49–50.

26  Barry, *Culture and Equality*, p. 62.

27  Barry, *Culture and Equality*, pp. 50–54.

28  Ronald A. Lindsay, *Future Bioethics: Overcoming Taboos, Myths, and Dogmas*, Prometheus, Amherst, NY, 2008, pp. 132–133.

29  Greenawalt, *Religion and the Constitution*, vol. 1, p. 415.

30  Rex Ahdar and Ian Leigh, *Religious Freedom in the Liberal State*, Oxford University Press, Oxford 2005, p. 300.

31  Lindsay, *Future Bioethics*, p. 145.

32  Lindsay, *Future Bioethics*, pp. 136–137.

33  Lindsay, *Future Bioethics*, pp. 138–144.

34  Lindsay, *Future Bioethics*, p. 144.

35  Lindsay, *Future Bioethics*, pp. 148–149.

36  Greenawalt, *Religion and the Constitution*, vol. 1, p. 58. Greenawalt also, quite rightly, acknowledges in a footnote that it may be very difficult working out when individual military personnel object in conscience and when they simply do not desire to participate.
37  See Abortion Law Reform Act 2008 (Vic), s. 8.
38  Ahdar and Leigh, *Religious Freedom in the Liberal State*, p. 300. Compare Greenawalt, *Religion and the Constitution*, vol. 1, p. 415.

CHAPTER SEVEN

PRIVATE POWER, RELIGIOUS COMMUNITIES, AND THE STATE

## Introduction

As Greenawalt puts it, legislators (and, I add, other public officials working in their official capacities) should not "consider the truth or falsity of religious ideas."[1] Religious freedom requires that the state abstain from deciding which religion, if any, is correct. It does not, however, require citizens, or private associations of citizens, to adopt the same neutral stance. While the might of the state should not be used to impose, suppress, endorse, promote, or disparage any religious view, private actors may become advocates for whatever views strike them as most compelling. This leaves the various religions in a state of mutual rivalry beneath the state's umbrella. Provided they maintain the civil peace, and don't jockey to obtain the power of the state in order to impose their views by force, religious organizations and individuals are free to advocate particular doctrines as vigorously as they wish, and to dispute or disparage others.

Rival religions need not regard each other as epistemic or moral equals, or even as benign. On the contrary, no political principle prevents religious adherents from viewing themselves as in a cosmic struggle to preach the capital-T Truth in competition with what they see as their rivals' deceptions. Not all will take such an adversarial stance, of course, but it is a choice that religious freedom leaves open to them. Likewise, they may teach contentious moral doctrines based on divine revelation or esoteric understandings of the universe – but they should not expect the state to enforce them.

In particular, individuals remain free to express biases, including religious biases, in such private matters as choosing their friends, sexual partners, dinner companions, and other associates. Nothing should, for example, forbid a Zeusist woman from preferring to marry a Zeusist man (rather than a man from some other religious background or a religious skeptic). If she does so, she is not denying non-Zeusists their religious freedom. In its essence, freedom of religion is freedom from *the state's* efforts to persecute certain religions or to impose others. It is not about requiring individual citizens, or the groups that they voluntarily form, to become religion-blind.

This accords with Brian Barry's insistence that liberalism is, in the first instance, about how states should treat people. The standards of conduct that we apply to the state do not apply to every individual or to every association, community, and privately established corporate entity. Though the government may be chosen by a popular vote, it does not follow that family decisions must be voted on. Though the government avoids most kinds of censorship, it does not follow that parents must provide for freedom of speech within their households: there is normally no problem with parents censoring the TV watching of their children. Citizens may belong voluntarily to associations whose rules and authority they accept, but an association such as a church can no longer call on the secular arm, or impose its own physical sanctions, to assert its authority.[2]

Nonetheless, the relationship between the citizen and the state is not the only "power relationship" that exists in modern societies. Various kinds of private power are exercised on a daily basis, often in ways that individuals experience as oppressive. When and how should the state interfere with this? That question provides the theme for this chapter.

## Private Power and the Secular State

We encounter many kinds of private power that are intermediate between individual citizens and the state. Consider, for example, the power of parents, employers, doctors, large (and small) businesses that supply goods and services to the public, landlords, trade unions, and educational institutions. In addition, we must add churches and other religious organizations, as well as traditional communities based on religion, culture, or ethnicity. Each of these can sometimes bully individual citizens, even though the might of the state theoretically dwarfs them all. I say "theoretically" because some transnational organizations, including some religious organizations, are very powerful indeed, and can sometimes bully national governments.

In many cases, it may be important for private power to be exercised with minimal interference from the state. It would be a nightmare if state officials tried to take command of every family, private business, church, or traditional community. Nonetheless, private power can be employed in ways that are destructive or oppressive. To protect the interests of its citizens, modern legislatures act in such areas as child protection, employment and labor relations law, consumer rights, and medical registration. The resulting panoply of legislation does much to allay our fears of the whimsically, abusively, or selfishly exercised power of non-state actors.

One obvious question is how far this should go, especially when it collides with actions that private parties might wish to take on religious grounds, or on grounds that are closely entangled with religion. Should the state take a more hands-off approach in some areas? Should it be more active in others?

For example, what attitude should the state adopt when confronted by traditional communities with their own standards of conduct, possibly at odds with the secular law? How far should it allow these communities to regulate themselves? Classic examples have arisen in the domain of family relations, as with Mormon polygamy, which was crushed in the United States in the nineteenth century in a much debated exercise of state power.[3] *Muslim* polygamy provides a current example: How should this practice be regarded in a liberal democracy? Should it be criminalized? Given a special accommodation (as an exception to the ordinary law of marriage)? Treated as legal (with whatever benefits that might entail) without being recognized as marriage? And what about "ordinary," that is monogamous, Muslim marriages? If a marriage between two devout Muslims breaks down, should they be permitted to settle disputed issues, such as property rights and custody of children, in accordance with what their community regards as Sharia law? If not, why not? Where does the public interest lie in a case such as this?

Some uses of private power are constrained by anti-discrimination legislation. This can be framed to deal not only with transactions involving powerful private actors, such as large business corporations, but also with some transactions that solely involve less powerful parties. Bear in mind how a cumulative impact can arise from many decisions, even if they are taken by parties who do not, taken one by one, possess great power. Without state intervention, people from certain racial backgrounds, for example, might suffer discrimination at the hands of employers and landlords, and from shop owners and proprietors of similar businesses that supply goods and services to the public. The cumulative effect of many discriminatory acts could have drastic impacts on the welfare of somebody from such a background. Some might, for example, find themselves excluded from the labor market, with all the hardship and humiliation this entails, even though they are competent and diligent workers.

For this reason, there is a strong secular case for legislation that forbids racial discrimination in such areas as employment, education, housing, and the supply of goods and services to the public. Over the last few decades, the enactment and enforcement of such legislation has become an accepted function of the state in modern society.

One area of concern, along with race, sex, and sexuality, is religion. Without anti-discrimination laws, people with religious (or anti-religious) views that are locally unpopular might find themselves severely restricted in their prospects for employment, education, housing, and even the most ordinary day-to-day economic transactions. But what if the state enacts legislation that prevents employers from discriminating against individuals in hiring and firing on the ground of religion? Might this not be seen as a restriction on religious freedom, since it prevents private actors, such as owners and managers, from engaging, for religious reasons, in conduct that would otherwise be lawful? Compare the less attractive prospect of the state enacting legislation that requires individual citizens to cease discriminating on the basis of religion in their choice of lovers or spouses.

One point that I hope to establish is that the state has a legitimate discretion to constrain the exercise of private power, insofar as it affects the secular welfare of citizens. But there are questions about how far this should go. Should the same rules apply to churches as to business corporations? Should some deference be given to the customs and self-organization of traditional communities? What lines should be drawn in this difficult area? I'll begin with issues of discrimination, particularly discrimination on the basis of religion, but we'll also need to consider discrimination on other grounds that may be *motivated* by religious doctrine.

## Anti-Discrimination Law, Religion, and the Workplace

In this section, I'll concentrate on the responsibilities of employers toward employees or potential employees who are motivated by religious beliefs. Similar issues can arise for others who exercise private power, individually or as a class: for example, shop owners, landlords, and educational institutions. However, special issues arise in employment given that religiously motivated conduct can interfere with an individual's work performance as part of a team. Nothing quite like this is applicable to "performance" as, say, a tenant, a customer in a supermarket, or even a student. Anti-discrimination law should be sufficiently nuanced to take such differences into account.

Employers, landlords, and so on exercise forms of private power that the state may have an interest in restraining. They may, of course, feel restricted by laws that impose such restraints – if they are prevented, for example, from refusing to employ, or to rent a property to, say, a Muslim, a Catholic, or an atheist. That, however, is part of the price of exercising power over others. The state has a legitimate discretion in how far it permits employers, landlords, and others who exercise private power, to act as if they were merely individual citizens deciding who to ask for dinner.

The sort of legislation we are contemplating in this section is enacted neither in pursuit of freedom of religion nor as an exception to it.[4] It is, rather, a matter of the state acting to protect citizens' civil interests by means of neutral, generally applicable laws. These laws are justified because employers, landlords, and such have voluntarily taken on roles in which they can no longer expect to be treated, always and for all purposes, simply as individual citizens. It should, therefore, be clear that the enactment of laws restraining certain uses of private power does not commit the state to a program of expunging all harmful discrimination by all private actors whatsoever. It need not, for example, forbid religious teachings that homosexual conduct is a sin or that men and women have different spiritual vocations (or even that those of men are, in some sense, superior). Indeed, liberal tolerance must accept the teaching of doctrines that may, viewed solely in worldly terms, have harmful effects.

Given the circumstances described in the previous section, it is reasonable that the subjective preferences of employers to hire, promote, or dismiss someone of, say, a certain racial background, sex, sexuality, age, or religion must give way to the interests of potentially disadvantaged workers. Accordingly, modern legislatures pressure employers into making rational decisions about a worker's ability to perform the functions of the job. In most jurisdictions, this involves anti-discrimination provisions that have two prongs, though the precise legal tests vary.

First, an employer may not discriminate *directly*, basing personnel decisions on a protected characteristic such as sexuality, race, biological sex, or religious belief, rather than on ability to perform the functions of the job. Second, it may not discriminate *indirectly*, establishing contrived or arbitrary requirements that tend to disadvantage individuals with a protected characteristic. For example, typical anti-discrimination provisions would prevent an employer from requiring that its office staff be over five foot eight and able to bench-press 150 pounds. These are *not* requirements that relate to a worker's ability to perform the job, and they would have the effect of excluding most women. Depending on the jurisdiction's precise legislative provisions, however, some such requirement might be legally acceptable in a job where physical strength is vital.

Let us consider how far religion should be protected by anti-discrimination legislation that applies to the context of employment. One possibility that such legislation addresses (and redresses) is that an employer may be unwilling to employ (or retain or promote) people of a certain religion that the owners or managers dislike or oppose. But there are other situations that the law should take into account. An employer might, for example, have a rational concern if an individual refuses, on religious grounds, to perform the lawfully required functions of the job, or even if conformity to religious canons of conduct merely hinders the ability of an employee to perform the job as well as others (particularly rivals for recruitment, promotion, or retention). Why should the employer not favor the worker who is, for whatever reason, the most efficient?

As a somewhat extreme case, consider the example of a Catholic nurse who seeks work at an abortion clinic. Perhaps she should not have to disclose her religious beliefs when she applies for work, but if they lead her to refuse to carry out her duties the employer is surely entitled to dismiss her from its staff. Numerous such situations are imaginable. Anti-discrimination law should not provide a sword for citizens to frustrate lawful activities of which they disapprove, or to claim payment for carrying out duties that they are not actually willing to perform.

The general rule in anti-discrimination law is that an employer does not have to employ someone who refuses to carry out lawful and essential job functions, for whatever reasons. Thus, in the American case of *Trans World Airlines v. Hardison*,[5] a Jewish employee was not able to obtain exemption from working on Saturdays in an airline's 24-hour stores department. This would have deprived other employees of their legitimate shift preferences and violated the terms of a collective bargaining agreement. An approach such as this gives employees considerable protection, but employers retain their ability to take decisions that are reasonably based on business efficacy. I submit that *Hardison* was correctly decided as a matter of law and in principle.

Note, however, that it is a policy matter for the state – and ultimately for democratic politics – exactly how protective anti-discrimination law should be in such a situation. Thus it is one thing for the state to insist that personnel decisions relate to job performance rather than an employer's subjective biases about people of a certain sexuality, race, sex, or religion, or an employer's wish to promote certain religions and discourage others. It is another thing to fill out the details of a regulatory code. Who should bear the burden of proof if an employer wishes to argue that an individual's religious beliefs impede her ability to work efficiently, or in a manner that conforms to the employer's safe and otherwise lawful system of operations? What evidentiary standard should be required for proving this one way or the other? How far should an employer be allowed a degree of discretion in establishing its work system, and conversely how far should the employer be required to modify it to accommodate an employee's religion-based canons of conduct?

It is not even clear that anti-discrimination law must apply to all employers. And if it should, should it apply to all employers for *all purposes*? In a society that is marred by racism, there may be a very powerful case for the state to require that all employers, however large or small, adopt race-neutral personnel practices, or even an element of "positive discrimination" to assist people from disadvantaged racial backgrounds. But religion may be rather different. If an employer is very small, perhaps it should be allowed some scope to act as an extension of the individuals who constitute it (perhaps as a partnership) or own it (perhaps as the sole shareholders in a family company). In that case, why should those individuals be totally precluded from advancing their religion by favoring co-religionists? Provided the labor market as a whole does not make life impossible for people with unpopular religious (or anti-religious) views, considerations of individual freedom and administrative simplicity might favor applying some laws only to employers above a certain size.

I do not propose to offer anything like a model statute to discourage religious discrimination in the employment setting. The point to be established is that the state has a considerable margin of appreciation in how it settles the issues I've sketched in the preceding paragraphs. We can't just *read off* the answers to difficult social and political questions by applying a principle such as: "Employers must not interfere with the free exercise of their employees' religions." Rather, the state (and by implication the electorate) has legitimate choices about what does and what does not go into anti-discrimination legislation.

## Religious Employers and Associations

Up to this point, I have focused on the protection of devout individuals who confront private power, perhaps as employees (or perhaps as customers, clients, students, residential tenants, etc.). What, however, if religious organizations, or wealthy religious adherents, set themselves up as employers (or as landlords, schoolmasters, providers of goods and services, etc.)? The general point to be made here is that they have no automatic expectation of being exempted from neutral laws of general application. Thus, a religious employer should not expect to be free of paying pay-roll tax, meeting occupational health and safety requirements, and generally conforming to the wide range of legislation that impinges on the activities of employers in general.

What about anti-discrimination law? Religious organizations and associated bodies such as church schools may be motivated by their doctrines to discriminate in various ways, such as by refusing to employ women in some positions or refusing to employ known gay men, lesbians, and bisexuals. Clearly this can run afoul of local anti-discrimination laws. Similar issues arise with religious landlords, shop owners, and so on. How should the state react?

The starting point should be that devout individuals, religious organizations, and related bodies have no automatic entitlement to exemption from these laws, should they decide to set themselves up as, say, landlords or employers. If this seems harsh, it should be added that the effect of such laws is not to suppress religion, though it may make some activities less attractive to certain organizations and individuals – activities such as renting out housing or employing members of the public. These activities will not usually be compulsory within the doctrines of the religion concerned, and there may be no particular policy reason for the state to go out of its way to enable religious organizations and individuals to take part in them.

Consider the case where a church that condemns homosexuality as a sin decides to buy a fishing fleet.[6] In those circumstances, it must comply with the general body of law that regulates the operation of fishing fleets, including any laws that forbid discrimination in employment on the ground of sexuality. Here, the effect is to make running a fishing business less attractive to this particular church, but running a fishing business is not something that the church is required to do either by its doctrines or by practical realities (there are many other ways to raise funds, if that's the issue). This is not even a case where individuals are prevented from enjoying aspects of their private lives, as with Barry's examples of meat-eating and riding a motorcycle, discussed in the previous chapter.

So, the starting point is one of no automatic exemptions. However, there are many situations that legislatures will need to consider on their merits. One is the situation that confronts the state when, for example, the Catholic Church restricts its priesthood to men. Here, the balance of considerations looks rather different from that in the fishing fleet example: although religious organizations are not usually bound by their doctrines to run fishing fleets, they most certainly are bound, in relevant cases, to provide the services of priests. Moreover, it seems clear enough that a religious organization needs scope to insist that its priests faithfully accept its doctrines – or at least seek to change them only in relatively marginal and incremental ways, and through the organization's own processes. Where it is a doctrine of the church that only persons of one sex or the other can engage in priestly rites, no one can seriously apply for the job, claim that she follows the church's doctrines, then complain if she is rejected for being of the "wrong" sex.

This is, then, an unusual situation where sex cannot be irrelevant to the job – not when, as Barry puts it, it is believed by all concerned to be essential: "If you believe that the sacraments have efficacy only if administered by a man you can scarcely regard the sex of the person administering them as irrelevant."[7] Something similar applies to membership in a church, sect, or religious faith. There is an interest in allowing these to have broad discretion as to who may join. Thus the state should tolerate, but not endorse, the refusal of the Roman Catholic Church to have female priests, that of the Nation of Islam to have white members, or that of a white supremacist religion to have black members.[8]

In case I seem to be inconsistent, let's look more closely at the status of churches as voluntary associations. A state apparatus devoted to protecting and promoting interests in the things of this world will look with concern on the cumulative effect of decisions made by parties that possess private power. However, it should also acknowledge the benefit in allowing people to form voluntary associations with like-minded others, such as co-religionists. Among other things, as Barry points out, "much of every normal individual's well-being derives from membership in associations and communities."[9] Thus, the state should not treat associations of co-religionists simply like business corporations. It is essential to private associations that they can determine who is eligible to join.

Voluntary organizations, religious or otherwise, should be able to structure themselves to carry on their activities and promote their teachings. A religious organization large enough to need full-time leaders, or a leadership hierarchy, should be able to appoint them in ways that are consistent with its doctrines. It will also need considerable freedom to determine those doctrines, including higher-level doctrines about how they are determined, and to organize its gatherings and rituals. All of this is reasonably necessary for religious associations to thrive.

By contrast, it is not necessary for them to buy or establish commercial operations. On one hand, the further we move from the hierarchy of leadership within the association itself to its employment of staff in peripheral activities, the less these special concerns should dominate and the more we should focus on the policy concerns that lie behind the general law. On the other hand, a secular government should realize the particular strength of religious feelings and attachments and the particular social risks of taking action that has the collateral effect of suppressing religion. That would be the situation if the Catholic Church were forced to defy the law or else renounce its doctrine that sacraments have efficacy only when administered by a man.

It is not my intention to rule definitively on when the state should and should not interfere with the operations of a body such as the Catholic Church. It seems clear enough (at least to me) that any sensible public policy must lean against requiring the Church to employ female priests. Likewise, it seems clear enough (to me) that a fishing fleet owned by the Catholic Church should be constrained by the same body of law as any other such fleet. There will, however, be intermediate cases where a line needs to be drawn, for example if the Church hires staff to teach its doctrines to seminarians. Can it require those staff to abide, in their personal lives, by its canons of conduct? If so, what about teachers employed in Catholic schools to teach secular subjects?

Nuanced decisions may need to be made by legislatures when anti-discrimination codes are drafted and enacted, and discretion may need to be exercised. As always with such discretionary decisions, they should be sorted out through the political process, rather than being made by bodies that exercise judicial power.

## How Free is Free Association?

It seems fine in theory to leave individuals to abide by the rules of associations that they have joined freely and whose rules they generally accept. In those circumstances, the individuals should be left to pursue any changes to the rules only through the association's internal procedures for making such changes. If those procedures are restrictive or grind too slowly, or if there is no real prospect of gaining the changes sought, the individual is free to leave.

Fine in theory, but how free is free association, particularly when we're talking about such things as churches and religious communities? Children may find themselves regarded as belonging to a church or a community, not because they have examined and agreed to its doctrines, and to the rules by which it organizes itself, but simply because their parents are part of it. Many adults may belong because they grew up in it as children and it has become their social world – or a large part of it. Again, for a wide variety of reasons, many people may have little opportunity to leave religious communities. These considerations at least weaken the argument that the state ought to adopt a laissez-faire attitude.

Children provide the subject of the next chapter. Briefly, the state has little practical choice but to accept parents as appropriate decision-makers for many aspects of their children's upbringing. This requires acceptance of the presence of children in religious communities – as de facto members, if not in all cases actually as believers. The state should not automatically assume that young children will take up the beliefs of their parents or that maturing minors actually embrace those beliefs. However, its main role should be in looking after children's more specific interests rather than simply assuming that churches and religious communities are, after all, involuntary. The presence of children in a community is virtually unavoidable, and does not in itself take away from the fact that the adults involved may voluntarily accept the community's authority and its rules. Nor does it detract from the benefit obtained by individuals in participating with like-minded people in communities whose rules they accept.

However, difficult issues arise even with adults. Should the state assume that membership in a church or religious community is involuntary because, as is often the case, the individual member has been socialized into the relevant body of beliefs from childhood? That is, should the state assume that individuals who have been taught religious doctrines and canons of conduct are showing some sort of false consciousness that justifies state paternalism and an interventionist approach to the internal affairs of churches and religious communities? That would be going too far. As far as possible, the state should take the commitments of adult citizens at face value, rather than inquiring into how they were formed and challenging their authenticity. Devout adults should not be treated by the state as if they don't know their own minds or their own interests. Prima facie, their consent to a community's doctrines and practices should be left unchallenged, even if their compliance sometimes appears not to be in their own best interests when judged from an external and purely secular viewpoint.

But that is not the end of the story. Often, the individuals who appear to suffer from cultural values and expectations that they (apparently) accept are women who are following rules that were created by, and apparently in the interests of, men. This creates a special sensitivity that ought to be acknowledged, but what follows from it? Karen Green warns that the women of past generations may have contributed to the community's values and that they – now joined by their present-day descendants – may have favored an ethic based on "care and love in the maintenance of culture, and in an acceptance of the subordination of individual desire to social duty." She asks us not to reject all this as merely foisted on women by men.[10] Further to Green's point, it is patronizing to a woman who actually does accept a community's expectations, values, and rules to assume that she does not know her own mind or her own spiritual interests.

Accordingly, I don't believe that the state should adopt a paternalistic and intrusive approach *merely* because individuals have been socialized to think in a certain way or even because of the restrictions that are often placed on women. But nor can we assume that all choices are made fully autonomously. Assumptions of false consciousness can seem arrogant and misplaced, but so can a callous assumption that all adults are living in ways that they chose autonomously, and for which they ought to take full responsibility. Many people who find themselves in religious communities, not least women who are relegated to a particular social role and faced with other restrictions, may have no real opportunities to leave, and so no real opportunities to do anything other than comply.

Ahdar and Leigh are right to worry that opportunities to exit a community may not be meaningful in practice, pointing out that a meaningful right to exit would depend on multiple conditions being met, among them "awareness of alternatives to the present way of life, the ability to assess these alternatives, the ability (financially, educationally etc.) to participate effectively in these alternatives."[11] Many people may not be aware of the possibilities for them in modern liberal democracies, perhaps because of language barriers or because they have been shielded from any extensive knowledge of life outside their communities, which may, in effect, wall them off from the wider society. Women who do not accept the community's demands can come under irresistible pressures to conform – from family members, religious authority figures, and peers. In some cases, the pressure may be backed by implicit or explicit threats of violence.

In any event, there may be considerable costs to leaving a community, ranging from what Barry calls the inherent costs (which might, at least in the minds of those concerned, include damnation), associative costs that are the lawful consequences of the action (e.g., former co-religionists may no longer want to associate with you if you leave), and external illegitimate costs (as when an employer unlawfully dismisses a former community member from employment, or a community organizes an unlawful boycott of a former member's business).

Even associative costs that arise solely from lawful actions may be sufficiently coercive from an individual's viewpoint to render community membership non-voluntary. Barry suggests that these costs might justify some compensation if a member is expelled and that it should be possible to challenge formal expulsions for breaches of natural justice or of a group's procedural rules.[12] I don't propose to pursue those points in the space available. However, they highlight the fact that – as an understatement – membership in religious communities, and compliance with their rules, is not always unproblematically voluntary. While groups such as churches and religious communities need some freedom to organize themselves in accordance with the beliefs of members and rules that members voluntarily accept as authoritative, there is also the risk that these groups can become oppressive to individuals who have little choice but to comply. What follows for state policy?

## Policy Implications

I cannot provide a definitive solution to the numerous issues confronting the state when it deals with churches and religious communities. The best I can offer are some observations that may open up some options and eliminate others. Once again, it is not the state's role to establish the correct worldview or canons of conduct, all things considered, or even to work out what, all things considered, is a good way of life or in the best interests of its citizens. At least where adults are concerned, its starting point should be one of non-interference with their voluntary associations, their self-regarding conduct, and any privately established rules that they voluntarily abide by.

Nonetheless, the state should recognize that supposedly voluntary communities often wield private power, and that individuals may be trapped into certain courses of action, not because they reflectively endorse a group's authoritative rules but because they have little choice. Communities should have the right to expel members for breach of their canons of conduct, including advocacy of views that are contrary to those of the group. It is, furthermore, essentially up to the group how broad a range of beliefs and actions it accepts from those who wish to be members. However, communities, including religious communities, should not be given the power to punish members other than by expulsion.

Even "mere" expulsion may be far harsher than it sounds. Consider, for example, a woman for whom it entails being ostracized by her family, kept from her children, and left with neither financial support nor skills that are valued in the wider labor market. A moment's thought reveals how some individuals are effectively captives of their communities. The state should not assume that this is *always* the case, but nor should it look the other way when it sees a group's rules threatening the interests of individuals in the most personal aspects of their lives. Thus the state has the option of intervening in exercises of private power involving religious communities. It may, for example, refuse to enforce agreements that would otherwise be legally binding – but which one party had little choice but to consent to.

This kind of question arises in current debates about the use of Sharia law within Muslim communities, particularly to regulate marital and parental relationships. Suppose a marriage between two devout Muslims breaks down: in that case, should they be permitted to settle disputed issues, such as property rights and custody of children, in accordance with what they understand to be the requirements of Sharia? In some situations this may be a non-issue: perhaps the parties agree outside of any court proceedings to an outcome that, in any event, seems fair by most secular standards. In such a case, the state may not even know whether principles derived from Sharia were invoked by the parties to the dispute or by their advisers.

In other cases, however, the use of Sharia law may be oppressive to women who have no real choice but to comply. Against that background, the state may be required to make policy judgments as to whether it will allow bodies such as Sharia courts to settle disputes by applying their own "law," rather than whatever body of secular law would normally operate. I submit that the state should not delegate its authority to bodies that are likely to use it in ways that the state itself would consider unfair. In addition, the state should satisfy itself that the secular interests of children are properly considered – these should take precedence over conformity to a body of religious law that is ostensibly consented to by the parties to a marital dispute.

The details of public policy on the private, consensual application of Sharia law would require a separate study. But justified fear of abuses of private power should persuade state officials to regard "consensual" application of Sharia law with some suspicion. For example, I suggest that the state should *not* enact legislation enabling binding arbitration of marital or family disputes in accordance with any system of law other than that used by the official courts of the jurisdiction. Even informal, non-binding arbitration can have its problems if carried out by an individual or body that is given official recognition and the prestige that goes with it, perhaps by being included on a government register. Family law policy should lean heavily in the direction of protecting the interests of women who are threatened with one-sided consideration of their interests under a community's traditional rules of marriage.

This leads me to a more general (but necessarily brief) consideration of the state's role in marriage.

## The Marriage Business

Contemporary debates about marriage often focus on the issue of same-sex marriages – whether these should be provided for by modern legislation and practice. These debates sometimes attract arguments about whether the state should be involved in the marriage business at all. Should it withdraw from that field, since marriage no longer functions to regulate who can engage in sexual relationships with whom? Generally speaking, laws relating to fornication and adultery have either been repealed or are not enforced. Perhaps the state should allow people to arrange the erotic and familial sides of their lives with few restrictions; allow couples (or larger groups who so wish) to regard themselves as "married" if that is important to them; and provide residual service in protecting the interests of children and settling property disputes that arise out of domestic relationships. No official marriage register is required.

It's not as if marriage as we now think of it is universal or inevitable. Today, the ideal is a union of two people based on love and intimacy, but that is a relatively recent historical development. It may be that people have had the experience of falling in love in most or all societies throughout history, but the Western ideal of marriage is more culturally specific. Stephanie Coontz sees it as evolving in Western countries only since the late eighteenth century, prior to which marriage had served less romantic purposes as an economic and political transaction.[13]

In recent decades, we have reached a point where there is far more choice as to whether to get married and whether to stay married. This creates new freedoms and new possibilities, but also new anxieties. In any event, marriage is not the primary institution of care-giving and commitment that it once was, and it is most unlikely that we could ever reinstate it in that role.[14] As Coontz points out, there is a tendency in many countries toward a blurring of the line separating married and unmarried couples. Governments and private employers often move to provide the same benefits to non-married couples and in some cases, as in France and Canada, to anyone who wishes to enter into a legally recognized arrangement to pool resources (this could be two siblings or friends, for example).[15] Indeed, liberal democracies can probably function quite smoothly if a time comes when no one opts for a formal, legally recognized marriage. That being so, why should the state provide for formal marriage at all?

For now, however, it is not a practical option for the state to withdraw from the field. As with the church establishments of such countries as the United Kingdom, current liberal democracies do not start with a clean slate when it comes to marriage. Though the institution has changed over time, it has a long history, very widespread public acceptance, and much emotional significance for the majority of citizens. As with church establishments, a move by the state to get out of the marriage business would have a different impact from merely declining to provide a system of state-recognized marriages in the first place.

For the foreseeable future, marriage will continue as an important institution. In most jurisdictions it provides a raft of legal benefits, including the many that follow from the parties becoming next of kin.[16] Though marriage is no longer assumed to be permanent, it remains an expression of strong commitment, and the legal formalities provide a way for the state to bless and glorify it. Given what marriage has become, and assuming that formal, legally recognized marriage will remain important in at least the medium term, should access to it be denied to those gay couples who want it?

One way of answering that question starts by interpreting it as "Is homosexual conduct immoral?" That, however, is the wrong approach. There is no need for legislators to concern themselves with whether homosexuality is morally wrong, all things (including otherworldly things) considered. Thus they need not adjudicate on, for example, the esoteric arguments of Catholic theologians and other natural law theorists. Given the state's role in protecting and promoting the things of this world, given that it cannot readily withdraw from the marriage business, and given the actual significance of marriage in contemporary societies, what policy position should liberal democracies move to from here?

In favor of doing nothing, it might be pointed out that homosexual relationships are now perfectly legal in most Western jurisdictions, and that any attempt to ban them would be unconstitutional in the US.[17] A mere failure to recognize and register these relationships as marriages is not of great importance, so the argument might run, and in some jurisdictions it might cause more trouble than it's worth. Against this, the valorization of intimate, loving relationships with the involvement of the state to give its blessing is currently denied to gay couples in a way that causes unnecessary hurt. Moreover, this can make it inconvenient, expensive, and downright difficult for gay couples to obtain the same secular goods as similarly placed straight couples. Writing in the US context, where there is no universal health care of the kind provided in other Western nations, Halwani sees the following as key and unquestionable facts:

> First, marriage is a glorified, crucial institution, and its being socially equated with other, similarly deep relationships seems remote. Second, marriage has been much reformed, with many states allowing unilateral divorce. Third, universal healthcare seems not to be in the horizon, let alone available in the near future. Fourth, many same-sex couples are in dire need of the benefits that marriage confers. Fifth, if same-sex couples do attain the right to marry, this will elevate gay people almost automatically in the general eyes of society.[18]

He argues that it is intolerable, in the American context, that gay couples facing emergencies, such as one partner being stricken with AIDS, are denied minimal legal rights such as access to joint possessions. Other solutions, such as drawing up a power of attorney, are, he suggests, not adequate. Halwani concludes that the best political strategy is for gay people and allies to agitate for gay marriage rights while simultaneously advocating marriage reform (such as universal divorce rights where these do not yet exist) and, where it does not exist as in the US, for universal health care.[19]

I find this persuasive and therefore support moves for liberal democracies to recognize same-sex marriages for those who want them. In current circumstances, the case seems strong enough, though it will be more compelling in some jurisdictions than others. Beyond this, however, what general policies should the state adopt in the area of marriage and family? For example, given this analysis of marriage's contemporary significance, should the state recognize and register traditional polygynous marriages, such as those allowed by Islam or those originally authorized by nineteenth-century Mormons (and still by some breakaway Mormon groups)?

Not obviously. One of the reasons for recognizing same-sex marriage is that the relationships concerned are likely to resemble the kinds of heterosexual relationships that are celebrated in the contemporary practice of marriage. There is no option, for now, of the state ceasing to be involved in those kinds of relationships; nor is there a need for it to move into relationships of very different kinds that often involve patriarchal notions of authority, arranged relationships, and little emphasis on romantic love and intimacy. As long as polygynous relationships do not involve abuses such as child brides, they should not be *illegal*, but there is no compelling reason for them to be given the blessing of the state by recognizing them as marriages. The sort of inequity that applies to refusing same-sex marriages is simply not present.

On the contrary, the state should be suspicious that women are pressured into polygynous arrangements by the actions of families and communities. Public policy should favor protection of women from abuses and pressures. One good starting point would be a publicly stated policy position that people who enter into polygynous relationships with the blessing of their families or communities will *not* be considered by the state to be married and that the state will not recognize rules that allegedly derive from Sharia law. However, even this is not the end of the story. There is one more twist.

Though contemporary societies valorize romantic love between couples, and the state is prepared to recognize and bless intimate loving relationships between two people, we can't assume that one kind of relationship suits all. In suggesting that traditional polygynous relationships not be banned, I was conscious that a significant number of people now negotiate non-monogamous or "polyamorous" relationships of one kind or another. These need not be patriarchal or in any sense the result of coercion; they may be free responses to the complex desires of the parties involved. They may come in different shapes and sizes, sometimes polygynous, sometimes poly-androus, sometimes involving still other forms ("open" relationships, com-munal arrangements, and so on).

I suggest that this is where the state really should withdraw from the field, except for a quite residual role if financial disputes arise when rela-tionships break up, or if the welfare of children is involved. There is no easy way to establish a legal template for what is potentially a bewildering variety of relationships and arrangements, and not all will be so closely analogous to typical heterosexual marriages that failure to recognize them in the same way has the appearance of an insult. Nor are the people involved in such non-traditional arrangements likely to press for the same sort of legal recognition as is sought by many gay couples. It may be dif-ficult for them to make the exact legal arrangements they want, but that is an almost inevitable outcome of entering into non-standard and uncommon arrangements that don't fit any template.

## The Battle of the Burqa

I am now in a position to consider one especially hot-button topic in current political debate: the ultra-conservative clothing for women associ-ated with certain strict forms of Islam. The garments concerned include the *jilbab*, *niqab* (a face veil), and *chadri*. Controversy about "the burqa" typically relates to any combination of clothing that envelopes the entire body, obscuring its shape and some of its movements, as well as veiling the whole face (except for the eyes, and even these may sometimes be hidden by mesh).

Sometimes it is suggested that a total ban should be imposed on wearing this sort of apparel in public. As of 2011, there are strong pressures in that direction, most notably in Western Europe, including Belgium, Spain, and the Netherlands. In 2010 France enacted a statute banning any headgear that covers the full length of the face, with effect from April 2011. This includes full-face veiling, and it applies to all almost all public places, including streets, parks, shops, and public transport.

Generally speaking, I oppose such developments. Assuming that "the burqa" is worn of her own free will by a sufficiently mature woman,[20] it should, I submit, be permitted in public spaces, even though it arouses paternalistic concerns. As to these, the garment is restrictive, uncomfortable, and perhaps unhealthy. Moreover, it hinders communication with others. Much everyday communication between human beings is *affective* (conveying attitudes and feelings), and much of this is carried out through facial expressions (often quite subtle but in most cases fairly easily read by others). Another component comes through gesture and expressive body language. To a large extent, the burqa hides both facial expressions and movement of the body.

The paternalistic concerns may be reinforced by a suspicion that wearing the burqa in public is not entirely or always voluntary. As we've seen, there is some reason to doubt the extent to which women in highly conservative traditional communities are truly able to make decisions about such issues of their own free will. Nonetheless, I assume that at least some women genuinely prefer to wear the burqa and would feel embarrassed, or worse, without it. If so, we should be reluctant to introduce paternalistic legislation, with its assumption that the state knows better than these women exactly what is good for them.

Perhaps the burqa conveys hostility to certain liberal values. It may even communicate specific messages that many people understandably find offensive (perhaps a message about the "place" of women, or perhaps a message that male sexuality is uncontrollable and demonic; there may be other possibilities). Accordingly, wearing a burqa may cause offense. Indeed, nobody has to react with approval when a burqa is worn in public, but the practice causes no significant direct harms to others. Nor does it cause the sort of high-impact offense to a captive audience that might reasonably justify bans on some kinds of images, odors, noises, and so on, in certain public spaces. Indeed, wearing a burqa can be interpreted, quite plausibly, as an exercise of free speech, since it communicates something of the wearer's religious and moral commitments – and that may be part of the point of wearing it.

What, on the other hand, if some women are in coercive situations, and are wearing the burqa involuntarily? A ban on wearing it in public may not assist their interests. The practical effect may be that more restrictive conditions will be placed on their movements. If family or community members can prevent you leaving your house without wearing a burqa, banning it in public places may have the effect that you will not be able to go out at all.

The state and its officials should tolerate the burqa; that is, there should be no comprehensive bans on wearing it in public. However, none of the above analysis entails that there should be a positive right to wear such garments even when doing so would fall foul of neutral laws of general application. Thus, it is one thing to permit (i.e., not prohibit) the wearing of burqas in public streets, parks, and similar spaces. It is quite another to grant an exemption from a generally applicable, religion-blind law that requires individuals to show their faces when they walk into banks – for security reasons – or from a law that requires them to have their faces photographed for such documentation as a passport or a driver's license. Consistent with the discussion in the previous chapter, it is a matter of discretion for the legislature just how far it is prepared to go to grant these sorts of exemptions. Failing to do so may cause anguish and practical problems, but this needs to be weighed against whatever secular concerns motivate the law in the first place.

In any event, let us stipulate that a comprehensive ban on wearing burqas in public would not be justified. What, however, if an employer decides that it will not enter into contracts of employment with job applicants who insist on wearing such garments in the workplace? Recall the earlier part of this chapter: such actions by an employer do not constitute religious persecution by the state, but, rather, an exercise of private power that the state may or may not choose to restrict by means of legislation. Recall, once again, how the cumulative effect of many employers using their power with the same bias – to discriminate against homosexuals, say – can be oppressive. In some cases, the state should step in and protect the worldly interests of vulnerable individuals who find themselves feeling the sharp end of private power. Is the burqa such a case?

Though the burqa should not be banned by law, we are not required to approve of it or of whatever messages it is thought to communicate. It is certainly not obvious that employers should be compelled by law to permit it in their offices or factories. Even in cases where they cause no outright safety issue, and so prevent the performance of essential duties, garments that envelope the body and hide the face may adversely affect morale and work performance.

Again, it is one thing for the state to allow forthright and divisive messages to be communicated in public spaces. It's another for it to compel employers to permit such messages in the workplace. Doubtless it should be legal to wear a T-shirt in the street or the park, even though it is decorated with words that express forceful and controversial messages about, say, the "proper" role of women or the demonic sexuality of men. It doesn't follow that an employer must allow such a T-shirt in the workplace. Furthermore, good workplace performance often requires face-to-face affective communication with clients, colleagues in a work team, and others, which must surely be hindered by wearing a burqa.

Martha Nussbaum would doubtless be skeptical at this point, since she emphasizes the degree to which people may be able to identify with, and exchange communications with, others who are wearing balaclavas, football helmets, or surgical masks. She even offers a personal anecdote about how she once made do when wearing a surgical mask while teaching during a period of dusty office renovations.[21] Nussbaum is correct that even people who are cooperating closely in, say, an operating theater can find ways to communicate with a minimum of facial expressions and bodily freedom. But that does not make it optimal. I doubt that employees can wear burqas, football or motorcycle helmets, balaclavas, or surgical masks at all times without creating at least some communication problems. Even surgeons do better not to wear masks when advising their patients or consulting with colleagues outside the operating theater.

I don't, however, mean to state definitively that anti-discrimination law should leave this situation untouched. There are important points to be made on the other side. For one thing, if all employers were left totally unconstrained in prohibiting burqas in their workplaces, it might have the effect of leaving conservative Muslim women unemployable. That would be undesirable for them and probably for society as a whole. At the same time, some jobs more than others involve soft people skills and significant affective communication. In the end, anti-discrimination law is a matter of weighing secular interests and employing craftsmanship. It is not a matter of requiring all employers to put up with all sorts of behavior, no matter how detrimental, so long as it has religious motivations.

## Religious Communities and the Angst about Islam

The state may offer churches and religious communities some leeway that it would not give, for example, a business corporation. But Stephen L. Carter goes too far when he characterizes religions as independent centers of resistance to government that should be promoted to avoid majoritarian tyranny.[22] *Many* organizations resist majoritarian tyranny from time to time, among them the courts, law firms, trade unions, universities, political parties, and even business corporations. That does not entail that they deserve exemptions from the general law. In any event, the main barriers to majoritarian tyranny can be found in constitutional limitations on government power, and (more importantly) in widespread acceptance of liberal principles such as freedom of speech, sexual privacy, and the harm principle.

Locke held that the state should suppress some views, including those of Muslims, those of atheists, and those of the Roman Catholic Church. In Chapter 3 I defended him to the extent of pointing out that this was not hypocritical, for Locke had *secular* reasons for the persecutions that he proposed. As I argued in that chapter, however, experience since Locke's time offers no plausible secular basis for persecuting Muslim, atheists, or Catholics. We should now be very reluctant to dream up reasons for persecutions from the comfort of our armchairs. It remains the case, however, that there could, in principle, be an adequate secular reason to crack down on a sufficiently fanatical atheist community, Catholic prelature, or Muslim sect.

Much contemporary angst relates to Islam, as can be seen with the controversies over polygamy, Sharia law, and the burqa. Deeper than any of these specific issues runs the fear that Islam may prove permanently hostile to a strictly secular state. As I noted in Chapter 2, Islam's historical record should not be sentimentalized, as it has shown a tendency toward absolutism, with many thinkers and leaders claiming that even non-believers must submit to its rules. As Bassam Tibi puts it, this led in the past to "violent Islamic proselytization by means of jihad wars."[23] Tibi believes that Islam has a "predicament with modernity," one whose solution must involve an agenda of internal reform, rather than a strategy of resistance to secularism.[24] He is concerned that intellectual debates within contemporary Islam are dominated by a view of the Sharia as immutable, inflexible, and of overriding, universal authority. On his account, this stands as an obstacle to Muslims' acceptance of secular government.

Tibi calls for education in Western ideas of democracy and for reform of inherited Islamic doctrine. The goal is for Islam to embrace pluralism and an attitude of equality with other systems of thought, extended not only to other monotheists but also to others. Without this, he says, Islam is doomed to conflict with the rest of humanity, which cannot be expected to submit to its requirements.[25] As a liberal thinker and a Muslim himself, Tibi does not call for persecution of Islam but for a process, within Islamic thought, of adaptation to modernity. Unfortunately, he is pessimistic about the current prospects.

Perhaps Tibi's pessimism will prove to be justified, but too much pessimism can be self-fulfilling, and these are still early days in the relationship between Islam and modernity. Though secular governments cannot give conservative Islamists what they want – if this includes such demands as recognizing Sharia law and forbidding blasphemy – historical experience should lead us away from ideas of inevitable conflict. Above all, we need to remember the unpredictable, but always severe, human costs of persecution. The answer to militant or illiberal forms of Islam is renewed commitment to liberal principles and the Lockean model of the state. While some Muslims may find liberal ideas alien to their tradition, much the same could have been said of Christians not so long ago. It seems reasonable to hope that Islam can adapt to a social environment in which the state acts for its own secular reasons, rather than in deference to religious teachings.

# Conclusion

Private associations, including religious communities, offer important benefits to their members, who should be accorded considerable freedom to live their lives in accordance with rules whose authority they voluntarily accept. However, communities also exercise private power, often over individuals who may not voluntarily accept it or may not be well informed about the alternatives. In promoting the secular interests of its citizens, the state should not claim to know the truth or falsity of any religious doctrines that communities teach and put into practice, but it can make its own assessment of secular benefits and harms – and act accordingly to rein in oppressive exercises of private power.

When the state imposes its standards on churches and communities, as when it requires church-owned enterprises to abide by anti-discrimination law, this should not be seen as an infringement of religious freedom. Speaking generally, churches and communities should obey the ordinary law, which should, in turn, be fashioned to protect and promote citizens' interests in worldly things. There may sometimes be a case for exemptions from the general law, but it will have to be made on each occasion based on secular considerations such as the benefit in allowing freely associating individuals to run their associations in accordance with rules that they all accept. Such an argument has force, but it also has its limits – not least because there are often question marks as to the degree of freedom in "free" religious associations.

Though Carter sees religions and associated communities as centers of resistance to majoritarian tyranny, they can often be centers of resistance to secularism, individual freedom, and liberal principles. The best answer to that resistance is a determined recommitment to such ideas as the Millian harm principle, the Lockean model of the state, and freedom of speech. The latter will provide my focus for Chapter 9, where I consider how freedom of speech applies to contentious issues involving churches and sects.

But first, I turn to the question of children's interests. Liberal principles are fine in dealings among competent adults, but what about children, whose secular interests may clash with the wishes of parents and communities, and even with their own developing ideas about worldly and spiritual matters? How should the state respond?

# Notes

1   Kent Greenawalt, *Religion and the Constitution*, vol. 1: *Fairness and Free Exercise*, Princeton University Press, Princeton 2006, p. 42.

2   Brian Barry, *Culture and Equality: An Egalitarian Critique of Multiculturalism*, Polity Press, Cambridge 2001, pp. 123–124.

3   For a highly critical account, see Martha C. Nussbaum, *Liberty of Conscience: In Defense of America's Tradition of Religious Equality*, Basic Books, New York 2008, pp. 179–198.

4   Greenawalt sees legislation forbidding religious discrimination by private parties as about extending religious freedom (*Religion and the Constitution*, vol. 1, p. 348). But that leads him into complicated, and in my view unnecessary, questions as to why the state is not actually *restricting* the religious freedom of employers, and others who exercise private power, to assist co-religionists and oppose religious rivals.

5   432 US 63 (1977).

6   Again, the fishing fleet example comes from Isaac Kramnick and R. Laurence Moore, *The Godless Constitution: A Moral Defense of the Secular State*, W. W. Norton, New York 2005, p. 59.

7   Barry, *Culture and Equality*, p. 174.

8   Greenawalt, *Religion and the Constitution*, vol. 1, p. 379.

9   Barry, *Culture and Equality*, p. 117.

10   Karen Green, *The Woman of Reason: Feminism, Humanism and Political Thought*, Polity Press, Oxford 1995, p. 150.

11   Rex Ahdar and Ian Leigh, *Religious Freedom in the Liberal State*, Oxford University Press, Oxford 2005, p. 337.

12   Barry, *Culture and Equality*, pp. 150–154.

13   Stephanie Coontz, *Marriage, a History: From Obedience to Intimacy or How Love Conquered Marriage*, Viking, New York 2005, pp. 4–5, 15–23, 145–160.

14   Coontz, *Marriage, a History*, pp. 312–313.

15   Coontz, *Marriage, a History*, pp. 278–280.

16   Coontz, *Marriage, a History*, p. 278; Raja Halwani, *Philosophy of Love, Sex, and Marriage: An Introduction*, Routledge, New York 2010, pp. 275–276.

17   This is a clear implication of *Lawrence v. Texas*, 539 US 558 (2003).

18   Halwani, *Philosophy of Love, Sex, and Marriage*, p. 310.

19   Halwani, *Philosophy of Love, Sex, and Marriage*, pp. 308–310.

20   There are legitimate concerns as to whether parents or communities should be permitted to require minors to wear such a restrictive garment. The only way to protect minors from private power may be to ban the garment in public and private schools and/or for girls and women below the age of majority.

21   Nussbaum, *Liberty of Conscience*, p. 350.

22   Stephen L. Carter, *The Culture of Disbelief: How American Law and Politics Trivialize Religious Devotion*, Anchor, New York 1994, pp. 125–126.

23   Bassam Tibi, *Islam's Predicament with Modernity: Religious Reform and Cultural Change*, Routledge, Oxford 2009, p. 71.

24   Tibi, *Islam's Predicament with Modernity*, p. 94.

25   Tibi, *Islam's Predicament with Modernity*, pp. 215–216, 232.

CHAPTER EIGHT

RELIGIOUS FREEDOM AND THE INTERESTS OF CHILDREN

# Introduction

In Locke's time, it made sense to imagine a relatively modest state apparatus. Unless the state engaged in active persecutions, there was relatively little
chance of its laws clashing with religious practices. Since then, the world
has changed. In the massively more complex reality of contemporary liberal
democracies, there is no serious alternative to active intervention by the
state in many areas of life. The state provides services, redistributes property
and income, and does much to ameliorate the harsher outcomes of capitalism – a productive, generally efficient, but potentially cruel, economic
system.

Increasingly, the state has become involved in the welfare of children, an
area of its activity that provokes many conflicts. These are not readily solved
just by applying liberal principles. Where adults are concerned, paternalism
is usually inappropriate – though not entirely ruled out – and the mature
citizens of a liberal democracy exercise a wide discretion to pursue their
own happiness. Before they interfere with adults' decisions, state officials
should consider the values of social pluralism and individual liberty. But
very different issues arise with children. As they mature, children and teenagers should doubtless gain their freedom, increasingly so as they approach
adulthood. It's assumed, nonetheless, that they need boundaries and guid-
ance, whether from parents or other sources. At what stage should they be
free to act for themselves? What should happen if parents make poor
choices? And what if parents base their choices on their children's assumed

*Freedom of Religion and the Secular State*, First Edition. Russell Blackford.
© 2012 John Wiley & Sons, Inc. Published 2012 by John Wiley & Sons, Inc.

spiritual interests, while harming them in purely worldly terms? When and how should the state interfere in parent–child relationships?

Such questions have no easy answers. Adults can weigh their own spiritual and civil interests, or so the state must assume. If they harm themselves, that is normally their own responsibility. Liberal principles do not, however, allow them to harm others who are not consenting. Parents are granted no license to act against their children's interests. Even when children reach sufficient maturity to understand and consent to parental actions, or simply to make their own decisions, the state has a role in ensuring their welfare. And yet it cannot make definitive judgments of what is best for individuals, *all* things considered, since it cannot inquire into otherworldly things. That sometimes creates dilemmas. Discussing medical treatment controversies, Ahdar and Leigh highlight the lack of a truly neutral perspective: these controversies "often reflect differing worldviews of the protagonists." The authors add: "to insist there is a neutral, objective basis upon which to judge these conflicts is to maintain the 'fiction of neutrality' as some medical ethicists call it. There is no 'View from Nowhere.'"[1]

Surely this is true, in the sense that nobody, including the state's officials, can find a neutral, all-things-considered, approach to controversies that involve religious claims. There are always some things that the state and its officials cannot claim to know. Accordingly, they must take the risk of acting in ways that are ultimately detrimental to citizens' spiritual interests. However, this is not something they can avoid or that we can reasonably complain about if we accept the arguments for the Lockean model of the state.

In this chapter, I'll discuss a number of current controversies where religious doctrine cuts across the secular welfare of children. These arise mainly in education, but also with medical treatment and parental rights in general. When child welfare is at stake, how far should parents' rights go? When should the state interfere for the sake of the children?

## Parental Rights and the Lockean Model

Modern societies grant parents extensive legal rights over their children, permitting them to make judgments about the children's spiritual as well as secular interests. If the state is not going to take sides in matters of religion, it can hardly prescribe what religious beliefs are or are not taught to children. It must leave this to someone else, and there are no plausible candidates other than the parents.[2]

That arrangement is fairly uncontroversial: as a rule, parents bond readily and strongly with their children, and it makes good sense for public policy to build on this. It is normally assumed, moreover, that the parents' rights include the freedom to socialize their children into their own religious faith. In the early phase of modernity, Locke evidently took this for granted. In arguing that oppression of religion breeds sedition and rebellion, he observes as follows:

> Suppose this Business of Religion were let alone, and that there were some other Distinction made between men and men, upon account of their different Complexions, Shapes, and Features, so that those who have black Hair (for example) or gray Eyes, should not enjoy the same Privileges as other Citizens; that they should not be permitted either to buy or sell, or live by their Callings; that Parents should not have the Government and Education of their own Children; that all should either be excluded from the Benefit of the Laws, or meet with partial Judges; can it be doubted but these Persons, thus distinguished from others by the Colour of their Hair and Eyes, and united together by a common Persecution, would be as dangerous to the Magistrate as any others that had associated themselves meerly upon the account of Religion?[3]

Here, Locke assumes that parents ought to have "the Government and Education of their own Children," and that interference by the civil ruler is intolerable. While this may reflect the time when he was writing – when there was little if any concept of "children's rights" – some things have not changed. We still assume that parents bear the main responsibility for their children's development and socialization. This approach is simple and efficient, giving most children obvious adult support.

Brian Barry acknowledges that a liberal state can allow much parental discretion in bringing up children, but only within limits:

> Children need to be protected against parents who would inflict physical harm on them, even if this is prescribed by the parents' beliefs or customs. A familiar example is that of parents whose religious beliefs would lead them to withhold life-saving medical treatment from their children. Another well-publicized example is the practice, or more precisely set of practices, often referred to under the names of female circumcision or clitoridectomy but more comprehensively and accurately described as female genital mutilation. There is nothing specifically liberal about the view that the state should override the wishes of the parents in such cases. Any doctrine that gives the state the duty to prevent physical injury and death from being inflicted on its inhabitants will have the implication that the state should intervene. All that has to be said is that a liberal state is such a state.[4]

At this stage, we should take note that parental rights over children exist for the sake of the children themselves; they are not a benefit for parents, akin to ruling over subjects or keeping slaves. The state accords parents wide discretion in child-rearing because parents are better equipped to bring up children than the state, but *not* because children are their parents' property or because "parents have a right to fly in the face of fundamental social judgments about children's welfare."[5] The highest English court ruled on this point in *Gillick v. West Norfolk Area Health Authority*:

> It was, I think, accepted both by Mrs. Gillick and by the D.H.S.S., and in any event I hold, that parental rights to control a child do not exist for the benefit of the parent. They exist for the benefit of the child and they are justified only in so far as they enable the parent to perform his duties towards the child, and towards other children in the family.[6]

However, more must be said where religious teaching is concerned. In Chapter 3 I described the problems with expecting adults to renounce their religious doctrines and practices, even in exchange for the benefits of social peace. For many people, religion is so important as to trump any loyalty to the state. For them, too much is at stake, possibly including their personal salvation and fate in an eternal afterlife. Naturally enough, this extends to their children, for what loving parent would risk her child's immortal soul? At the very least, a loving and devout parent will want maximum freedom to raise her child in her own faith.

In many cases, perhaps most, this causes no problems: generally speaking, parents have the best interests of their children at heart, and act accordingly; religion adapts to the modern world; and society avoids rigid expectations of how children should be socialized. In general, we don't require that each child receive an optimal upbringing – if that could ever be defined in pluralist societies. Though parents exercise control in the interests of their children, they are not expected to do everything possible to maximize the children's prospects. It is usually considered sufficient if children are raised to be productive, well-adjusted, and peaceful citizens, with skills that give them a reasonable range of life choices.

When parents do more than this to improve their children's life prospects, it may be seen as praiseworthy or virtuous – except where it strays into "over-parenting," with undue pressure on all concerned. But in any event, extra efforts are not normally demanded, either by commonsense morality or the provisions of the law. In practice, we adopt a rather lenient standard: children should be nurtured, treated kindly, and given life's necessities, such as food and water, clothing, shelter, and essential health care. The state also sets some compulsory school requirements. Within those constraints, however, parents are given much choice in how to bring up their children. The law gives them space in which to act, a broad margin of discretion.

Even so, cases arise where parents' wishes, perhaps motivated by religious beliefs, clash with their children's welfare, at least if this is viewed as ordinary human flourishing. These cases can arise within the home, in the health-care system, in education, and in many other contexts.

## Indoctrination and Punishment

Against this background, Ahdar and Leigh are able to state: "There can be no doubt that religiously devout parents are vitally interested in the successful transmission of their faith to their offspring. This is one of the prime incidents of religious liberty."[7] That remark is consistent with the Lockean model – at the least, state officials should not impose a religious view on children or persecute parents for their attempts to "transmit their faith." Prima facie, the state has no opinion about the existence or character of any otherworldly order of things, and has no interest in what parents choose to teach their children about it. Furthermore, it needs to understand that much is at stake in the minds of parents who seek their children's spiritual welfare.

Thus the state should not attempt to transmit its preferred religion to the next generation; nor should it block the transmission of disfavored religions. It should *not*, for example, reason like this: "The doctrines of Santeria are false; people are better off not believing in false doctrines; therefore people are better off not believing in the doctrines of Santeria (and we'll forbid their transmission to children)."

We should, however, pause to note the skeptical remarks of A. C. Grayling. Grayling accepts that liberal political principles and the view that parents "have a right to determine their children's faith and education" point to an acceptance of indoctrinating small children into their parents' religious beliefs. But, he asks, might society actually have a duty to protect children from proselytization? He worries about children being taught what he regards as falsehoods, fantasies, and absurdities from an early age, and so being rendered incapable of challenging what they were taught. Grayling's discussion of the issue is inconclusive: he proposes this approach as something to consider; while we're thinking about it, he suggests, we need strong arguments to be made against religion.[8]

The state should not be acting on the basis that it considers religious doctrines to be fantasies, falsehoods, or absurdities. Nonetheless, Grayling's point about autonomy is well taken. In any event, parents do not have an absolute right to reproduce their religious views at all costs, and the state has a responsibility to consider the secular welfare of children. This, in fact, should be its starting point: it has a role in protecting children's civil interests, and this gives it reason for enacting general laws requiring that parents meet at least minimum standards of provision for their children's physical and psychological welfare. If parents are motivated by religious concerns to act in ways that fall short of these standards, enforcing them should not be seen as religious persecution – the purpose and primary effect of the relevant laws relate to child welfare, not to suppressing religion.

The real issue here is what degree of accommodation the state should offer to devout parents. As I explained in Chapter 6, claims for accommodation require a balancing of interests. Here the interests involve the secular welfare of children versus the liberty of parents to teach their religious beliefs (in many cases accompanied by anxiety if, for example, a child is not considered "saved"). Where these interests genuinely clash, the state has little choice but to favor the secular interests of the children. If, for example, parents declined to provide their children with food, the state would have every reason to intervene. The motive might be religious, and any intervention might cause parents anxiety if they considered some kind of food deprivation necessary for a child's spiritual welfare. But the anxiety suffered by parents cannot be allowed to outweigh their children's need for food. Recall that the broad discretion given to parents is intended to benefit children and cannot otherwise be justified.

Mere indoctrination in the tenets of a faith might be thought to raise no secular concerns such as to justify state intervention. Even here, however, there could be extreme, or even less extreme, examples that to concern us. Many religious traditions include doctrines, narratives, and images that children could find distressing. Consider, for example, the biblical story of Noah's Ark. However edifying, harmless, or merely quaint this might seem to adults, the story of global drowning for almost all humans and other animals might be terrifying for at least some young children.

At the more extreme end, there are doctrines of hellfire and eternal torture, sometimes backed up by the use of so-called "Hell Houses," where the sufferings of the damned are simulated by actors. These were given wide public exposure by Richard Dawkins's 2006 television program *Root of All Evil?* (first broadcast on Channel 4 in the United Kingdom). Dawkins went on to reflect about the experience in his popular book *The God Delusion*, which describes the presentation of Hell House enactments to frighten children into repentance from sin and acceptance of born-again Christian doctrine.[9] This sort of exposure of children to supernatural terrors underpins Dawkins's view that some kinds of religious indoctrination of children are tantamount to child abuse.[10]

Doubtless the state should be reluctant to interfere with children's religious upbringings, and I am not suggesting a ban on the story of Noah's Ark, or that it be declared out of bounds for children. But the state may well have a role if a particular child's behavior is seriously disturbed by exposure to supernatural terrors. Similar issues arise with punishments. As with all parental rights, the right to punish is not intended for the benefit of the parents. Its primary justification is that it benefits the children concerned, though there is doubtless a secondary benefit to others who might be harmed by a particular child's behavior. In effect, the state delegates to parents some of its responsibility to protect its citizens from harm.

Doubtless the state should allow parents considerable discretion to make judgments about when punishment is appropriate and what form it should take, but the discretion cannot be unlimited. At least some constraints must be imposed on physical or psychological ill-treatment of children, even where administered for the purpose of socializing them and protecting others. The modern trend is toward gentler forms of upbringing, with many jurisdictions banning or significantly constraining corporal punishment. The state has a legitimate secular reason to enact such laws: once again they are not intended to restrict the religious beliefs and practices of parents, and that is not their primary effect. They aim at protecting the civil interests of children.

In setting the boundaries to parental discretion, state officials cannot depend on passages contained in holy books. They should first obtain the best available expert advice on child development and whatever is known of the effects of various punishments. Untoward effects from corporal punishment need to be weighed against the obvious difficulties inherent in disciplining children. Educational campaigns may be needed to teach parents effective but less harmful methods. In the first instance, this deliberation should be religion-blind. After deciding on the general law, the state can consider any accommodations of religion. As always, it should not be too willing to grant exemptions from a generally applicable law that it considers justified.

What then? The state cannot decide whether harsh punishment serves children's otherworldly interests: some religions may teach this; others may not; and the truth of it all is simply not available to the state's officials, acting in their official capacities. Instead, the children's secular interests should be weighed against those of parents, bearing in mind the underlying purpose of parental rights – again, these are essentially to benefit the child, not the parents. Parents may feel anxiety if they believe they are disobeying the command of a god, or that their children are thereby put at spiritual risk. However, the children's secular interests, as best as the state can assess them, must be weighed against parental anxieties.

Ahdar and Leigh discuss the right to smack children as a religious freedom claim: there is, they say, a direct link between this "right" and the practice of religion, since some religious viewpoints explicitly require corporal punishment.[11] Though these authors offer a detailed, valuable, and even-handed discussion of the issue, they miss the essential point that this is not an issue of freedom from religious persecution, but merely one of accommodation for the practices of a religion that is *not* actually being persecuted. Anti-smacking laws apply generally and neutrally to religious and non-religious parents and to religious parents of all faiths. The state does not enact such laws out of disapproval of a religion, but for its own good and sufficient worldly reasons. Admittedly, such laws may *feel* like persecution to parents who are restrained from putting some of their religious views into practice. They may feel aggrieved, but it does not follow merely from this that they are actually being persecuted.

Unfortunately, the state cannot guarantee that no one will ever feel persecuted by neutral, generally applicable laws, enacted for good secular reasons. It can grant accommodations, or exemptions, if the secular argument for doing so is sufficiently strong, but that is all.

How strong, then, is the claim by some religious parents that they should be exempted from laws that restrict the corporal punishment of children? As I've suggested, the state must balance the worldly interests of parents and children. Once it has reached the conclusion that such laws are generally required, it is unlikely to grant an exemption. Strictly speaking, this will depend on its assessment of just how damaging corporal punishment is. The likely conclusion, however, is that a case for exemption is weak – that is always likely when the purpose of a law is to prevent individuals from physically hurting others.

## Health and Medical Issues

Religious belief and practice can intersect in a number of ways with issues of medical treatment. Where the patient is a mature adult, she is generally accorded the right to make her own decisions about accepting treatment, and the state will not intervene on paternalistic grounds. This is a relatively clear-cut example of the harm principle in action. If the patient refuses medical treatment on religious grounds, that is generally not the state's business: the patient is the best judge of what is in her interests, all things considered, and the state should not exercise paternalism merely because it cannot assess whatever spiritual interest she is pursuing.

The state has a clearer role when the case involves a child's illness or injury. One possibility is that a maturing child may seek medical treatment that the parents object to on religious grounds. Another is when children and/or their parents object to necessary medical treatment – medical treatment that may be life-saving in many cases. Of these the first is relatively (though *only* relatively) straightforward.

Much of the burden of *Gillick* was to the effect that children become more mature and independent as they grow older. Over time, parents' rights gradually yield as a child gains sufficient understanding to make her own decisions. The case involved prescriptions for the contraceptive pill for teenage girls under 16, but its reasoning went far wider to expound a "mature minor" doctrine. As a child grows in maturity, she can properly consent to medical treatment in consultation with her doctor. In such a case, parents' rights must give way; parents have no right to countermand the

decisions of sufficiently mature minors. This legal approach gives the maturing child an increasing ability to make decisions that her parents might
disapprove of, such as a decision to use contraception or a decision by a
Jehovah's Witness to have a blood transfusion.

The more difficult, sometimes heartbreaking, cases come in two forms.
In some, the parents refuse to agree to medical treatment for a young and
dependent child. The child may side with her parents, insofar as she understands the situation. The parents may not seek medical help at all, believing
that prayer or faith healing is sufficient. These situations can, and often do,
lead to disastrous outcomes, sometimes including the death of a child. Even
more difficult are the cases where a mature minor deliberately refuses treatment on religious grounds.

In one oft-cited case, the US Supreme Court expressed disdain for parents
who would, in effect, sacrifice their children to religion. *Prince v.
Massachusetts* dealt with child labor laws, not with a medical issue, but the
majority judges stressed that parents, who might lawfully make martyrs of
themselves, cannot, "in identical circumstances . . . make martyrs of their
children before they have reached the age of full and legal discretion when
they can make that choice for themselves."[12] This is, I submit, the correct
approach. Where parents fail, for whatever reason, to protect the ordinary
secular interests of their children, the state may act for the children's benefit.
The case is stronger where life and death are at stake, even if the parents
have religious motives. The balance here is exactly the reverse of an adult's
self-regarding decision, where the presumption is against state paternalism.
Where children are concerned, the state cannot decline to act for fear of
spiritual harms that it knows nothing about: "The state should not abandon
its determination about secular welfare in the face of such beliefs, and it
properly requires medical treatment that is essential for life, even against a
parental claim that the treatment is harmful religiously."[13]

The ordinary law should require that parents provide full medical care.
If they feel unable to do so, an efficient process is needed to override their
decisions. This is not religious persecution, merely protection of children's
interests by a generally applicable law. The courts should *not* look on such
cases as infringing on religious freedom, and then consider the issue of
compelling justification. Under the Lockean model and the US Supreme
Court's approach in *Smith*, no persecution arises, there is no infringement
of religious freedom, and no process of balancing rights should be attempted
by the courts. The remaining issue is whether, nonetheless, the legislature
ought to make some accommodation for the parents' religion.

As with corporal punishment, the state must consider the secular interests of those concerned. Strictly speaking, it has a broad discretion to weigh
these up and reach a policy conclusion. What might be done in one jurisdiction does not bind another that weighs the interests differently. Normally,

however, solicitude for conscience and religious sensibilities should not outweigh the state's more clear-cut role in protecting young citizens from physical harm. This is a situation where exemptions should *not* be granted – or so it seems to me.

Tragically, cases where parents deny medical treatment often lead to the death of a child – with consequential criminal charges for crimes such as manslaughter. In those circumstances, should parents be accommodated by some kind of statutory defense? Writing in 2005, Ahdar and Leigh report that over 40 American states have enacted some sort of religion-based defense to child-neglect laws.[14] In practice, the legal situation in the United States is a nightmare, with conflicting cases and often contradictory statutes in the same jurisdiction.[15] Despite all that, the policy choice is reasonably clear. The parents concerned are doubtless well intentioned, and seek the best for their children, but that can be raised as a mitigating factor in sentencing. Neither statutory provisions nor the courts should hold them innocent of crime.

Consider, too, a health measure such as vaccination. This does not treat a pre-existing medical condition, but it grants the individual an additional resistance to harmful infection by particular microscopic life forms. Parents who refuse to vaccinate their children, whether on religious or other grounds, thereby place them at unnecessary risk of illness. Again, the state has a discretion to exercise and in principle a range of policy choices may be open to it, but once again I suggest that its choice should be clear: though the parents may be well intentioned, seeking the best for their children, that should not give them an exemption from the law.[16] With vaccination programs, the case against exemptions is especially strong: these programs typically bolster herd immunity, where a high proportion of protected individuals hinders the spread of disease even to those who cannot be vaccinated. Where herd immunity is an issue, parents who refuse to take part in government programs create avoidable risks, not only for their own children but also for others who may need to rely on the immunity of the "herd."

What about older children who may be mature enough to give and refuse consent to medical treatment? While there are variations from jurisdiction to jurisdiction, *Gillick* states the common position on children's developing competence. Children do mature, and at some point before full adulthood a child is likely to be capable of making her own decisions about medical treatment. What if she refuses potentially life-saving treatment on religious grounds – possibly fearing for her spiritual salvation if she accepts certain treatment? These cases are especially heartbreaking. If we allow a mature teenager to refuse treatment, on religious or other grounds, we thus allow her to die at an early age. No matter how intellectually mature she may be, no matter how well she understands the consequences, this is the loss of a young life, just beginning to bloom. To say the least, that is a distasteful outcome. What's often not appreciated, at least in my experience, is that the alternative is also distasteful.

We are considering a young person who understands that her life is at stake, but knowingly accepts the likelihood of death – rather than disobeying her god or harming what she sees as her spiritual prospects. From her point of view, death may better than damnation. Nor need such a person be deranged or fanatical; her choice may be perfectly logical given the religious doctrines that she accepts, and which the state cannot disprove. Forcing her to accept the treatment may terrify her – perhaps she'll need to be forcibly strapped down if she resists, physically struggling and screaming. Afterwards, she will have to live with the feeling of sin and deep violation, and the fear of spiritual consequences. As a society, should we really use force to overbear such a person's will? After all, her liberty and peace of mind are *also* things of this world that merit protection. We wouldn't use force on an adult who refuses treatment, so why should we with a mature minor? The only difference is that adults are presumed to be mature, whereas minors need to demonstrate it in a situation like this. *Ex hypothesi*, however, the young person whom we're discussing has done exactly that.

When such situations come before the courts, they often take the view that the minor is insufficiently mature.[17] In some cases, this is probably a fiction. Young people with strong religious convictions may understand the issues as well as anyone else, and, recall, it is not up to the courts to declare that otherworldly beliefs are false. The reality, however, is that there is great social resistance to allowing young people to lose their lives. Perhaps this can be rationalized as follows. Some young people are sufficiently mature to accept medical treatment or to reject it when the consequences are relatively minor. We can accept this much, but it's a further step to allow them make final, irrevocable decisions about life-saving medical care – throwing away their lives, as it may seem. In such an extreme situation, so the thinking runs, we must favor life over liberty and conscience, so paternalism toward minors must prevail. For *this* special purpose, we won't treat them as adults until they reach the statutory age of majority.

Such reasoning is not entirely satisfactory. If we are so opposed to a 15-year-old or a 17-year-old "throwing her life away," why not also a 19-year-old – or, if it comes to that, someone much older? The difference cannot be that the others are sufficiently mature, while the 15- and 17-year-olds are not: we are contemplating a situation where these young people are "Gillick competent": they understand what they are doing. It would seem more principled to apply a notion such as Gillick competence to all cases where minors make health decisions, or else abandon it entirely and rely on an arbitrary cut-off point where competence is assumed.

This may, however, be an area of the law where values conflict and compromise is necessary. We have a special solicitude for young people, and perhaps a doubt as to whether any of them can really make such an extreme decision. At the same time, our respect for the autonomous decisions of adults forces us to allow people who have reached official adulthood to make their own decisions – even where their lives are at stake. This leaves an area between the onset of Gillick competence and the attainment of the age of majority where we feel impelled to impose *some* restrictions on autonomy. I join with Ahdar and Leigh and others who tend to see this as the best available policy option,[18] but it is not truly satisfying. For such situations, when they arise, there is simply no comfortable answer.

## Education

In Chapter 4 I argued that the state, through its employees such as teachers, should not be endorsing or imposing any form of religion, and should certainly not be proffering a religion to children via the public education system. That, however, leaves plenty of room for controversy about how religion should be approached in education policy. Note at the outset that children cannot make all educational decisions for themselves and that, as Barry emphasizes, the state does not have quite the same reasons to take a hands-off approach and leave important decisions to parents as it does with children's general nurture. In the latter case, ongoing state interference would involve many imponderables, be highly intrusive, and seldom lead to improvements if the state substituted its discretion for that of parents. These factors are not so apparent with education.[19]

In discussing the celebrated *Yoder* case, which I'll come to later in this chapter, Greenawalt identifies five purposes for education beyond the relatively basic level of the eighth grade. It increases the child's skills that she may need for a career; enhances her ability to choose how to live; assists her to enjoy culture, especially written culture such as novels, biographies, and works of philosophy; helps her to understand the principles of government and to participate in citizenship and democratic processes; and assists in more general moral development.[20]

The last of these is, I suggest, somewhat problematic, and should be treated with care, since the state makes no claim to know what is morally best when everything is taken into account. Nonetheless, there are powerful secular reasons to require that all children be educated to some substantial degree in the sciences and humanities, the fine arts, and socially acceptable conduct – and not merely in generic or specialized job skills. If religion, with its otherworldly claims did not exist at all, we would still have good reasons to teach these subjects. We would, moreover, ask the public school system to reinforce at least some basic moral ideas that are needed for social harmony: ideas such as the value of tolerance, cooperation, and honesty.

Amongst all this, the state may have good secular reasons to teach children information about the many and varied religions of the world. Apart from its importance for a child's understanding of human cultures, this kind of knowledge may reduce intolerance and assist with social peace and harmony. Once again, the aim is not to promote a favored religion, or to subject disfavored religions to disparagement or persecution. Instead, it is a practical and worldly one. As with many educational initiatives, provision of comparative religion classes might be interpreted as persecution by some parents, should they wish to raise their children in ignorance of other views. Some may even think that their children's salvation is at stake.

Similar issues can arise with other educational programs. For example, the state may provide school students with information about drugs, calculating that this is best for harm reduction. It may provide information on sexuality and contraception, based on similar reasoning. Some parents may resist these programs, or accept them only with resentment. Ahdar and Leigh complain as follows:

> Compulsory sex education programs that focus on contraceptive techniques yet consider a religious commitment to abstinence until marriage to be so unrealistic as not to be worth mentioning, or drugs education that devotes excessive attention to the types and effects of different substances (so that pupils can make "informed" choices) are examples of the sort of "citizenship" training that many devout parents would prefer to do without.[21]

However, consider the context of sex education (similar considerations apply to education about drugs). The state must act on a secular basis, not on the basis that sex of some kinds is sinful. Presumably, it aims at a low teenage pregnancy rate. This is plausible as a secular goal, in order to protect the interests of young teenage girls.

In contemporary circumstances, pregnancy confronts a teenager with two obvious alternatives. On the one hand she can make the potentially career-stopping choice of becoming a mother long before she has finished her own education. On the other, there is the grim decision to have an abortion. I am not suggesting here that abortion typically leads to a "post-abortion syndrome" involving depression and feelings of loss. This common claim by anti-abortion activists lacks scholarly support, and may best be seen as scaremongering. Nonetheless, the decision whether or not to go through with an abortion is surely one that we want few girls of high-school age to face. As long as modern societies are structured with very long educational periods, extending well into adulthood for some careers, this dilemma can arise.

If the goal is to protect the secular interests of teenage girls, rather than to deter or punish sin, the state must answer an obvious policy question.

Is it more likely to be successful if it moralizes against teenage sex, instills guilt in young people (or attempts to, with mixed success), and treats pregnant teenagers harshly? That approach may seem intuitive to adults who already regard teenage sex as wrong. Or would success be more likely with a different policy? This could provide teenagers with reliable information about sex and contraception, encourage them to use the information intelligently, and attempt to reduce the trauma in those cases where teenage pregnancy does occur. A secular policy on teenage sexuality might involve easy access to contraception and abortion, a non-moralistic approach to girls and women who choose abortions, and a sufficient economic safety net to ensure that having a child is not a complete career-stopper for anybody who makes that choice. Sex education classes might combine information about sex and contraception with frank discussion of the difficulties of adolescent pregnancy.

Different jurisdictions have taken different policy paths, and there is a wealth of data available on the outcomes. My aim here is not to analyze that data, but merely to suggest that the state should adopt whichever policies appear more likely to achieve its secular purpose. If it adopts the less moralistic policy mix, it may find itself in conflict with the wishes of many parents who regard teenage sex as sinful, or in any event morally forbidden. Thus, the state may have to weigh the emotional impact on parents if they are frustrated in their attempts to inculcate certain moral beliefs in their children.

Related to sex education is the state's attitude to homosexuality. Ahdar and Leigh claim that schools unavoidably take some sort of attitude to this. If heterosexuality is presented as the norm, this will be perceived as discriminatory. If the school is even-handed, this carries the implicit message that what some parents see as immoral behavior is acceptable.[22] So yet again, some deeply religious parents may feel persecuted where no persecution is intended. But once again the way forward suggests itself. The state knows nothing of "sin," but merely seeks to protect the secular interests of citizens. Laws against homosexual conduct should be ruled out by liberal principles, and the state has no reason to disparage its citizens' lawful sexual behavior. It may, however, have good reasons to protect the civil interests of gay citizens. When it comes to education, considerations of social harmony and inclusion may favor treating homosexual relationships as "no big deal." This approach may concern parents who view homosexual conduct as a sin, but the state does not promise never to cause concerns, only that it will act for worldly reasons.

Again, there is no persecution in these cases. The issue that arises is what, if any, accommodation should be provided for parents' religious views. As with many cases discussed in this chapter, that may not be an easy decision, but let us recall, once again, that the authority of parents over children is meant to benefit the children rather than the parents. The state must make its own judgment about the weight of the secular interests involved, but it cannot be assumed that the parents should be accommodated.

Many other issues can arise across the school curriculum, and I can't even list them, let alone discuss them all. To take just one example, what if the religious poetry of Gerard Manley Hopkins were taught in English literature classes? Should it be taught from a specifically religious viewpoint? Surely not. Rather, the teacher must help students to enter the historical context and the poet's mindset, and to gain a lively sense of the poetry's imagery, style, and rhythms. The emphasis is on understanding and enjoying poetry, and on expanding students' imaginations, not on a commitment to Hopkins's Catholic worldview. However, that kind of neutrality in teaching will leave some parents dissatisfied: does it convey a message that religion is unimportant?

Or what if students were introduced to irreligious or anti-religious authors such as A. E. Housman or Jean-Paul Sartre? In such a case, ideas must be identified, but again without endorsement or disparagement. Students may have to grapple with them for themselves. Clearly, all this requires sensitivity from teachers, but the main aim of studying literature is to deepen students' understanding, not to proselytize for one or another worldview. A teacher who bears that in mind will not go far wrong.

Before turning to the general issue of accommodation in education, I need to discuss a major site of debate between educational values and the concerns of some religious adherents. At least in the US, this is a hot-button issue: the teaching of biological evolution in public schools.

## The Evolution Debate

Modern evolutionary theory is a synthesis of scientific developments since the mid-nineteenth century. It draws on Charles Darwin's masterpiece *On the Origin of Species* (1859), but also on more modern work in paleontology, genetics, and many other fields. Many lines of inquiry converge to give the theory empirical support, and it is now the central organizing theory in the biological sciences.

Evolutionary theory explains life's diversity and the complex functioning of earth's vast number of life forms. These are seen as the products of gradual change that required many millions of generations. On this picture, as elaborated since Darwin's time, the first life forms appeared three to four billion years ago, and have since evolved through the stages shown in the fossil record, up to the present day. Evolutionary scientists investigate a number of mechanisms by which life may have evolved and branched into numerous taxa, but the central mechanism remains that proposed by

Darwin, that is natural selection. As understood by contemporary biologists, this involves the differential success of different combinations of genes in reproducing themselves through the generations. Less accurately, but perhaps more intuitively, we can think of some life forms out-competing others for survival and reproduction. We, for example, are descended from unbroken sequences of animals that lived long enough to pass down their genes.

The main propositions of contemporary evolutionary theory are robust – they have so much empirical support that they are almost certainly true. They fit, moreover, within an emerging scientific picture of the universe in space and time, a picture that has been built up by such fields as geology and astrophysics. Unfortunately, evolution conflicts directly with some religious claims, as do other robust scientific findings that inform the overall picture. Many of these relate to the vast depth of time – it is now clear that the planets and the stars are billions of years old. That, however, is not accepted by all religions.

In particular, some popular kinds of Christianity take a literal approach to the Bible, and postulate that our planet was created about 6,000 years ago, or perhaps a bit more on some theological accounts. This view proposes that each kind of living thing (particularly, but not only, human beings) was specially and separately created by God. That theological claim is not merely an add-on to an essential core. Rather, it is part of an integrated system that also includes a literal fall from God's grace at a more or less identifiable time, the historical introduction of sin and corruption into the world, Jesus Christ's sacrificial atonement for sin, and an ultimate victory of good over evil.

Other religions, of course, have different views. Some may be consistent with the scientific picture, while others may be inconsistent with it only in subtle, indirect, and debatable ways. As discussed in Chapter 1, scientists cannot directly investigate a transcendent order, though they can test sufficiently specific claims about how it affects events in this world. In most cases scientific testing of claims about a transcendent order is not a practical prospect; religious claims about another world may be vague, certain gods may be capricious, and so on. But where a religious doctrine claims an age for the earth, or a chronological sequence of creation, it can plainly and openly contradict scientific theory. Both cannot be true.

The dilemma for the secular state is that evolutionary biology is a major and fundamental scientific theory. No child has a good scientific grounding unless she understands the basics of evolution. From a religion-blind viewpoint, then, the state should teach evolution in its public schools, and perhaps even require it in private schooling. It would do so if religion did not exist at all. The key value here is the welfare of children in a modern world that increasingly depends on science, and where scientific illiteracy closes off many careers. Indeed, the secular case for teaching evolution is so powerful that opposition to it is difficult to explain except on religious grounds.

In the US, disputes about the teaching of evolution have frequently reached the courts – and sometimes the judicial apex of the Supreme Court. *Epperson v. Arkansas*[23] concerned a state law that banned all teaching of evolutionary theory, insofar as it involves human descent from earlier animals, in public or publicly funded schools. The Supreme Court had no difficulty in invalidating this provision, seeing it as an attempt to protect biblically literalist religion. In *Edwards v. Aguillard*,[24] the Supreme Court upheld lower court decisions that struck down a Louisiana statute as unconstitutional. The statute would have required that evolution be taught in public schools only if accompanied by teaching in "creation science," an alternative developed to conform with biblical literalism.

The majority of judges in *Edwards* held that the Louisiana statute breached the Establishment Clause in having no secular purpose. On the court's interpretation, the statute attempted to discredit evolutionary theory and to advance a religious position. I can only add that any such laws are best explained as attempts to shore up the credibility of a particular body of theology – one that happens to conflict directly with robust findings from modern science. Even if the state could find a secular reason not to teach evolutionary theory, or not to teach biological science at all, it is difficult to find such a purpose in teaching it but casting doubt on it by one device or another. As the courts have recognized, the motivation for that must be religious. I submit that the American cases have been correctly decided, insofar as they've taken this approach.

Another case was *Tangipahoa Parish Board of Education v. Freiler*,[25] decided by the United States Court of Appeals for the Fifth Circuit. *Tangipahoa* concerned the policy of a school board in Louisiana that had ordered that a disclaimer be read immediately before any presentation of evolutionary theory to students. The case has received some criticism from legal scholars, so let us consider why. In their discussion, Eisgruber and Sager quote from the disclaimer, which they seem to consider innocuous: "It is hereby recognized by the Tangipahoa Board of Education, that the lesson to be presented, regarding the origin of life and matter, is known as the Scientific Theory of Evolution and should be presented to inform students of the scientific concept and not intended to influence or dissuade the Biblical version of Creation or any other concept." Eisgruber and Sager argue that the courts may have gone a step too far in striking this down, and suggest that public schools could go further in presenting arguments both for and against evolutionary theory.[26]

For their part, Ahdar and Leigh complain that the US courts have embraced "a liberal form of rationality" by treating evolution as "an objective theory (lacking in religious assumptions or foundations), rather than a rival, quasi-religious worldview, as many of its critics maintain."[27] Referring to *Tangipahoa*, they add that the courts do not provide a level playing field if a school teaching evolution cannot offer a disclaimer that involves calling it a theory and advising students to form their own opinions. Ahdar and Leigh view the *Tangipahoa* disclaimer as a "mere invitation to exercise critical rationality and the reminder of [the students'] right to hold differing beliefs."[28]

With respect, all these criticisms miss the mark. The Lockean model of the secular state does not require that it be neutral between "liberal rationality" and some other kind of rationality. Rather, the state disclaims expertise in otherworldly matters and supernatural transformations, such as those involving the salvation of souls. Thus, it has no basis to doubt robust findings from modern science, such as those involving evolution. If presented with proper evidence from scientific experts, the courts should, indeed, treat evolution as an objective theory, rather than as a "quasi-religious worldview." In particular, evolutionary biology was not contrived for the purpose of discrediting religion. Rather, it is the result of incremental investigation of nature using the ordinary methods of rational inquiry supplemented by the more precise "scientific" methods that have become increasingly available during the past four centuries – such as instruments that extend the human senses, mathematical modeling, and equipment that enables many decisive experiments to be done.

Evolution is well-established science, not quasi-religion. That's not to say, however, that it has no implications for philosophers and theologians: obviously, it casts serious doubt on those religious views that plainly contradict it. Yet it may even support other religious views – that is a matter for philosophical debate. For example, some thinkers, such as biologist-theologian Francisco Ayala, argue that Darwin's theory provides a solution to the age-old problem of evil (why does an omnipotent and benevolent deity allow suffering and evil in the world?).[29] Others, such as philosopher of science Philip Kitcher, have suggested that it makes the problem worse.[30] But this is all a matter for argument outside the science classroom. Whether evolution and religion (of one kind or another) are ultimately incompatible, mutually compatible, or even mutually supportive is a deep issue for the consideration of philosophers, theologians, and other interested persons.

I have already discussed why these debates are so inconclusive in practice (see Chapter 1). Meanwhile, it is not the role of the state to determine the broader philosophical and theological implications of evolutionary theory, one way or the other. Its role, in this instance, is simply to advance the civil interests of children by teaching them well-established science.

*Pace* Ahdar and Leigh, it is tendentious to teach evolution with a specific disclaimer, without doing likewise for other well-established scientific theories that are taught in schools. Although evolutionary biologists talk about the "theory" of evolution, this does not mean that they consider evolution to be a mere conjecture or speculation. As Jerry A. Coyne explains, the word "theory" is used within the profession of science to denote "a well-thought-out group of propositions to explain facts about the real world."[31] A point can arrive where such a body of propositions has been overwhelmingly supported by evidence, and is considered robust by scientific practitioners. In principle, it could be falsified by new data – the propositions of science are accepted provisionally. But in some cases, as with the heliocentric description of local astronomical bodies and their orbits, it is vanishingly unlikely that the main propositions will ever be falsified.

In that respect, Eisgruber and Sager miss the point. It is one thing to engage sufficiently advanced students in the pros and cons of genuine scientific controversies, such as the balance of importance between natural selection and other evolutionary mechanisms. It's another to single out a particular scientific theory for disclaimer whenever it is taught in public schools. If the state were merely encouraging freedom of individual thought, why not compose similar disclaimers for, say, the germ theory of disease or for heliocentrism? The irresistible conclusion is that Tangipahoa's school board sought to give comfort or assistance to literalist Christians.

Eisgruber and Sager make things difficult for themselves by promoting a constitutional theory that downplays the state's purposes, or motivations, as a constitutional issue.[32] Thus, they struggle even to defend *Epperson*, where the state of Arkansas obviously sought to strengthen the position of biblical literalism by hiding inconvenient knowledge from school children. For Eisgruber and Sager, the outcome in *Epperson* is best explained as a rejection of state-enforced orthodoxy in education.[33] But if we keep our eye on the Lockean model of the secular state, no constitutional gymnastics are required. Rather, the religious object of the Arkansas legislation is clear and plain to see, and identifying it falls well within the competence of the courts. The secular state has no business in assisting the cause of religion – or of any preferred religion – and the First Amendment forbids it. To borrow contemporary slang, *Epperson* was a no-brainer.

As I write, the most recent such case to reach the American courts was *Kitzmiller v. Dover Area School District*,[34] which was decided in the US District Court for the Middle District of Pennsylvania (the case was never appealed to a higher court, at least in part because of a change of membership on the relevant school board). Like *Tangipahoa*, *Dover* involved an attempt to employ a disclaimer to undermine the teaching of evolution. In this case, the disclaimer involved the alternative of "Intelligent Design": the idea that life as we see it is best explained via the operations of a designing intelligence. The disclaimer blatantly sought to discredit evolution as a robust scientific theory and to encourage students to explore Intelligent

Design as an alternative. In December 2005 it met the same ignominious fate as the disclaimer debated in the *Tangipahoa* case. Judge Jones found that it breached the US Constitution's Establishment Clause.

Cases such as *Epperson*, *Edwards*, *Tangipahoa*, and *Dover* show the school curriculum being manipulated for essentially religious reasons. In each situation, the aim was to discredit a body of scientific theory that blatantly clashes with certain popular religious views. The state should not involve itself in such exercises, and state officials should certainly not be involved in a game of testing or stretching the envelope: seeing how much religious endorsement or promotion they can get away with. Once the state decides to teach the theory of evolution – and the case for doing so is very strong – it should do so in good faith.

The only issue is how far public policy should accommodate the sensibilities of objecting parents, perhaps by excusing attendance in certain classes. That brings me back to the broader question of educational accommodations.

## Educational Accommodations

At several points in this chapter, I've commented that the real issue is one of accommodation for parents who disapprove of certain educational content for their children. Let's review the logic of this. First, decisions about the public school curriculum should not be based on support of or hostility toward religion in general or a particular religion, but on secular concerns – essentially, the socialization and ordinary flourishing of children. If the resulting regulations or guidelines are neutral and generally applicable, no religious establishment or persecution is involved.

Second, however, as with many other issues relating to state action, some parents may understandably *feel* persecuted even by acts that have no persecutory intention. The state's requirements may impact (sometimes even severely) on parents' religiously motivated plans for bringing up their children. That is not a reason to alter generally applicable educational requirements, but should the law allow specific students to be exempted from them at the request of their parents? This might depend on what the parents can propose as an alternative, and on just what is lost if exemptions are granted.

The high point for parental accommodations in education was another American case, *Wisconsin v. Yoder*,[35] which was treated as a breach of the Free Exercise Clause. Here, the Supreme Court accommodated the concerns of the Old Order Amish, a Protestant Christian group who separate themselves from the larger society in North America and shun much of its technology. The court allowed Amish families to withdraw their children early from Wisconsin's education system, which compelled school attendance until the age of 16. The rationale was that an extra two years of schooling would undermine children's commitment to the Amish teachings and culture – perhaps eventually destroying the Amish as a recognizable group.

Greenawalt has defended the outcome of *Yoder* in an analysis which concludes that the reasons for imposing an extra two years of education on Amish children (or an associated obligation on their parents to send them to school for an extra two years) were outweighed by the reasons against. His main consideration is the value of religious communities being able to practice their forms of life,[36] but this is not a compelling point. Whether a particular religious community will be able to practice its form of life indefinitely into the future depends on many things, including how attractive it can remain to potential converts and to young people who have a choice whether or not to leave.

The state may, indeed, allow participants in free associations of members a margin of discretion to accept rules that are not necessarily in their best interests. Where adults are concerned, there is a secular case for this. Interference would be offensively paternalistic, and competent adults should be able, to a large extent, to determine what is good for them, all things considered. However, this reasoning does not transfer to the treatment of children. Nor should the state be deciding which communities or entire ways of life are so valuable, all things considered, as to be preserved in the face of social changes. It is not the state's responsibility to frame laws affecting children in such a way as to keep Amish communities attractive or viable.

The state's responsibility here is to make its decisions on worldly grounds, without adverting to otherworldly considerations. Those grounds might include the hardship that is created for parents and other adults when children are educated in a way that could lead to conflict, rebellion, and parental fears about the children's spiritual well-being. But the state should also consider the interests of children in obtaining a sound education. Exactly where the balance is to be struck is a matter for political judgment. In the *Yoder* case, there seems to have been no evidence that any improper considerations about otherworldly matters infected the judgment of the secular authorities.

Notwithstanding Greenawalt's view and the 7–0 outcome at Supreme Court level,[37] I submit that *Yoder* was wrongly decided. Though it has never been formally overruled, it cannot stand consistently with *Smith*, decided almost 20 years later, and with cases that have followed, such as *City of Boerne v. Flores*.[38] The majority in *Smith* distinguished *Yoder* rather unconvincingly, referring to parental rights as an issue in addition to religious freedom, but parents' rights are usually subject to the state's basic educational requirements. The case is, therefore, shaky whether viewed as a matter of parental rights or as a matter of religious freedom, and it is difficult to see how the combination can be any stronger.

Hamilton provides a concise summary of the Supreme Court's current doctrine, within which *Yoder* is now an anomaly: "(1) the courts are to apply a default rule in favor of applying duly enacted, neutral, and generally applicable laws to religious conduct and (2) that default rule is only overcome in the face of evidence of persecution of religion."[39] On this approach, the Amish parents should have failed. Wisconsin's law was duly enacted, had general application, was neutral, and was not persecutory – its objects had nothing to do with harming or suppressing any religion. Its adverse effect on the plans of Amish parents was purely incidental to its purpose. The circumstances were remote from those arising much later in *Lukumi Babalu*, where a legislative intent to persecute was clearly apparent. More importantly, *Yoder* was wrong as a matter of political principle: the Lockean model of the secular state supports a constitutional doctrine such as Hamilton identifies.

In retrospect, *Yoder* should have been decided differently in the courts, but that is a claim about constitutional law. Assuming I am right about that, should a *legislative* exemption have been granted to the Amish in the circumstances that arose in *Yoder*? This is a more difficult question, and in a sense it is not my task to decide it. I've argued that legislative accommodations of religion can be justified when secular reasons for and against it are weighed up. If, however, it were a simple question of the welfare of children versus the peace of mind of parents, the welfare of children should usually prevail. Why should it be different for the Amish?

The Amish presented to the courts as a model community: industrious, prosperous, stable, peaceful, and with a low crime rate. They even permitted older teenagers some opportunity to leave, though this was surely difficult if they had not been educated for life in the outside world.[40] In short, they were well placed to demonstrate the success of their system, even in secular terms. They could almost guarantee their children achieving various secular goals: economic security; skilled and engrossing work; and life in a peaceful community. As Carter points out, the opinion of the court was heavily qualified, emphasizing the special character of the Amish way of life, and no other group has ever gained such a wide exemption from basic schooling.[41] Perhaps the judges saw benefit in allowing a "good" community, such as the Amish in Wisconsin, to survive, unhindered by the state's education policy, and legislators might well take a similar view.

In some ways, this looks like a particularly strong case for a group to be left alone and allowed its own educational system, one focused on practical skills rather than theoretical knowledge. It is not, however, any sort of no-brainer. The Amish could, perhaps, bring up a child "to perform his part well in life towards others and himself," as Mill puts it,[42] but don't we want something more than this when children are raised to adulthood? Modern education attempts to equip them with the knowledge and skills to open up a varied array of possible life plans. At least to some extent, it offers each child the possibility of an open future. This concept was formulated by Joel Feinberg in a 1980 article, the "The Child's Right to an Open Future," which he wrote in response to the *Yoder* case.[43] Clearly enough, the Amish could not provide this for their children. Then again, as the court clearly recognized in *Yoder*, an extra two years might not make much difference.[44] The state's policy already gave parents considerable scope to curtail their children's educations. Perhaps the Amish were not asking for all that much more.

How should this be decided by the legislatures of liberal democracies? My own bias favors more education, but it's a matter for the state's discretion, and for democratic decision-making. If, after weighing the secular considerations, the state frames the law to give certain groups a measure of exemption from ordinary educational requirements, that is democratically legitimate. It is not legitimate when exemptions are crafted by the courts, supposedly as a matter of religious freedom. Note, too, that even if the state does grant exemptions, it may do so with conditions. It need not, for example, free the exempted parents of taxes that nominally go to state schools. Nor need the exemption be permanent; if the state grants a partial exemption from a law enacted for good secular reasons, it may need to monitor the outcomes with some concern.

Should parents be permitted to withdraw their children from compulsory sex education lessons, or from lessons in biological evolution? What about classes that seek to teach tolerance (perhaps of homosexuals, perhaps of varied religious and cultural points of view)? Should parents be permitted to send children to private schools, or to "home school" their children, rather than enroll them in the public system? If they are, how closely should the curriculum in private schools (or the home) be specified and monitored by the state? Should the state require, for example, that parents or private school teachers teach legitimate science – including evolutionary theory?

I don't claim that there are clear answers to these questions. Pluralism may favor the existence of private schools, and parents should have opportunities to pass on their own religious beliefs, whether at home or through schooling that they have paid for themselves. In the real world of practical politics, detailed compromises are necessary, the cases can't all be solved in advance, and any compromise that is brokered should stay open for review as evidence of its effect gradually emerges and society continues to change. Conservative religious parents will not, and should not, have everything their own way, but nor must all children be brought up and educated identically. Private schools can be given some room to depart from the public curriculum, or at least to add a religious perspective that would be unacceptable in a public school system. Different jurisdictions might experiment with varied approaches, and the evidence can then be collected and analyzed.

Consider sex education. Greenawalt presents a subtle argument for the conclusion that failure by a public school system to teach about contraceptives in high-school sex education courses would be an establishment of religion, and accordingly unconstitutional within the US. In essence, his argument is that only religious grounds could be provided to conclude that sex among teenagers is grossly immoral, and while there might still be secular public policy reasons to discourage adolescent sex, failure to teach about contraception has been shown not to have the required effect.[45]

Greenawalt seems to overreach – not necessarily in his view of what is desirable educational policy, but in converting an essentially discretionary matter of public policy into one of constitutional law. A government may well be *wrong* to conclude that excluding information on contraception will advance its policy goals, and here I agree with Greenawalt, but that does not entail that it has thereby acted for a religious purpose. Surely governments should be able to make decisions that are merely unwise or based on poor information without having breached the constitution.

At the other end of the spectrum of views we find theorists who insist that parents be able to withdraw their children from sex education classes that don't accord with their moral views (for example, classes that do not explicitly teach an ethic of sexual abstinence). The apparent strength of their case lies in the fact that what is best as a general policy for discouraging early teenage pregnancies may not be needed for every single child. Parents are given wide discretion to do what is best for their children's interests, secular as well as sacred, and the state should not micromanage this process. Carter, for example, wishes to teach his children an ethic of abstinence, and surely parents are entitled to do so – though teenagers are also entitled to reject their parents' teaching.

Carter is entitled to his view that teenagers should be discouraged from sex. Should he, however, possess a right to insist that this ethic be taught in schools, or to withdraw his children from sex education classes in which it is not taught? He suggests that there is something offensive about the alternatives: "There are only two plausible responses to my concern, and both are deeply offensive. First, I could be told, 'We know how to reach your kids and you don't'; second, the message might be, 'Because we need to do it this way to reach other kids, yours will just need to suffer.' "[46]

But how, exactly, will Carter's children *suffer* if he is unable to withdraw them from sex education classes? *Ex hypothesi*, they will not get the teaching about an ethic of abstinence if they go to the classes, but that omission hardly qualifies as *suffering*. It sounds more as if *Carter* will suffer, thinking that his children may learn information and attitudes that he disapproves of, perhaps using the information to think for themselves and reject what he teaches them at home. That may be unfortunate for him, but it is far from clear that the state should place more weight on this interest than on society's interest in preventing the spread of AIDS and reducing pregnancies among girls of high-school age.

Why should the state and its officers not agree with Brian Barry that this social interest is too vital for parents to be allowed to withdraw children from sex education classes, or for schools or local authorities to opt out?[47] Even if sex education classes take a relatively non-moralistic approach, it remains open to parents such as Carter to supplement it by teaching their children an ethic of abstinence in their own time. What the state cannot guarantee, of course – and should never wish to – is that Carter's children will be prevented from thinking for themselves.

More generally, exemptions from a basic school curriculum should not be given too lightly, too broadly, or as a matter of right. It bears repeating that the rights of custody and control accorded to parents should be exercised for the benefit of their children. Parents have an important say in what their children come to know or believe, but not the only say and not always the final say.

# ✗ Conclusion ✗

*This is how he constructs his argument*

As I discussed in Chapter 1, referencing the work of Charles Taylor, religion typically postulates and asserts an order of things beyond this world – together with a higher good beyond ordinary human flourishing. It involves personal transformations, to ensure that the higher good is achieved. Religion, then, is about the transcendent: an order beyond the immanent order; a good beyond our worldly interests; and a dimension to human life extending beyond what we see as life and death. Religious claims may be true or false, and in theory some are testable. In practice, however, disputes about religion defy resolution by reason. Wherever it can, the secular state should step back from all this, neither promoting nor discouraging religion – or any particular form of it. The secular state should not concern itself with religious truths or hopes, but merely with the things of this world.

The state's historical turn to secular interests and reasons removes its main motive for religious persecutions, but it does not remove all sources of tension between it and religious groups. As the state's secular role expands – as it did, dramatically, in the last century and a half – it leads to new areas of potential conflict with religious aspirations. Religion and the state propose canons of conduct aimed at achieving their different purposes, and needless to say these will not always be compatible. Conduct that contributes to ordinary human flourishing may clash with what is said to promote salvation or rightness with God. How should this be resolved?

Where the conduct of adults is at issue, the state should avoid enacting laws based on moralism or paternalism. This leaves its citizens wide scope to pursue their earthly happiness, but also to seek transcendent goods such as salvation. Seen from a worldly viewpoint, devout adults may sometimes appear to martyr themselves, but that is their decision to make, one way or the other. This, however, is not a satisfactory approach where children are involved. Children cannot be assumed to know or accept the full implications of their decisions, and adults don't have the same latitude in harming children's worldly interests as they do in harming themselves. Not surprisingly, then, the interests of children provide a constant source of tension between governments with a worldly focus and various religions that aim at higher goods.

The dilemma has no clear-cut solution. It arises from the different functions of church and state, together with the nature of childhood. We can consider the issues clearly, take the range of concerns into account, sometimes make accommodations, and manage the dilemma as kindly and intelligently as possible. But it won't go away entirely unless and until the churches and the state promote the same interests – meaning a complete overlap of goals. In the nature of things, that will not happen and should not be expected: it would require a theocratic state or subservient churches. Neither of those is something to wish for.

# Notes

1   Rex Ahdar and Ian Leigh, *Religious Freedom in the Liberal State*, Oxford University Press, Oxford 2005, p. 279.

2   Brian Barry, *Culture and Equality: An Egalitarian Critique of Multiculturalism*, Polity Press, Cambridge 2001, pp. 202–203.

3   John Locke, *A Letter concerning Toleration*, 1st pub. 1689, Hackett, Indianapolis 1983, p. 52.

4   Barry, *Culture and Equality*, p. 124.

5   Kent Greenawalt, *Religion and the Constitution*, vol. 1: *Fairness and Free Exercise*, Princeton University Press, Princeton 2006, p. 94.

6   [1986] 1 AC 112, 170 (per Lord Fraser).

7   Ahdar and Leigh, *Religious Freedom in the Liberal State*, p. 193.

8   A. C. Grayling, *To Set Prometheus Free: Essays on Religion, Reason and Humanity*, Oberon, London 2009, pp. 19–20.

9   Richard Dawkins, *The God Delusion*, Transworld, London 2006, pp. 319–320.

10  Dawkins is frequently said to regard the teaching of religious ideas to children as child abuse. His actual views are, however, considerably more nuanced – the details need not concern us here, but see *The God Delusion*, pp. 311–344.

11  Ahdar and Leigh, *Religious Freedom in the Liberal State*, pp. 218–219.

12  321 US 158, 170 (1944).

13   Greenawalt, *Religion and the Constitution*, vol. 1, p. 402.
14   Ahdar and Leigh, *Religious Freedom in the Liberal State*, p. 271.
15   Ahdar and Leigh, *Religious Freedom in the Liberal State*, pp. 272–274.
16   Though, once again, the parents' good intentions might be a mitigating factor in sentencing if a child actually suffers from a preventable disease and the parents are subsequently convicted of a criminal offense.
17   See, for example, the cases cited in Ahdar and Leigh, *Religious Freedom in the Liberal State*, pp. 276–278.
18   Ahdar and Leigh appear to endorse this view, or at least sympathize with it: see *Religious Freedom in the Liberal State*, p. 278. Compare Greenawalt, *Religion and the Constitution*, vol. 1, pp. 404–408. However, Greenawalt reluctantly countenances a teenager's rejection of life-saving treatment if her parents agree.
19   Barry, *Culture and Equality*, pp. 210–211.
20   Greenawalt, *Religion and the Constitution*, vol. 1, pp. 90–91.
21   Ahdar and Leigh, *Religious Freedom in the Liberal State*, p. 231.
22   Ahdar and Leigh, *Religious Freedom in the Liberal State*, p. 253.
23   393 US 97 (1968).
24   482 US 578 (1987).
25   185 F 3d 337 (5th Cir. 1999). Subsequently, the US Supreme Court refused to hear an appeal: 530 US 1251 (2000) (certiorari denied).
26   Christopher L. Eisgruber and Lawrence G. Sager, *Religious Freedom and the Constitution*, Harvard University Press, Cambridge, MA 2007, pp. 194–196.
27   Ahdar and Leigh, *Religious Freedom in the Liberal State*, pp. 250–251.
28   Ahdar and Leigh, *Religious Freedom in the Liberal State*, p. 252.
29   Francisco J. Ayala, *Darwin's Gift to Science and Religion*, Joseph Henry Press, Washington, DC 2007, pp. x–xi, 2–5, 21–23, 154–160.
30   Philip Kitcher, *Living with Darwin: Evolution, Design, and the Future of Faith*, Oxford University Press, New York 2007, pp. 125–126.
31   Jerry A. Coyne, *Why Evolution is True*, Viking, New York 2009, p. 15.
32   By contrast, Kent Greenawalt agrees with the position argued in this chapter, that if an alternative theory such as Intelligent Design "is pushed *because of* its religious content" this is an unconstitutional purpose. See *Religion and the Constitution*, vol. 2: *Establishment and Fairness*, Princeton University Press, Princeton 2008, p. 152.
33   Eisgruber and Sager, *Religious Freedom and the Constitution*, pp. 190–194.
34   400 F Supp 2d 707 (2005).
35   *Wisconsin v. Yoder* (1972) 406 US 205.
36   Greenawalt, *Religion and the Constitution*, vol. 1, p. 98.
37   Or 6–1, since Justice Douglas dissented in part.
38   521 US 507 (1997).
39   Marci A. Hamilton, *God vs. the Gavel: Religion and the Rule of Law*, Cambridge University Press, Cambridge 2007, p. 216.
40   Barry emphasizes that the basic level of education that the Amish wished to keep their children to in *Yoder* would not equip them well for life outside Amish communities, thus hindering a choice to leave as adults (*Culture and Equality*, pp. 242–244).

41   Stephen L. Carter, *The Culture of Disbelief: How American Law and Politics Trivialize Religious Devotion*, Anchor, New York 1994, pp. 172–173.
42   J. S. Mill, *On Liberty*, 1st pub. 1859, Penguin, London 1974, p. 176.
43   Collected in Joel Feinberg, *Freedom and Fulfillment: Philosophical Essays*, Princeton University Press, Princeton 1992, pp. 76–97.
44   406 US 205, 233–234 (1972).
45   Kent Greenawalt, *Religion and the Constitution*, vol. 2, pp. 155–156.
46   Carter, *The Culture of Disbelief*, p. 202.
47   Barry, *Culture and Equality*, p. 225.

CHAPTER NINE

RELIGIOUS FREEDOM AND FREEDOM OF SPEECH

# Introduction

As I suggested in Chapter 1, the "liberal" part of "liberal democracy" implies a degree of restraint by the apparatus of the state, a reluctance to impose a template, or a narrow set of templates, for the good life. The idea is that the political framework will allow people with many differing views to live in harmony, or at least with mutual forbearance. Liberal democracies are especially willing to tolerate a wide range of speech and expression (for convenience, I'll henceforth abbreviate this idea as simply "freedom of speech" or "free speech").

All this is, for better or worse, inherently messy. Within a liberal political framework, no single worldview, however precise or vague, is imposed by state coercion, but many views are allowed to compete. Some may be mutually hostile, but the state will not normally silence these unless they lead to violence or impossibly hostile conditions for citizens to live their lives. Citizens may influence the social environment through their speech and expression, but they forgo the power to suppress the speech and expression of others – even others who reject a social consensus. In most situations, this framework is more productive than groups trying to gag one another by making threats of punishment.

However, no jurisdiction allows complete freedom of speech, totally without protections from such things as threats, defamation, and fraudulent representations. One critical consideration here is that such protections should be based on the state's role in protecting worldly interests, not on an imperative to promote otherworldly systems or their canons of conduct.

---

*Freedom of Religion and the Secular State*, First Edition. Russell Blackford.
© 2012 John Wiley & Sons, Inc. Published 2012 by John Wiley & Sons, Inc.

Approaching this from one end, protection of worldly interests may require some restrictions on fraudulent or reckless commercial speech. There is also a need for carefully circumscribed protection of individual reputations from lies that could ruin careers or lead to individuals' social ostracism. This does not necessarily entail support for defamation law in its current form: in at least some jurisdictions, it may be far more protective than could be justified by any plausible secular rationale. Still, *some* kind of defamation law appears essential, even if it ought to be pared down.

Starting from the other end, some forms of speech are of such value to the speaker that the state has good reason to consider them almost entirely out of bounds for regulation. This might include much in the way of artistic speech and much everyday personal expression. Most relevant to current purposes, it includes speech aimed at producing religious conversions (which may, in the mind of the speaker, make a crucial difference to a listener's eternal fate).

In this chapter, I'll argue for an ideal of minimal interference by the state with its citizens' speech. That ideal is constantly challenged, however, and it requires defense. Importantly for this book, there are various ways in which religious organizations become involved in the dispute. For example, some wish to restrict speech that they regard as obscene, indecent, or blasphemous. Some oppose the ability of others to seek converts, especially where smaller groups attempt to convert members of a religious majority. Finally, secular reasons are often provided for restricting hate speech of various kinds. If this is done, how expansive a concept of hate speech should we use? One question that defies a satisfactory answer is when extreme hostility to religious doctrines or organizations becomes, in effect, hatred for the adherents themselves.

I do not pretend to be comprehensive in what follows. Much could, for example, be written about laws restricting the availability of pornography, where religious adherents sometimes line up in support alongside secular communitarians and advocates of certain feminist positions – while other feminists help provide the opposition. While I'll have something to say about broader free speech issues, my main focus will be on anti-religious speech, religion-based hate speech, and religious vilification. Here, free speech advocates have frequently been placed on the defensive. Contemporary forms of religious and cultural intolerance have led many academics, commentators, and politicians to call for strict limits on what we can say, all in an effort to promote harmony and reduce sectarian tensions. Sometimes this is even defended in the name of religious freedom.

I'll argue against the tendency to restrict freedom of speech, and in support of a broadly Millian position. A good starting point is to identify the deeper considerations that underlie freedom of speech. Why is it so important?

## The Rationale for Freedom of Speech

To some extent, freedom of speech can be defended as merely a special case of the harm principle. Most forms of speech are not directly harmful: any harms will usually be indirect, as when people are persuaded to endanger themselves or others. Now, directness should not be made a fetish, and the real issue may not be whether a harm is, strictly speaking, "direct" so much as whether some kinds of speech create an urgent risk of harm or something like a clear and present danger. Even Mill thought it permissible to punish words that were likely to incite immediate violence, such as a demagogue's claim, made to an angry mob outside a corn dealer's house, that corn dealers are starvers of the poor.[1] Still, most speech-related harms can be addressed by means that fall short of absolute prohibition of the speech itself.

Similarly, many forms of speech may cause offense, but seldom of such intensity as to shade into harm. Where speech has a high emotional impact for only some people, that may not be sufficient cause to prohibit it – especially if the immediate impact is relatively brief, if the speech has value to others, or if it can be avoided by those who don't wish to be exposed to it.[2] For most of us, most of the time, high-impact offense is difficult to achieve with mere words and requires the use of images or smells, though some vividly realistic or "gritty" prose can doubtless produce nausea or shock, at least in some readers. In any event, the most high-impact material can usually be controlled without absolute prohibition. It might be reasonable to prohibit the display of viscerally shocking images in public buses, for example, where there is a captive audience, while permitting display of the same material in an art gallery, accompanied by appropriate warnings.

It seems that relatively little government interference in freedom of speech could be justified by the harm principle – even if extended cautiously to deal with a limited range of technically indirect harms and with some kinds of high-impact offense. In many cases, that might be a decisive consideration, but it is not the only one. Various positive justifications can be provided for governmental toleration of *speech* in particular. Paul Cliteur has recently summarized some of the considerations in a twofold justification for freedom of speech. First, following Mill, he offers the idea that free development of the human personality would be frustrated if others could control what we think or say. There would be little room to express our ideas if expressions of them could be suppressed when others take offense. Secondly, free speech has fruitful consequences for the development of science and culture (including religion). Indeed, new ideas, including the foundational doctrines of Christianity and Islam, were once offensive, hurtful, and even blasphemous, and required opposition to the beliefs of the existing order.[3]

In her judgment in *R v. Keegstra*, a 1990 Canadian Supreme Court case on hate propaganda, Justice McLachlan provided an accessible and concise synopsis of the main considerations: (1) free speech promotes "the free flow of ideas essential to political democracy and democratic institutions" and limits the ability of the state to subvert other rights and freedoms; (2) it promotes a marketplace of ideas, which includes, but is not limited to, the search for truth; (3) it is intrinsically valuable as part of the self-actualization of speakers and listeners; and (4) it is justified by the dangers for good government of allowing its suppression.[4] Such justifications may each be developed in different ways, and they are not mutually exclusive.

Though other justifications are sometimes adduced, such as the need to obtain information about products and services, in order to make enlightened choices in a consumer society, those stated by Cliteur and by Justice McLachlan cover the most persuasive considerations. Some relate to free speech's political role in a liberal democracy (I shall call this "the political justification"). Others involve the particular importance of language, symbolism and representation for our lives, self-actualization, and autonomy. These can be developed further by referring to the importance for individuals of communicating deeply held religious and similar beliefs, and to the value of creativity as expressed in literature, art, and many other ways, including personal presentation or "style" (this can be called "the self-actualization justification"). Still other considerations relate to the need for free speech in the pursuit of rational inquiry. If we value this, we should also advocate the liberty to articulate potentially unpalatable or unpopular ideas (this may be termed "the rationalist justification").

*On Liberty*, Mill's classic defense of political freedoms, is based essentially on self-actualization arguments, but the bulk of its second chapter, entitled "Of the Liberty of Thought and Discussion," is devoted to the rationalist justification of free speech. Mill favored the freedom to develop and discuss ideas in the search for truth or understanding, a defense of the marketplace of ideas.[5] This is very powerful as far as it goes, but inevitably somewhat elitist, for relatively little speech and expression in real-world societies appeals primarily to the intellect.

Still, the rationalist justification can be extended beyond the speech of academics, scientists, and other intellectuals. To some extent, it merges with the self-actualization justification, insofar as it involves our *individual* need to pursue truth and understanding in our own ways, necessarily reliant on resources available through language. It also encourages us to protect serious literature and art, especially narrative forms such as prose fiction, theater, and cinema, one function of which is to open minds by appeals to the imagination. The rationalist justification also merges with the democratic justification, insofar as debate about political ideas – with attempts to find the best kinds of political structures, principles, and policies – forms a large component of the general pursuit of truth in modern societies. Moreover, it supports the importance not just of speech but of all methods of inquiry into the nature of the world, such as those used by science.

In arguing against unrestricted free speech, Alan Haworth suggests that Mill pictured society not as a marketplace of ideas, but as something like a large-scale academic seminar.[6] A seminar, of course, is an effective forum for refining and testing ideas only because its participants can rely upon tacit standards of conduct and interaction, including some degree of mutual respect. Note, however, that no entire society can operate like a seminar. If too much weight is given to Haworth's point, free speech will be a far more narrow thing than is usually understood by the concept. It normally includes freedom for robust, sometimes even offensive, kinds of interaction that would be strongly inhibited, if not actually forbidden, in the confined space of an academic seminar.

It is usually accepted in liberal societies that there is a public interest in permitting debate that is not so restrictive of the parties involved. This allows them to express themselves passionately, emotively, and loyally on subjects that arouse passion, emotions, and competing loyalties – all without fear of retaliation by state agencies, or of narrow constraints being imposed to preserve decorum. Further, it allows the participation of individuals, perhaps the majority, who may not have been socialized or trained to express themselves with the detachment and urbanity that might be expected in a seminar for, say, middle-aged philosophy professors. If freedom of speech is confined too closely to decorous speech, this is likely to disadvantage young people, working-class people, and many other groups.

At this stage, the analysis suggests a number of conclusions. First, the harm principle provides adequate reason in most cases for the state to avoid restrictions on freedom of speech. Second, there are powerful overlapping arguments, going beyond the harm principle, for government deference to citizens' freedom of speech, and thus for enshrining free speech as an important political principle in any liberal democracy. Third, however, free speech is not a simple and absolute concept but a liberty that is justified by even deeper values. Fourth, the values implicit in the democratic, self-actualization, and rationalist justifications for free speech will not apply equally strongly to all speech in all circumstances. For example, these "free speech values" may not be at stake to their fullest extent when there are proposals to regulate purely commercial advertising or entirely cynical works of pornography. Nonetheless, it may still be worth permitting these to go uncensored unless direct, secular harms can be identified.

If freedom of speech is to operate as a political principle that imposes practical restraints on the coercive power of the state, it needs to be formulated in a relatively simple and sweeping way. It cannot track the precise relevance of underlying free speech values in every circumstance where speech might be suppressed. It follows that a constitutional restriction on state interference with free speech might give practical protection to some speech that has little to do with democratic, self-actualization, and rationalist values. This creates a buffer zone around the more central areas where free speech values apply. In particular circumstances, other values might be more important than free speech, especially in situations where the underlying free speech values have little bearing. Nonetheless, exceptions to the principle of freedom of speech must be defined carefully and applied sparingly. Otherwise, they will soon eat up the rule.

There is a strong case to define the powers of governments so that they are prevented from restricting any serious artistic, literary, scientific, or philosophical speech (on rationalist and self-actualization grounds) and almost any spontaneous speech of natural persons (on self-actualization grounds). Exceptions can be justified where a restriction prevents significant harms that could not be averted by less liberal means. We should, however, use extreme caution before prohibiting speech that is merely offensive: what offends one person may be of value to another.

Even if we resist the full implications of this argument, the Lockean model of the state lends much of it direct support. It seems clear enough that a secular state should not suppress speech merely in an attempt to enforce religious canons of conduct. It should not, for example, suppress speech – including images of various kinds – that are condemned by an Augustinian morality in which sex and the body are considered shameful. If some kinds of pornography are to be prohibited or severely restricted, a secular case will need to be made out, relating perhaps to effects on the physical safety of women. Since any such effects would be highly indirect – perhaps by way of a coarsening of sensibility of pornography users, making them more willing to engage in sexual assaults – careful and convincing research would need to be done to support the case.

Once the Lockean model is accepted, the secular value of free speech soon becomes apparent. This is an example of secularism tending toward liberal political principles. In modern liberal democracies, freedom of speech is a widely accepted principle, and exceptions will not be justified easily in any particular instance. Nonetheless, might requirements such as those of social harmony require some limits on the freedom?

## The Limits of Freedom of Speech

The secular state exists to protect and promote the things of this world – it should not enforce religious canons of conduct, except where this can be justified independently on worldly grounds, and a fortiori it should not protect any religious viewpoint from competition or criticism. As I have argued, the secular state has good reasons to develop into a *liberal* state, permitting a wide range of individuality and social pluralism, and particularly extensive freedom of speech. However, the latter must have some limits. I have already mentioned Mill's example of a demagogue arousing an angry mob against a corn dealer, an example where the speech is intimately part of a possible course of events involving violence.

Cliteur offers the Ayatollah Khomeini's notorious fatwa of 1989 against the novelist Salman Rushdie as a modern example of the proper limit to free speech. As Cliteur points out, the problem here is not that Khomeini's speech showed a lack of respect for Rushdie, or that it failed to stimulate dialogue, or even that it was socially divisive. Rather, it incited murder. As events demonstrated, such speech creates a clear and present danger to its victim's life. As I write these words, Rushdie has not been killed, but his Japanese translator, Hitoshi Igarashi, was stabbed to death in 1991 and his Italian translator, Ettore Capriolo, was seriously wounded in the same year.[7] Although Khomeini was not in Rushdie's geographical proximity when he announced the fatwa, which distinguishes the situation from Mill's corn dealer example, the fates of Igarashi and Capriolo demonstrate the power of this kind of incitement, by figures who are accorded religious authority.

Such horrific events as the Rwandan Genocide of 1994, in which approximately 800,000 Tutsis were massacred over a period of about three months, demonstrate the power of the modern media to deliver messages of hatred. In particular, much of the incitement to violence came from messages on Radio Rwanda and Radio Télévision Libre des Mille Collines. Such examples show the power of hate propaganda calling for violence against identifiable groups, which could be ethnic, cultural, racial, or religious. Dehumanizing propaganda campaigns can support acts of discrimination, violence, and even genocide. The state doubtless has an interest in deterring this kind of hate propaganda, as well as incitements against particular individuals (such as Rushdie) by those (such as Khomeini) who are likely to be heeded by fanatics.

Amos M. Guioroa argues that the state should be especially concerned about speech that contains explicit or implicit calls to violent action in the service of religious extremism. He defines this to cover any form of religion where "the actor believes that his or her tenets and principles are infallible and that *any* action, even violence, taken on behalf of those beliefs is justified."[8] Guioroa is concerned that many religious extremists possess real power to provoke their followers to violent actions against those whom they see as enemies. Though he is generally concerned to protect free speech, he concludes that extremist religious speech should not receive constitutional protection.[9]

Cliteur and Guioroa make powerful points. In modern circumstances, fanatics are frequently addressed through the mass media by other fanatics whom they accord moral authority. With many forms of communication that can reach fanatics of one kind or another everywhere in the world, it would be too much to require that the state restrain incitements to violence only where the speaker is in close physical proximity to the victim. Nonetheless, the state should not move too far from the *spirit* of Mill's corn dealer example. That is, the purpose is to protect citizens from harm, not from offense caused by the speech itself. Nor is the purpose to advantage any particular religion, or any non-religious or anti-religious viewpoint, in competition to obtain and retain adherents. As a first approximation, the limits should be drawn to protect ordinary secular interests, such as those in life, limb, and property, not to protect feelings or truth, and not even to impose a regime of forced civility.

We should not accept the idea that the state may legitimately ban any speech at all that might tend, via an indirect process, to cause hostility or acts of violence. For example, some passages in the New Testament and some long-established Christian doctrines doubtless contributed, historically, to anti-Semitism, and indirectly to persecutions, pogroms, and the Holocaust.[10] Recognition of this is not, however, sufficient reason for censorship of the New Testament or for banning such Christian doctrines as the supersession of God's covenant with Israel. Where the teaching of certain doctrines encourages hostility only by an indirect and uncertain process, there are many other ways for the state authorities to combat it, whether through education, inclusive gestures toward religious communities, or campaigns for mutual toleration and respect.

This pretty much rules out the imposition of laws relating to proselytism, blasphemy, and criticism of religion. Should they be ruled out in total? I turn first to the issue of proselytism.

## Proselytism

Some religious organizations resent attempts by others to convert their adherents to another faith, leading to laws that prohibit or restrict proselytism. One example can be found in *Kokkinakis v. Greece*,[11] the first case relating to freedom of religion to be determined by the European Court of Human Rights. This court, based in Strasbourg, enforces the European Convention on Human Rights, to which all the nations of the Council of Europe are party. Many of the cases brought before the court over the past two decades have involved alleged violations of the freedoms of religion and speech contained in the convention. Some cases have involved the interaction of the two freedoms.

Article 9 of the convention provides for "freedom of thought, conscience and religion," including a right to change religion:

1. Everyone has the right to freedom of thought, conscience and religion; this right includes freedom to change his religion or belief and freedom, either alone or in community with others and in public or private, to manifest his religion or belief, in worship, teaching, practice and observance.
2. Freedom to manifest one's religion or beliefs shall be subject only to such limitations as are prescribed by law and are necessary in a democratic society in the interests of public safety, for the protection of public order, health or morals, or for the protection of the rights and freedoms of others.

This does not refer specifically to a right to convert others, though it does refer to a right to manifest one's religion or beliefs via, among other things, teaching.

Article 10 of the convention provides broad protection for free speech, though this is somewhat weakened by the lengthy list of grounds for over-riding it provided in 10.2:

1. Everyone has the right to freedom of expression. This right shall include freedom to hold opinions and to receive and impart information and ideas without interference by public authority and regardless of frontiers . . .
2. The exercise of these freedoms, since it carries with it duties and respon-sibilities, may be subject to such formalities, conditions, restrictions or penalties as are prescribed by law and are necessary in a democratic society, in the interests of national security, territorial integrity or public safety, for the prevention of disorder or crime, for the protection of health or morals, for the protection of the reputation or rights of others, for preventing the disclosure of information received in confidence, or for maintaining the authority and impartiality of the judiciary.

*Kokkinakis* should be read against the background that Greece has long adopted measures to hinder the activities of religious faiths outside the Orthodox Church, particularly the Jehovah's Witnesses, who actively seek to recruit from other religions, and Islam. The special relationship between church and state in Greece may be attributed, in part, to the Orthodox Church's role in preserving a Greek national identity during the country's centuries-long Ottoman occupation. The establishment of the Greek Orthodox Church is provided for in the Greek Constitution, where it is referred to as the "prevailing" religion, and is defended strongly by both church and state. Hindrances to non-Orthodox faiths have softened to some extent only in very recent times, after international criticism of the Greek administrative and ecclesiastical authorities, including from the European Court of Human Rights.[12]

In *Kokkinakis*, the applicant was a retired businessman who had become a Jehovah's Witness in 1936. Thereafter, he was arrested many times under Greece's anti-proselytism legislation. In March 1986, he and his wife were arrested once again after calling on Mrs. Kyriakaki, the wife of the cantor of the local Orthodox church, and engaging her in a conversation to try to convert her to their faith. In doing so, they also raised broader political issues relating to the Jehovah's Witnesses, such as pacifism. Subsequently, Mr. and Mrs. Kokkinakis were convicted of the crime of proselytism, though this was later quashed in the case of Mrs. Kokkinakis. In finding Mr. Kokkinakis guilty, the Crete Court of Appeal described his crime as one of attempting to undermine Mrs. Kyriakaki's religious beliefs "by taking advantage of her inexperience, her low intellect and her naïvety."[13] This fell under a provision that prohibited proselytism and defined it as follows:

> By "proselytism" is meant, in particular, any direct or indirect attempt to intrude on the religious beliefs of a person of a different religious persuasion, with the aim of undermining those beliefs, either by any kind of inducement or promise of an inducement or moral support or material assistance, or by fraudulent means or by taking advantage of his inexperience, trust, need, low intellect or naïvety.

When the case eventually found its way to the European Court of Human Rights, the majority of the judges were unwilling to hold that the Greek provision was, in itself, inconsistent with the convention. Following the existing Greek jurisprudence, however, they held that it applied only to "improper" proselytizing.[14] On the facts of the particular case, it was held that the Greek courts had failed to specify sufficiently the improper means by which Mr. Kokkinakis had attempted to convince his neighbor, and that none of the factual findings warranted a finding of improper means. Accordingly, the conviction was not justified by a pressing social need, was not proportionate to the legitimate legislative aim, and was not necessary to protect the rights and freedoms of others.[15]

The outcome of *Kokkinakis* is, I submit, obviously correct, and it reflects the stance toward proselytism that should be taken in a liberal democracy. To the extent that the presence of Mr. and Mrs. Kokkinakis was unwelcome, their neighbors could simply have asked them to leave their house; instead they called the police, invoking Greece's illiberal anti-proselytism law. Up to that point, the court's determination of the case should be welcome. Not so welcome is its broad acceptance of the concept of "improper" proselytizing by citizens, almost as if this itself could amount to a breach of Article 9:

> It may . . . take the form of activities offering material or social advantages with a view to gaining new members for a Church or exerting improper pressure on people in distress or in need; it may even entail the use of violence or

brainwashing; more generally, it is not compatible with respect for the freedom of thought, conscience and religion of others.[16]

On the other hand, Ahdar and Leigh appear to overreach in their discussion of the case. Their concern is that the concept of improper proselytism necessarily suggests that "the state can take sides in a religious controversy to criminalize the latter."[17] This is a genuine concern, and is appropriately raised by authors from an evangelical Christian background, who require freedom to preach the gospel as they understand it. Nonetheless, there can be circumstances where the state has good secular reasons to prohibit certain forms of proselytism. *Larissis v. Greece*[18] illustrates this.

In this case, the European Court of Human Rights upheld convictions of Jehovah's Witness airmen for proselytism of military subordinates, though it found a breach of Article 9 relating to convictions for proselytizing civilians. Although the Greek law was illiberal and cast in overly broad and imprecise terms, the actual outcome appears defensible. Where military superiors attempt to convert their subordinates to a religious viewpoint, this gives the impression that state power is being used to promote religion. Even if the situation had not involved any abuse of power within the military arm of the state, a secular government could have legitimate reasons to restrict boss–subordinate proselytism. If the action had taken place within a private business corporation, it would still have involved a questionable of exercise of private power. Consistent with the argument of Chapter 7, the state might wish to control this in an effort to prevent religious discrimination within the ordinary labor market. It is worth noting that *Larissis v. Greece* also reached the correct conclusion that there was no "improper" proselytization when the airmen concerned spoke to civilians over whom they had no authority.

It now appears likely that the European Court of Human Rights will uphold restrictions on proselytizing or evangelizing only where some legitimate secular reason can be found, as with restrictions on outright brainwashing techniques or on pressuring subordinates in the workplace. This is commendable. Nonetheless, the court has shown an unnecessary readiness to embrace the concept of "improper" proselytizing, and even the idea that mere attempts to persuade individuals to change their beliefs are somehow an assault on their political rights. I'll return to this in the next section, where I discuss the issue of blasphemy.

At this stage, I emphasize that freedom of religion and freedom of speech point in the direction of maximum liberty for individuals to express their religious beliefs and attempt to persuade others to adopt them, though not to impose them through political coercion.[19] Religious dogmatists should even be free to advocate that laws be enacted to suppress rival religions. There are, of course, difficult issues about how far we should tolerate the intolerant. However, the general assumption in the area of free speech is that the advocacy of intolerant laws should itself be given a broad measure of tolerance. That doesn't mean, however, that I should receive any *credence* if I ask for rival religions to be suppressed by state power.

By analogy, I submit that we should give no credence to claims that the state should enforce a religious morality; but that is far from saying that making such claims should be *unlawful*. Writing in the American context, Nussbaum puts the point well:

> If people seek to torture children, or to enslave minorities, citing their religion as their reason, their claims must be resisted even though they may be sincere. If they simply *talk* in favor of slavery or torture, their freedom to speak must be protected, up to the point at which speech becomes a threat. They will not, however, be able to present their ideas in the political sphere on an equal basis with other ideas, since the Constitution (in the case of slavery) and the criminal law (in the case of torture) forbid the practices they recommend. So: *people* are all respected as equals, but actions that threaten the rights of others may still be reasonably opposed, and opinions that teach the political inequality of others, while they will not be suppressed, will still be at a disadvantage in the community, since their advocates would have to amend the Constitution to realize their program.[20]

It should be added that, even if it is not necessary to amend a nation's constitution to realize an intolerant program, the program's advocates will (rightly) be at a disadvantage because they will need to overthrow political principles that are widely accepted within liberal democracies. Within such a society, they cannot expect equal consideration of their intolerant views in the public sphere. They can, however, expect to be permitted to express their views.

More generally, nothing should stop an individual or organization with one religious viewpoint from attempting to convert other people from theirs, even though the long-run tendency of such activity might be the (peaceful) destruction of some religions. All that individuals and organizations need to do in respect of tolerating rival religions is recognize that they should not be suppressed by an exercise of state power.

## Blasphemy

In the British legal tradition, the offense of blasphemy was originally more about protecting public order than protecting the dignity of God. In the seventeenth-century legal cases, challenges to Christianity were seen as politically subversive.[21] More recently, however, this has seemed implausible, and attention has turned more to the offensive character of blasphemous speech. Ahdar and Leigh note that the type of expression that has provoked most offense in recent decades has involved artistic appropriation of venerated religious symbols or persons. But, they add, punishment for blasphemy cannot literally protect Christ or his reputation: "When people claim to be doing so they are best understood as expressing the strong nature of the offence which *they* have suffered."[22]

Nonetheless, the European Court of Human Rights has sometimes upheld blasphemy laws, notably in two cases from the mid-1990s, in which government action was challenged on free speech grounds under Article 10 of the European Convention on Human Rights. *Otto-Preminger-Institut v. Austria*[23] and *Wingrove v. United Kingdom*[24] both involved the banning of blasphemous or disparaging films involving Jesus and other iconic Christian figures.

In *Otto-Preminger-Institut*, the Innsbruck diocese of the Roman Catholic Church had successfully requested the local public prosecutor to commence criminal proceedings against the manager of the Otto-Preminger-Institut on a charge of "disparaging religious doctrines," contrary to section 188 of Austria's penal code. The film concerned, *Das Liebeskonzil* ("Council in Heaven"), was based on a satirical play by Oskar Panizza, originally published in 1894. In 1895 Panizza was found guilty of "crimes against religion" and sentenced to a term of imprisonment. The film, directed by Werner Schroeter and released in 1981, begins and ends with scenes depicting Panizza's trial. In between, it shows a performance of the play by the Teatro Belli in Rome. This shows God the Father as a senile old man and Jesus Christ as mentally defective. It contains numerous controversial scenes involving the interactions and antics of these figures, along with the Devil and the Virgin Mary.

The European Court of Human Rights held that there had been no breach of Article 10. On its analysis, religious adherents must tolerate and accept the denial by others of their religious beliefs and the propagation of doctrines hostile to their faith – but only within limits:

> The manner in which religious beliefs and doctrines are opposed or denied is a matter which may engage the responsibility of the State, notably its responsibility to ensure the peaceful enjoyment of the right guaranteed under Article 9 . . . to the holders of those beliefs and doctrines. Indeed, in extreme cases the effect of particular methods of opposing or denying religious beliefs can be such as to inhibit those who hold such beliefs from exercising their freedom to hold and express them.[25]

Furthermore, the court condemned what it called "provocative portrayals of objects of religious veneration"; these, the judgment suggests, can be seen as violating the respect for believers' religious feelings as guaranteed in Article 9. It adds: "such portrayals can be regarded as malicious violation of the spirit of tolerance, which must also be a feature of democratic society."[26] The court found that the Austrian courts had held the film to be an abusive attack on Roman Catholicism, and had showed due regard for freedom of artistic expression. In the end, so it was said, the Austrian authorities were within their rights to ensure religious peace in a predominately Catholic region and to prevent some people feeling "the object of attacks on their religious beliefs in an unwarranted and offensive manner."[27]

This approach is, I submit, dangerous and misguided, but it has echoed through the court's later jurisprudence. In *Wingrove*, the eponymous Mr. Wingrove was the writer and director of an 18-minute video entitled *Visions of Ecstasy*, based loosely on the life and writings of St. Teresa of Avila. It depicted a highly erotic encounter involving the saint, her externalized psyche, and Jesus on the cross. Wingrove insisted that the video was a serious treatment of St. Teresa's ecstatic raptures, but the British Board of Film Classification refused to issue a classification certificate for the work – essentially on the ground that it was criminally blasphemous. This effectively banned it in the UK.

Following its own lead in *Otto-Preminger-Institut*, the European Court of Human Rights held that the law of blasphemy was intended to protect against the treatment of a religious subject in such a manner that would outrage individuals with "an understanding of, sympathy towards and support for the Christian story and ethic." It added that this aim corresponded to "the rights of others" within Article 10.2 and was "fully consonant with the aim of the protections afforded by Article 9 . . . to religious freedom."[28]

More recently, in *İ.A. v. Turkey*,[29] a majority of the court sustained a conviction against the managing director of a publishing house that had published *Yasak Tümceler* ("The Forbidden Phrases"), a philosophical novel by Abdullah Rıza Ergüven. The applicant, referred to as Mr. İ.A., had been prosecuted successfully under section 175 of Turkey's criminal code, which provided that, "It shall be an offence . . . to blaspheme against God, one of the religions, one of the prophets, one of the sects or one of the holy books . . . or to vilify or insult another on account of his religious beliefs or fulfilment of religious duties." Ergüven's novel was condemned in the Turkish courts for passages that promulgated a materialist philosophy, expressed scorn for religion, and contained trenchant criticisms of Islam and the Prophet Muhammad. Particular attention was given to a passage with the following wording:

> Look at the triangle of fear, inequality and inconsistency in the Koran; it reminds me of an earthworm. God says that all the words are those of his messenger. Some of these words, moreover, were inspired in a surge of exulta-

tion, in Aisha's arms. . . . God's messenger broke his fast through sexual intercourse, after dinner and before prayer. Muhammad did not forbid sexual relations with a dead person or a live animal.

Of course, lifting particular passages from a novel, out of context, may entirely alter their meaning and literary effect. But in any event, opposition to ideas, including religious ideas, often involves an element of robust denunciation, satire, or mockery – think of the treatment routinely meted out to political opponents within liberal democracies. It is not to the point to note that Mr. İ.A. had ultimately been fined only a derisory amount in the Turkish courts and that copies of *Yasak Tümceler* were not confiscated. Doubtless the Turkish authorities could have acted in more draconian ways, but that does not suggest that the law they'd enacted and invoked was either necessary or desirable. It should also be remarked that the applicant was initially sentenced to two years' imprisonment and had to fight his case over a long period in the Turkish courts to avoid heavy punishment.

Unfortunately, the jurisprudence of the European Court of Human Rights tends to elevate freedom from religious impositions or persecutions by the state to something more like a right against other citizens not to be outraged by their anti-religious speech. In some passages, the court goes close to seeing Article 9 as including a positive right to hold and express religious beliefs without inconvenience from the speech of other citizens. All this creates an unnecessary tension between the concepts of freedom of religion and freedom of speech. As long as both are viewed essentially as negative rights against the state – or as limitations on its powers – freedom of religion in Article 9 and freedom of speech in Article 10 cannot conflict. This is, I submit, the natural meaning of the European Convention and is consonant with any reasonable historical understanding: each of the provisions provides a partial remedy to the state's long-standing penchant for imposing a preferred religion, persecuting the adherents of dis-preferred religions, and suppressing inconvenient speech.

The crime of blasphemy was finally repealed in the UK in 2008, but a hate speech provision, the *Racial and Religious Hatred Act* 2006, was enacted in its place, coming into effect in late 2007. Meanwhile, some cases in the European Court of Human Rights have shown a more liberal direction. Arguably, however, this merely reflects the court's involvement with cases involving less extravagantly anti-religious speech. Most sensationally, a unanimous court struck down the French courts' finding of defamation of Catholics in the 2006 case *Giniewski v. France*.

In 1994 Paul Giniewski, an Austrian historian and journalist, published an article in a French newspaper, *Le quotidien de Paris*. Using the occasion of the publication of a papal encyclical, *Veritatis Splendor*, in 1993, he argued for a thesis that I endorsed earlier in this chapter: that an element of anti-Judaism in the New Testament, together with the Catholic theological doctrine of the fulfillment of the Old Covenant in the New, had contributed to anti-Semitism in Europe and "prepared the ground" for the horrors of Auschwitz (and the Holocaust more generally). Publication of this thesis led to successful litigation against Giniewski by a Catholic organization called *Alliance générale contre le racisme et pour le respect de l'identité française et chrétienne* (AGRIF), which is a frequent litigant in the French courts, challenging what it sees as insults to Catholicism.

AGRIF took legal action under a provision of France's *Freedom of the Press Act* 1881 relating to individual and group libel. This provided: "It shall be defamatory to make any statement or allegation of a fact that damages the honour or reputation of the person or body of whom the fact is alleged." The case then took a tortuous path through the French criminal and civil court systems, culminating in two hearings before *le cour de cassation*, France's highest court, which held that the article was defamatory and published in bad faith. However, the European Court of Human Rights took the opposite view, holding in favor of Giniewski. In doing so, it emphasized that it is essential for democratic societies to allow free debate about the causes of crimes against humanity, such as those perpetrated by the Nazis.

A similar result was reached in *Aydin Tatlav v. Turkey*,[30] in which the court reviewed a criminal case relating to *The Reality of Islam*. This was a blatantly atheistic and anti-religious book by Turkish journalist Erdogan Aydin Tatlav. The Turkish courts had found Tatlav guilty of profanation of Islam, though he had ultimately been sentenced to no more than a moderate fine. In finding in Tatlav's favor, the European Court of Human Rights observed that a criminal penalty, with the risk of a custodial sentence, could deter writers and editors from publishing non-conformist opinions on matters of religion. This was contrary to what the court saw as a need to safeguard the pluralism essential for the healthy evolution of a democratic society.

While the outcomes of these, and other, recent cases are commendable, they do not show a full acceptance of merely verbal or symbolic attacks on religion. In the *Giniewski* case, it was considered important that the impugned article did not contain attacks on religious beliefs as such – but what if it had? Likewise, in *Aydin Tatlav v. Turkey* the court noted that the book included caustic comments about Islam that could offend Muslims, but that it did not directly insult Muslims or their sacred symbols. Thus, the court continues to accept what is, in effect, a concept of blasphemy. This, I submit, is the wrong approach. In a liberal democracy, the claims of all religions – whether to truth or to social utility and moral authority – should be open to challenge, whether through intellectual argument or more direct expressions of repudiation. Given that high-impact offense can shade into harm, there may legitimate scope to regulate the placement of extreme sacrilegious imagery, but even here care must to be taken to avoid a tyranny of the sensitive.

## Blasphemy and Islam

The publication in September 2005 of the notorious Danish cartoons – a set of satirical cartoons depicting Muhammad, printed in the newspaper *Jyllands-Posten* – led to widespread violence, political debate, high-profile litigation, and numerous attempts to explain the depth of anger among (at least some) Muslims.

One such attempt is that of Talal Asad, who offers an explanation of distinctively Muslim attitudes to free speech, blasphemy, and anti-religious satire. His analysis stresses the sanctity of private thought in the Islamic tradition – religious and government authorities will not inquire into individual's hidden motives and beliefs, scrutinizing them for heresy – as opposed to freedom to express thoughts in public. According to Asad, Islam differs from Christianity in its commitment to the privacy of thought. However, it does not protect attempts to seduce the thoughts of others away from their bond with God, their responsibility to co-religionists, and what it sees as metaphysical and moral truth. In Islam, so Asad assures us, such "seduction" is regarded as a kind of violence; it is dangerous to individuals and the social order, threatening discord and violence.[31] For Muslims who take this seriously, "it is impossible to remain silent when confronted with blasphemy . . . blasphemy is neither 'freedom of speech' nor the challenge of a new truth but something that seeks to disrupt a living relationship."[32]

Saba Mahmood takes a different, though perhaps complementary, approach. She describes a special form of pain felt by (some) pious Muslims, which amounts to a sense of personal loss and sorrow when confronted by ridicule of the Prophet.[33] On this account, the loss and sorrow relate to Muhammad's role as a moral exemplar, someone to be imitated in many of the quotidian aspects of life – such as how he walked, slept, spoke, ate, and dressed. Thus, these Muslims respond to ridicule of the prophet not with anger that a moral interdiction has been violated, but with a sense of having been personally violated and wounded. Like many other commentators, Mahmood also insists that such phenomena as the Danish cartoons involve an element of "racism" – extending this idea beyond biological notions of race to groups marked by religious and cultural characteristics.[34] This characterization tends to undermine the value of satire directed at Islam, or at radical forms or manifestations of Islam, associating it with worthless racial slurs.

How should a secular state respond to these analyses? First, Asad and Mahmood do not seem to be suggesting that the considerations they raise provide a basis for censorship of supposedly blasphemous speech, including images such as the Danish cartoons. They seem more concerned to foster an understanding of Muslim viewpoints, and perhaps to create a more sympathetic response from non-Muslims in Western societies. Nonetheless, it is worth considering whether the issues they discuss should affect state policies.

In that respect, there is a clear danger if the state acts on the basis of Asad's description of Muslim attitudes. The Lockean model does not propose that the various religions cease teaching their ideas, and arguing for them, but only that they cease jockeying for the power to impose their doctrines and practices by fire and sword. While some Muslims may find this model alien to their tradition, much the same could have been said of Christians not very long ago. It seems reasonable to hope that Islam can adapt to a social environment in which it is open to criticism, and in which it is relatively routine for individual citizens to change religious faiths or lose religious faith altogether.

What about Mahmood's suggestion that Muslims experience attacks on the Prophet in a uniquely painful and personal way? This point may have more merit as a consideration for public policy, but again it has its dangers if pressed too far. I have no way of assessing the accuracy of Mahmood's claim, though it seems plausible that devout religious adherents would feel something of the pain she describes when attacks are made on iconic figures.

An explanation such as Mahmood's may help non-Muslims to understand what is at stake, emotionally, when satirical attacks are made on Islam, and especially on the person of the Prophet. Perhaps something similar explains the passionate responses of others, such as devout Catholics, to what they see as sacrileges (e.g. Andres Serrano's photograph *Piss Christ*, which portrays a small crucifix submerged in the photographer's urine). This is consistent with the militancy and litigiousness that we see from some Catholic organizations, such as AGRIF in France.

Perhaps, then, we need to absorb the lesson that certain images, and perhaps mere words in some cases, can have a very high emotional impact not only for Muslims but also for adherents of other religions. That hardly excuses violent retaliation, such as occurred in many parts of the world following publication of the Danish cartoons, but it could play a limited role in public policy. If it's correct that high-impact offense shades into harm, then the state has a legitimate role in protecting citizens from exposure to images and smells (for example) that produce this type of offense. However, there's a catch. There would be very few situations where exposure of others to nauseating smells has any communicative value. The situation is very different with movies, artistic photographs, satirical cartoons, philosophical novels, and so on. These are protected by the free speech values discussed earlier in this chapter. Moreover, they can usually be avoided – even a newspaper can be closed.

The Danish cartoons caused great offense to many people, but the readers were not a captive audience. The immediate impact could be shut off by turning the page. A ban on such images would effectively mean that Islam was placed beyond satirical comment, since the images were not extreme as satirical cartoons go – no more so than run-of-the-mill cartoons that are published every day making fun of political proposals, events, and participants. What seems to have been most offensive about the cartoons was their *ideas*, for example of a linkage between Muhammad and modern-day Islamist terrorism. But opposition to certain ideas cannot provide a ground for censoring newspapers.

Think, too, of the erotic video that was in dispute in *Wingrove*: public policy might well favor that this not be shown on open-air screens in city shopping centers, or to captive audiences in buses and trams, and that it not be broadcast on television without some warning of its content. Most, if not all, jurisdictions already do this much to protect individual sensibilities in such ways. However, issues of high-impact offense cannot justify the total prohibition of such a video, keeping it even from people who might search it out on the Internet, watch it on television after being warned of its mixed sexual and religious imagery, pay to obtain a copy, or otherwise consent to view it at their own risk. Exactly similar considerations would apply if, for example, such a video were made about one of the wives of Muhammad rather than a Christian saint.

Finally, the issue of racism needs to be addressed. This demands some consideration of the much debated word "Islamophobia" and the concepts that lie behind it.

## Racism and Islamophobia

Islam is, of course, not a "race," or even an ethnicity. It is a belief system that posits an otherworldly order, with an almighty god (Allah) and numerous other supernatural beings, such as angels, Satan, and demons; a means of spiritual transformation (via submission to Allah); an eschatology (with hell, paradise, and a final judgment); and associated rituals and canons of conduct. Nothing in this is confined to any specific race, and it is noteworthy that Islam has many millions of followers all over the world, the largest number in Indonesia. How, then, is satire directed at Islam, or at its iconic figures and symbols, in any way comparable to racism?

Mahmood does little to make the comparison stick, beyond suggesting that religion, like biology or ancestry, is not simply a matter of choice.[35]

That is obviously true, as far as it goes: religion is, in very many cases, a matter of socialization from parents and other elders in one's community, rather than one of individual judgment based on the seemingly superior evidence for one or another set of claims ("Jesus was the Son of God," "Muhammad was God's prophet," etc.). But nothing follows from this as to the wisdom or moral propriety of criticizing or satirizing Islam.

The true contrast with race is not that race is unchosen, whereas religion is unproblematically *chosen*. It is that racism is not, generally speaking, based on objections to doctrines, associated practices, and canons of conduct. Even where racism has been fueled by doctrinal disagreements, a distinction can be made between doctrinal disagreement and racial hatred. That is not to say that they can always be disentangled in practice, merely that they are not the same thing and that either could, in principle, exist without the other.

At the same time, I do not doubt that some dislike of Islam, or impatience with Muslims and their spiritual leaders, has a quasi-racist character, grounded in parochialism and xenophobia, and perhaps a dislike of Arabs in particular. It is not coincidental that much of the public criticism of Islam as a religion, and of Muslims and their practices, emanates from European political parties and associated groups found on the extreme right, such as the Front National in France and the British National Party (BNP) in the UK. These organizations typically promote an intense, even bigoted nationalism – combined with what they portray as a defense of Christian traditions and values, and an endangered "Christian identity." They thrive on a fear of strange cultures and a fear of change – fears that are somewhat understandable in a new century overshadowed by the massive terrorist acts carried out in the name of Islam on September 11, 2001.

An obvious problem for critics of Islam who do not share the values of the European extreme right is that they may find themselves painted with the same brush. Conversely, extreme-right critics of Islam have gained a degree of respectability by co-opting issues and adopting stances that many politicians and members of the public find compelling. In making this point, José Pedro Zúquete refers to arguments about the situation of women within Islam:

> When the situation of women in Islam is discussed, the European extreme right puts forward arguments that, in a not-so-distant past, were considered to be positions exclusive to progressive and feminist groups in the West. The extreme right has been visibly active in its rejection of several cultural practices associated with Islam – ranging from the use of the headscarf and forced marriages, to honour-killings and female genital mutilation – by using arguments similar to those employed by mainstream groups that denounce inequalities and discrimination against women.[36]

Indeed, as Zúquete details, extreme-right groups have also co-opted such notions as secularism and animal rights, in their campaign against what they see as an Islamic threat to European and Christian identities.[37]

At the same time, many Muslims in Western countries continue to suffer from suspicion, cultural and personal misunderstanding, discrimination, and outright intolerance that sometimes rises to the level of harassment and violence. The extreme right exploits and encourages an environment where all this is possible. In the circumstances, it is unsurprising when a phenomenon such as Islamophobia is identified by academics, political commentators, and public intellectuals – and steps are taken to combat it.

This situation creates a complex set of advantages, disadvantages, and risks. The extreme right benefits from the availability of politically respectable criticisms of Islamic thought and associated cultural practices. As this goes on, there is a risk that the word "Islamophobia" will be used to demonize and intimidate individuals whose hostility to Islam is genuinely based on what they perceive as its faults. In particular, we should remember that Islam contains *ideas*, and in a liberal democracy ideas are fair targets for criticism or repudiation. Religious doctrines influence the social and political attitudes of their adherents in ways that merit public comment (favorable or otherwise), and many religious leaders and organizations exert vast power. It is in the public interest that all this be subjected to monitoring and criticism.

Even attacks on Islam that are made opportunistically, motivated by something like racist thinking, or by extreme kinds of national or cultural supremacism, cannot be dismissed out of hand as worthless. After all, there are *reasons* why extreme-right organizations have borrowed arguments based on feminism, secularism, and concepts of animal rights. These arguments are useful precisely because they have an intellectual and emotional appeal independent of their convenience to extreme-right opportunists. Regardless of who uses these arguments, they apply plausibly to certain elements of Islam, or at least to attitudes and practices associated with it. Whether or not they are put in good faith by organizations such as the BNP, nothing precludes them being put sincerely, and perhaps cogently, by others who are genuinely passionate about the issues.

Thus, there are legitimate reasons for some people who are not racists, cultural supremacists, or anything of the sort, to criticize Islam, or certain forms of Islam, or to express hostility toward it. These relate to their disapproval of various doctrines, canons of conduct, associated cultural practices, and so on, and to the power wielded by Islamic leaders and organizational structures. In this situation, expressions of disapproval or repudiation cannot simply be dismissed, a priori, with the assumption that they are racially motivated. Such dismissals are, moreover, all too convenient for those who wish to stifle genuine criticism of Islam.

A number of lessons can be drawn from all this. One is that opponents of Islam, or some of its forms, cannot reasonably be expected to keep quiet when accused of racism or the quasi-racism of "Islamophobia." When these accusations are misdirected, they are likely to inflame passions even further, though they may intimidate some individuals into silence. This suggests that commentators such as Mahmood would do well to understand that quasi-racism does not underlie all attacks on Islam. In particular, it would be wise to avoid painting critics of Islam as members or dupes of the extreme right without additional evidence.

There is also a lesson for critics of Islam, and associated practices, who do not identify with the extreme right. For a start, they need to understand the situation, including the extreme right's co-option of mainstream issues and arguments. This may lead to greater patience with opponents who make the charge of Islamophobia, though it hardly makes the charge more palatable. At a more practical level, opponents of Islam who do not wish to be seen as the extreme right's sympathizers or dupes would be well advised to take care of the impression that they convey. Where practical, they should explain their positions with as much nuance as possible, distance themselves from extreme-right figures making similar arguments, and avoid sharing platforms with them.

Note, however, that these are voluntary choices and that there may be limits. The words "where practical" are important, because what is practical in, say, a philosophical essay may not be practical in a satirical cartoon. In any event, beyond a certain point there is a disadvantage to walking on eggshells. It can make a message seem bland and exclude the talents of many people whose training or temperament does not suit hedged, half-apologetic communication.

Finally, how should the state react to criticism and satire targeted at Islam? The state is not well placed to tease apart motivations: since Islam, particularly its more aggressively political forms, attracts hostility because of its ideas and its impact on the world, the state has little choice but to take anti-Islamic critique and satire at face value. Accusations of racism, or something similar, may be true when applied to Islam's extreme-right opponents, but they do not provide a good basis for suppressing, demonizing, or marginalizing anti-Islamic speech. I don't rule out the possibility of extraordinary circumstances where it may be necessary to suppress a sufficiently violent or otherwise dangerous extreme-right group. But even then, it would be wrong to equate all hostility to Islam with racism or Islamophobia.

State officials need to keep the peace. In doing so, they may be tempted to suppress some kinds of speech and to demonize the speakers. However, this can be counterproductive. If an impression is created that political power is being used to silence opposition to Islam, this will add to the resentments against Islam in Western societies. In the current situation in the West, we do well to scrutinize ourselves as individuals, and to be alert to possible racism, even unconscious, somewhere within our motivations. That, however, is no reason for the state to treat anti-Islamic criticism and satire as *ipso facto* worthless forms of speech with improper motives behind them.

## The Limits Reconsidered

Some of the European case law appears to propose that religious ideas, practices, and canons of conduct, and the images and individuals who symbolize them, should be insulated from the robust give and take of ideas in liberal democracies. In such cases as *Otto-Preminger-Institut*, it seems that speech which conveys forthright opposition to religion – or a particular religion – is granted only a dubious, and easily defeasible, claim to protection. But religious freedom is essentially a freedom from state persecution, not a guarantee of a religion's ongoing credibility or its success in the contest of rival ideas.

Whatever the intention of the European court, anti-religious speech is often criticized in a way that goes beyond attempts at refutation to a suggestion that it is somehow socially unacceptable. Consider Tom Frame's recent attack on what he calls "contemporary anti-theism," in which he includes such books as *The God Delusion*, by Richard Dawkins: "When it becomes acceptable, and even admirable, to mock and ridicule a person's religious convictions and customs – and especially when the intention is to provoke an indignant reaction – the next step is to prohibit the expression of religious sentiment in all public places and forums.[38]

But this claim verges on paranoia. Frame is Australian, and he should be well aware that there is no prospect in his (and my) home country of any prohibition of public expressions of religious sentiment – though he claims, vaguely, that there are "signs" to the contrary.[39] If he were writing in the US context, where the presidency is intimately linked with religious ritual and involved in interaction with religious leaders, the claim would appear even more bizarre. The freedom of speech enjoyed by "contemporary anti-theists" is more than matched by that of their religious counterparts and opponents.

Accordingly, Frame is legally free to liken these examples of "contemporary anti-theism" to religious fundamentalism. However, although this slur is perfectly legal, it is unfair. Frame suggests that the "anti-theism" he identifies has "some of the characteristics of fundamentalism and, like all fundamentalisms, needs to be opposed."[40] But which characteristics of fundamentalism is this anti-theism supposed to display? Frame does not tell us, and it is not at all clear. For example, the "anti-theists" he refers to have no holy text that they treat as inerrant: they may give respect to each other's writings or to classics of science such as Charles Darwin's *On the Origin of Species* (1859), but that is a very different thing. They do not show extreme resistance to modernity through acts of violence, resistance to science and scholarship, and subordination of women. Dawkins and others may be confident of their positions, but not with the extreme dogmatism that clings to a position even when it is plainly contrary to robust scientific findings.

In short, Frame appears to use the word "fundamentalism" for its hurtfulness rather than its accuracy. That is, of course, his legal right in a liberal democracy. However, his analysis exemplifies the illiberal view that satire and robust criticism are illegitimate forms of speech when directed at religion.

Once again, the limit of free speech is reached, not when certain ideas, practices, and so on, are subjected to criticism and satire, but when violence is incited. In contemporary circumstances, unlawful incitements to violence need not be physically proximate to the victim, as with Mill's corn dealer example. They should, however, create some imminent and specific danger, as with Khomeini's death sentence against Rushdie, knowing that many would be glad to do his bidding.

As blasphemy laws have fallen out of favor, they have been replaced by laws against hate speech or vilification. How well do these track the proper boundary? As previously mentioned, repeal of the law of blasphemy in the UK was accompanied by the passage of the *Racial and Religious Hatred Act* 2006. In the form passed by the House of Commons, this caused a public outcry, including from religious leaders who were troubled by its breadth. Amendments were subsequently passed in the House of Lords, and eventually accepted in the House of Commons by razor-thin majorities. As a result of these amendments, the prohibitions in the act apply only to "threatening" forms of speech with intent to stir up religious hatred. This does not exactly follow the line I've suggested, but the references to intent and to "threatening" speech *should* ensure that the legislation catches only a narrow range of material that deliberately endangers the civil peace. Section 29J provides an important protection that should be included in any such law, irrespective of the jurisdiction:

> Nothing in this Part shall be read or given effect in a way which prohibits or restricts discussion, criticism, or expressions of antipathy, dislike, ridicule, insult or abuse of particular religions or the beliefs or practices of their adherents, or of any other belief system or the beliefs or practices of its adherents, or proselytising or urging adherents of a different religion or belief system to cease practicing their religion or belief system.

Unfortunately, tribunal members, judges, and others in authority take widely different attitudes to hate speech legislation and to the relative importance of freedom of speech. The remaining fear, therefore – a rational one in the circumstances – is that the authorities in the United Kingdom will still find ways of reading the legislation expansively, in a misguided effort to ensure that it has "teeth."

Laws relating to hate speech or vilification can vary widely between jurisdictions, defy legal interpretation, lead to tortuous and expensive litigation, and prove counterproductive in promoting mutual tolerance. In some cases, well-resourced and determined defendants may be able to resist legal actions initiated under these sorts of laws, but not all potential respondents are well resourced or determined. Laws such as these are intended to supersede the Enlightenment liberal concern with individual freedom. They are meant to work against the demonization and scapegoating of vulnerable minorities, to support inclusion and social harmony, and to heal community divisions. It is likely, however, that they have the opposite effect.

Consider AGRIF's persistent efforts in France to obtain court orders suppressing images and other expression that it considers defamatory of Catholics. It is difficult to see how this does anything to ease social tensions. When religious organizations try to prevent certain speech from being heard or certain images from being seen, this adds to the layers of distrust and resentment. Ahdar and Leigh note that prosecutions have seldom been brought under the relevant legislation in Northern Ireland for fear of inciting sectarian hatred. They cite the eminent Indian jurist, Soli Sorabjee, India's Attorney-General from 1998 to 2004, for the view that equivalent provisions in that country only encouraged intolerance and divisiveness.[41] Attempts in the Netherlands (during 2010 and 2011) to prosecute outspoken anti-Muslim politician Geert Wilders merely seemed to add to his popularity. I submit that a more hands-off attitude should be adopted in all these cases, with the limit set at speech which deliberately incites violence and produces an immediate and credible risk.

As Cliteur acknowledges, one might ask whether the publication of a book such as Rushdie's *The Satanic Verses* does not itself create a danger, given the violence that happened in response to it. But as he adds, such an approach would mean that bold new ideas could not be published. For example, Martin Luther, Giordano Bruno, and Galileo could all have been censored on the basis that their ideas were provocative to the Vatican.[42] The line should be drawn so as to allow bold speech that might offend, while protecting those who merely give offense from threatened violence. Such a liberal attitude might permit some ugly speech, but the long-term effect would be to reinforce a valuable lesson: ideologically opposed groups of whatever kind – religious, political, or philosophical – must make their own way, enduring criticism, and even satire, from their opponents, without asking the state to interfere.

## Conclusion

The secular state has good reasons to tolerate a wide range of speech, and it should not be in the business of censoring speech merely because it fails to conform to religious requirement. Nonetheless, it cannot ignore the fact that many, perhaps most or almost all, of its citizens will maintain an allegiance to one religion or another. In some cases, this may justify the state in regulating expression that is likely to have a high emotional impact on religious adherents. More generally, the state may be concerned that high-impact expression in public spaces, such as city streets and shops, and in the mass media, can damage citizens' quiet enjoyment of their environment.

This provides a justification for such regulatory responses as classification codes for television and cinema, restrictions on the content of billboards, and approval processes for images displayed within buses, trams, and other spaces with essentially captive audiences.

There is, however, a risk that the state will use this rationale to interfere unnecessarily with individual self-expression. Some things with an offensive sensory impact, such as the smell of feces or vomit, may be nauseating to almost everyone of any cultural background. But many other things that initially seem shocking (at least to some) become less so over time: consider nose-piercings; mixed-race or homosexual couples holding hands; flimsy summer clothing on men or women; long hair on men; and so on. In cases such as these, the wisest response favors liberty and a zeitgeist of increasing tolerance and acceptance.

Above all, protection should be given to speech that expresses opposition to religious doctrines or canons of conduct, or to religious organizations and leaders, or the social influence that they wield. All of these are legitimate matters for public discussion, and it is almost inevitable that such discussions take place within modern societies. As Malik suggests, it is better to deal openly with clashes of religion and ideology than to try to suppress their public expression. Widespread freedom to discuss such matters should be seen as healthy. If it is constrained, this will silence not only artists, and others who may be seen as privileged, but also the weaker voices within traditional communities.[43]

Malik argues, I believe plausibly, that a political culture which defends freedom of expression, rather than suppressing expressions of ideological conflict, provides extremists with few resources to draw upon. If it is considered unacceptable to give offense, and politicians and intellectuals are terrified of doing so, this makes it easier to *take* offense and gives extremists a false moral legitimacy for their violent actions.[44] It is far better to permit robust debate, including satire and mutual criticism.

Whatever limits might be imposed should be consistent. The proponents of blasphemy laws often make much of the offense suffered by religious believers if their beliefs are criticized or mocked. But what about the offense caused to others by the aggressive rhetoric of some religious persons. I am thinking here not only of calls for violence but also of threats to unbelievers and "sinners," who are portrayed as worthy of eternal suffering in hell (not to mention persecution on earth). Discussions of blasphemy rarely acknowledge any symmetry here, or call for mitigation of such rhetoric. If some level of offense is taken into consideration in public policy, it needs to be considered across the board. Offense can, indeed, shade into psychological harm, but might this not be more likely if children are threatened with hellfire than if religious doctrines and icons are treated disrespectfully? A fair debate about the limits would need to include such issues.

Meanwhile, various churches and sects retain feelings of mutual suspicion – based on opposed beliefs and ideals, and often on historical grievances. Freedom of speech allows this to be expressed, even through satire or mockery. In a tolerant, liberal society, however, the churches and sects need not fear the worst from each other: none is able to gain control of the coercive power of the state to punish or silence others. Over time, they may set aside their differences and learn to cooperate. To a large extent, that has already been the experience among the mainline Christian churches. Although the West faces new challenges, not least from assertive forms of Islam, it is far too early to abandon trust in the Lockean model and continued extension of liberal freedoms.

## Notes

1  J. S. Mill, *On Liberty*, 1st pub. 1859, Penguin, London 1974, p. 119.
2  Joel Feinberg, *Harm to Others*, Oxford University Press, New York 1984, p. 26.
3  Paul Cliteur, *The Secular Outlook: In Defense of Moral and Political Secularism*, Wiley-Blackwell, Oxford 2010, pp. 138–140. See also Kenan Malik, *From Fatwa to Jihad: The Rushdie Affair and its Legacy*, Atlantic Books, London 2009, pp. 175–176.
4  (1990) 61 CCC (3d) 1, 78–82.
5  Mill, *On Liberty*, pp. 77–96.
6  Alan Haworth, *Free Speech*, Routledge, London 1998, pp. 24–29.
7  Cliteur, *The Secular Outlook*, pp. 134–135.
8  Amos M. Guioroa, *Freedom from Religion: Rights and National Security*, Oxford University Press, New York 2009, p. 10.
9  Guioroa, *Freedom from Religion*, p. 57.

10 The legality of making a claim such as this in France was tested before the European Court of Human Rights in *Giniewski v. France*, Jan. 10, 2006 (discussed later in this chapter).

11 *Kokkinakis v. Greece*, May 25, 1993.

12 See *Manoussakis v. Greece*, Aug. 29, 1996, particularly §48.

13 *Kokkinakis v. Greece*, May 25, 1993, §10.

14 *Kokkinakis v. Greece*, May 25, 1993, §49.

15 *Kokkinakis v. Greece*, May 25, 1993, §50.

16 *Kokkinakis v. Greece*, May 25, 1993, §48.

17 Rex Ahdar and Ian Leigh, *Religious Freedom in the Liberal State*, Oxford University Press, Oxford 2005, p. 388.

18 *Larissis v. Greece*, Feb. 24, 1998.

19 As Kent Greenawalt notes, the point of religious freedom is not that religion be confined to an entirely non-public sphere, but merely that it be kept out of politics (*Religion and the Constitution*, vol. 2: *Establishment and Fairness*, Princeton University Press, Princeton 2008, p. 499).

20 Martha C. Nussbaum, *Liberty of Conscience: In Defense of America's Tradition of Religious Equality*, Basic Books, New York 2008, p. 24 (emphasis original).

21 Ahdar and Leigh, *Religious Freedom in the Liberal State*, pp. 366–368; Kenan Malik, *From Fatwa to Jihad*, p. 157.

22 Ahdar and Leigh, *Religious Freedom in the Liberal State*, p. 370.

23 *Otto-Preminger-Institut v. Austria*, Sept. 20, 1994.

24 *Wingrove v. United Kingdom*, Oct. 22, 1996.

25 *Otto-Preminger-Institut v. Austria*, Sept. 20, 1994, §47.

26 *Otto-Preminger-Institut v. Austria*, Sept. 20, 1994, §47.

27 *Otto-Preminger-Institut v. Austria*, Sept. 20, 1994, §47.

28 *Wingrove v. United Kingdom*, Oct. 22, 1996, §48.

29 *İ.A. v. Turkey*, Sept. 13, 2005.

30 *Aydin Tatlav v. Turkey*, May 2, 2006.

31 Talal Asad, "Free Speech, Blasphemy, and Secular Criticism," in Talal Asad et al., *Is Critique Secular? Blasphemy, Injury, and Free Speech*, Townsend Center/University of California Press, Berkeley 2009, pp. 20–63, pp. 36–46.

32 Asad, "Free Speech, Blasphemy, and Secular Criticism," p. 46.

33 Saba Mahmood, "Religious Reason and Secular Affect: An Incommensurable Divide?" in Tala Asad et al., *Is Critique Secular? Blasphemy, Injury, and Free Speech*, Townsend Center/University of California Press, Berkeley 2009, pp. 64–100, pp. 74–78.

34 Mahmood, "Religious Reason and Secular Affect," pp. 79–80.

35 Mahmood, "Religious Reason and Secular Affect," p. 81.

36 José Pedro Zúquete, "The European Extreme-Right and Islam: New Directions?" *Journal of Political Ideologies*, 3 (2008), pp. 321–344, pp. 331–332.

37 Zúquete, "The European Extreme-Right and Islam," p. 333.

38 Tom Frame, *Losing my Religion: Unbelief in Australia*, University of New South Wales Press, Sydney 2009, p. 267.

39 Frame, *Losing my Religion*, p. 267.

40   Frame, *Losing my Religion*, p. 268.
41   Ahdar and Leigh, *Religious Freedom in the Liberal State*, p. 386.
42   Cliteur, *The Secular Outlook*, p. 137.
43   Malik, *From Fatwa to Jihad*, pp. 172–174.
44   Malik, *From Fatwa to Jihad*, p. 196.

Very
IMPORTANT!

CHAPTER TEN

BACK TO LOCKE
CONCLUDING REMARKS

Throughout this volume, I have defended and elaborated upon a Lockean model of the state, updated for modern circumstances in which both the state and the churches carry out a far wider range of activities than Locke would ever have imagined. For Locke, the state should concern itself with protecting worldly interests, while the churches offer rival paths to spiritual salvation. On this approach, the state should not favor particular doctrines relating to the salvation of souls, or anything analogous, while the churches should not seek the power of the secular ruler.

As we've seen, religion typically postulates an order of things beyond this world – together with a higher good beyond ordinary human flourishing. It involves personal transformations, to ensure that the higher good is achieved. It is about the transcendent: an order beyond the merely immanent order; a good beyond our worldly interests; and a dimension to human life extending beyond what we ordinarily understand as life and death. Very often, it specifies canons of conduct; these may conduce to salvation or to rightness with a god. Religious claims about a transcendent order may be true or false, and in theory some are even testable. In practice, however, disputes about religion defy resolution by reason. Wherever it can, the state should step back from all this, neither promoting nor discouraging religion (or any particular form of it).

On this conception, religious freedom does not require that religion be held in high esteem or that the survival of particular religions be underwritten by public resources. Nor, on the other hand, does it require an attitude of skepticism or hostility to religious claims. Rather, freedom of religion can be seen as a negative right against the state. Reduced to its essence, it

*Freedom of Religion and the Secular State*, First Edition. Russell Blackford.
© 2012 John Wiley & Sons, Inc. Published 2012 by John Wiley & Sons, Inc.

is a right that the state *not* impose its own favored religious doctrines and practices, or persecute those that it disfavors. Locke explains why the state should not be motivated to impose or persecute religion – because it simply does not concern itself with otherworldly things.

Three centuries later, this model still has much to offer. It implies political arrangements in which the state will be religion-blind, as far as possible. It will make decisions for its own secular reasons, without claiming any transcendent backing – or even claiming that its actions are morally best, all things considered. There is always the theoretical possibility that the state's actions are morally wrong by some transcendent standard or other that may turn out to be true, but law-makers cannot concern themselves with that. It would require an inquiry, potentially interminable and inevitably divisive, into the truth of religious and perhaps other esoteric teachings.

In Chapter 5 I explained why a secular state logically develops into a liberal state that embraces social pluralism and permits its citizens a vast range of individual and cultural differences. In consequence, modern liberal democracies assume that harmony is better produced through accommodation of differences than by an attempt to impose uniformity. While allowing room even for the advocacy of illiberal ideas, liberal democracies favor liberal political principles such as freedom of speech, sexual privacy, the harm principle, and a rejection of arbitrary punishments. Enforcement of religious canons of conduct for its own sake can never be a legitimate purpose of public policy. That is, at least, the ideal.

Most liberal democracies give additional support to liberal political principles by establishing binding limits on government power, typically in instruments such as bills and charters of rights. These limits are maintained by a system of independent courts.

If the state confines its reasons for action to worldly matters and interests, this removes its main motive for religious persecutions but does not remove all possible sources of tension between the state (on one hand) and various churches, sects, religious communities, and devout individuals. As the state's secular role expands – as it did, dramatically, during the past century and a half – new areas of potential conflict open up. Religious organizations and the state authorities may advocate mutually inconsistent canons of conduct aimed at their different purposes, and needless to say these will not always be compatible. Legislative or executive acts that are intended to contribute to ordinary human flourishing may clash with religious aspirations.

Throughout this volume, I've argued that religious actors – religious organizations, devout individuals, traditional religious communities, and so on – cannot claim to be persecuted if they are inconvenienced or restricted by laws that are enacted for secular purposes and apply to everyone in the jurisdiction. The state may enact neutral laws with general application, and it may expect the religious to abide by them like everybody else.

Imagine, therefore, a devout individual who holds a position of leadership in her sect – we'll call her Helena. Within a liberal democracy that supports freedom of religion, Helena should be able to believe what she wants, express her beliefs, teach them to others, take part in associated rituals, and so on. But what if her sect's rituals involve human sacrifice? In that case, she had best lead a reform movement to modify them, because no one's religion exempts her from the ordinary law applying to murder. Ordinarily, the state will not need to enact any non-neutral laws aimed specifically at her sect or its practices; it need only enforce the ordinary law. If human sacrifice seems like too extreme an example to be persuasive, consider a more mundane aspect of Helena's religious activities. If the objects used in her sect's rituals attract some kind of sales or consumption tax, then the sect should pay it when it purchases paraphernalia in the marketplace – just like anyone else buying the same items. This is not persecution; it is simply being treated impartially.

It has, however, been one of my themes that the state is *not* left with no reasons at all to accommodate religious sensibilities. The state's officials should be able to understand how some laws could feel like persecution to religious adherents, even though harm to religion is in no sense their purpose or their principal effect. Once again, consider Locke's example of a ban on all slaughter of cattle, enacted for a secular purpose relating to stock replenishment. This could have a severe impact on a religious sect that believes the sacrifice of cattle is required by its deity and necessary for spiritual salvation. Without endorsing the sect's actual belief, the legislature can reasonably conclude that it has a secular reason not to create this dilemma for sect members, and thus to grant them a limited exemption from the law.

Still, such an exemption tends to undermine the law's original purpose, to shift a greater burden onto others, and perhaps to breed resentment. In deciding whether to grant an exemption, the state needs to weigh up its own secular reasons, for and against the exemption, without taking a view on the underlying merits of the religious belief itself. Given that exemptions have their downside, they should be tailored narrowly and crafted with care. If state officials conduct that exercise sincerely, not showing more leniency to some religions than others when analogous circumstances arise, then they are doing their proper job.

The attractions of secularism and liberalism cannot be demonstrated to all possible opponents with all manner of starting points. The concept of a secular state, such as described by Locke, provides good prospects for a reasonable and peaceful political order, for "putting an end to the worst consequences of fanatical sectarianism – of the 'clash of orthodoxies' – such as senseless persecution and bloodshed."[1] It does, moreover, have independent support from arguments that the real *point* of the state is secular: it provides peace and security, facilitates large and complex societies, and makes possible a wide range of worldly goods. Once the idea of a secular state is embraced, it leads to a broader form of liberalism. But for all that, someone who starts with deeply held theocratic beliefs will probably not be moved. Such a person relies on different premises, and may be immune to any argument in support of the Lockean model and liberal political principles.

We should not be too quick to brand fellow citizens as beyond the reach of reason. It may be that most people can be brought to see the benefits of religious freedom and individual liberty. Secular liberals should not, for example, conceive of Islam as simply an enemy to be opposed by force: modern ideas of freedom may be alien to the Islamic tradition, but it remains reasonable to hope that Islam can reform and adapt. Though theirs may not always be the loudest voices in their communities, most Muslims living in liberal democracies may have already embraced much in the way of liberal ideas.

Nonetheless, extreme members of the Christian Right and proponents of radical Islam continue to demand that we institute theocracies. They do not explain why this is not a recipe for perpetual religious warfare or why citizens who reject their views should give up their demands for religious freedom. From a theocratic perspective, however, those may not be the crucial questions. Hard-line theocrats place a higher value on rightness with God, and they expect to *prevail*, eventually, perhaps even with divine assistance. They do, indeed, occupy an intellectual position that puts them beyond persuasion, and we certainly cannot give them what they want. Open conflict with such people is a last resort, but it can never be ruled out entirely. Meanwhile, we can hope it never comes to that as we renew our commitment to secular and liberal principles, advocating them strongly, as is our right in a liberal democracy.

That advocacy must continue. This volume makes one small contribution.

# Note

1   J. Judd Owen, *Religion and the Demise of Liberal Rationalism: The Foundational Crisis of the Separation of Church and State*, University of Chicago Press, Chicago 2001, p. 168.

# INDEX

*Freedom of Religion and the Secular State*, First Edition. Russell Blackford.
© 2012 John Wiley & Sons, Inc. Published 2012 by John Wiley & Sons, Inc.